Governing under Stress

Globalization and the Semi-periphery:
Impacts, Opposition, Alternatives

*Series editor: Gordon Laxer, Director, Parkland Institute,
University of Alberta, Edmonton*

This series presents research from an international network of writers, all based in four carefully selected middle-ranking powers – Canada, Mexico, Norway and Australia – who are studying neo-liberal globalization with a view to understanding the social forces at work which may have the potential to transform it. Starting from the unique vantage point of resource-rich countries located in the semi-periphery, these scholars reject as ideologically loaded the idea of the historical inevitability of globalization, arguing instead that it is in reality a political project whose proponents are seeking a form of economic and ecological recolonization of the world.

In analysing the impacts of globalization in the semi-periphery and the potential effectiveness of sources of opposition, they seek to identify and explore emerging alternative conceptual, political and ecological paradigms. The working assumption is that the condition of semi-peripherality, whether defined in social, cultural, economic or spatial terms, provides the citizens of these countries with both the consciousness of subordination and the means of resistance and transformation – unlike the countries of the core which may lack the consciousness, and the countries of the periphery which may lack the required means. The result of this ongoing inter-disciplinary research effort will be the identification of social forces and ideas that hold out the hope to humanity of political choice, and of alternative social paths not totally constrained within the current parameters of globalization.

Governing under Stress

Middle Powers and the Challenge of Globalization

**Edited by Marjorie Griffin Cohen
and Stephen Clarkson**

ZED BOOKS
London & New York

FERNWOOD PUBLISHING
Nova Scotia

Governing under Stress was first published in 2004 by
Zed Books Ltd, 7 Cynthia Street, London N1 9JF, UK,
and Room 400, 175 Fifth Avenue, New York, NY 10010, USA

www.zedbooks.co.uk

First published in Canada in 2004 by Fernwood Publishing Ltd,
8422 St Margaret's Bay Road (Hwy 3) Site 2A, Box 5,
Black Point, Nova Scotia, B0J 1B0

Research for this book was supported by the Social Sciences
and Humanities Research Council of Canada

Designed and typeset in Monotype Bembo by Illuminati, Grosmont
Cover designed by Andrew Corbett

A catalogue record for this book is available from the British Library
Library of Congress Cataloging-in-Publication Data available
Canadian CIP data available from the National Library of Canada

ISBN 978 1 84277 302 4 (HB)
ISBN 978 1 84277 303 1 (PB)

Contents

Tables and Figures

Preface

Gordon Laxer

Long before the attacks on the World Trade Center on 11 September
2001 and the Bush doctrine of pre-emptive war, the Clinton administration had linked US security interests to other countries'
compliance with its agenda of opening their economies to transnational corporate ownership and control. As early as 1996, Lawrence
Summers, Clinton's under-secretary of the Treasury, contended that
'globalist economic policy ... is the forward defense of America's
deepest security interest.' Denouncing critics of the 'Bretton Woods
consensus' as 'separatists', Summers proclaimed 'our ideology, capitalism, is in ascendance everywhere.' The authors of the Globalization
and the Semi-periphery book series challenge this 'consensus' from
the perspective of the semi-periphery, which has produced, and
continues to produce, unique insights and political standpoints.

Canada, Australia, Mexico, and Norway – the semi-periphery
countries in question – are neither major drivers of global power, nor
simply its victims. They occupy positions where they are dominant
in some areas, but subordinate to core countries overall. Critics from
these countries have produced significant assessments of globalization
and neo-liberalism, of neo-imperialism and sovereignty, and of the
concentration of transnational corporate ownership in core countries.
Drawing on ideas from democratic citizens' movements and critical
thinkers in the semi-periphery, our volumes will present readers with
a range of measures to help economies develop under democratic
control, and to do so in harmony with living environments. Three
main issues guide us: first, the impacts of neo-liberal globalism on

societies; second, the actions citizens in the semi-periphery and their governments are taking to reshape their countries and contest globalism; and third, the alternative paradigms emerging around popular democratic proposals and practices, and the role of challengers from the semi-periphery in this shift.

This Preface highlights key arguments, concepts, and debates in the Globalization and the Semi-periphery series and this its lead volume.

A note on concepts

Our studies critically examine the paradigm which dominated the 1980s and 1990s, 'neo-liberal globalism', that is the norms, institutions, and laws that support corporate profitability at the expense of collective rights. Also known as structural adjustment programmes (SAPs), the Washington consensus, the Wall Street–Treasury complex, liberal productivism, and the New World Order, the prescription for every country is consistent: encourage foreign ownership, remove foreign exchange protections, slash public services, cut corporate taxes, and sell government-owned enterprises.

The neo-liberal prescription challenges democratic assumptions about the sovereignty of countries, as states turn away from citizens' concerns to focus on exports and enshrine transnational corporate rights. Structural adjustment programmes in the South, international agreements such as NAFTA in the North, and international institutions such as the World Trade Organization lock countries into neo-liberal principles. Those wishing to withdraw from such agreements and create international agreements premissed on different, more democratic lines, face threats of economic sanctions by the G7 and the World Bank or even military retaliation by the US and its allies.

Neo-liberal globalism adopts as its model American and British capitalism, an ideology of governance that spreads through persuasion, diplomacy, and economic power. The writers in this series call it 'globalism' for short. Portrayed as common sense and inevitable, this globalism is a self-serving approach that favours rich countries and rich corporations, while its internal structural contradictions eliminate the delivery of material benefits and livelihoods to many in the world. Globalism's challengers range across political boundaries from reformed capitalists and neo-traditionalists to a tide of popular-democratic movements attempting to build alternatives to capitalist societies. As the US and its allies lose the battle for ideas, they turn to force – a shift that suggests the instability of globalism's hegemony. As the Globalization and the Semi-periphery series develops, some authors will explore whether the 'disciplinary liberalism' of the 1990s is being replaced by a new kind of empire, centred on the US military–industrial complex and its allies.

The second term, 'semi-periphery',[1] emerged from ideas developed by dependency theorists in the 1960s. They argued that the development and economic autonomy of rich Western countries was not reproducible elsewhere and that the very advances and power of the West held back development in the periphery and locked the latter into subordinate roles. Because their surpluses were drawn off to the rich countries, periphery countries became perpetual sources of raw materials and cheap labour, unless they partially delinked from Western capitalism and transformed themselves through 'inwardly directed development' and 'import substitution industrialization'. The language of core and periphery in dependency theory captured these relations of unequal power, and provided a powerful counter-discourse in the developing countries.

Views from the semi-periphery of power and resources are again providing a perspective that is distinct from that of either the core or the periphery. Among new insights in this series, three stand out. First, an approach called the new constitutionalism[2] interprets international 'trade' agreements as external constitutions, which restrict government actions. Discussed as constitutions, these agreements would not likely have been approved by voters, if given the chance. Second, several authors identify how contemporary anti-corporate globalization contestations are often continuations of long-standing national and popular-democratic sovereignty movements rather than the creation of a new 'global civil society'. Third, a number of authors are developing a post-globalism paradigm through concepts around claiming popular-democratic sovereignties over eco-social commons.

Canada, Australia, Norway, and Mexico have long been described as in-between countries: go-between nations, semi-satellite countries, intermediate-development countries, resource-exporting economies, fringe countries, hinterlands, and dependencies. Margaret Atwood called Canada a 'rich colony'. While Mexico has a huge 'informal

sector' and high productivity in pockets which are highly integrated
with the US, Australia, Canada, and Norway have productivity levels,
pay rates, and class formations that are indistinguishable from core
countries. Why, then, do we still call them semi-peripheral?

Historically the four countries have paid their way in the world
by continually shipping part of their non-renewable heritage to
more powerful countries. They still do. Their resource-exporting
relationships tend to retard the development of more diverse activities
for their citizens. Resource-exporting dependency reflects power
differentials with dominant states and transnational corporations that
are reminiscent of classical colonial relationships. Resources are the
neo-liberal term for nature, but they are about more than economics.
Natural resources are treasured in non-economic ways as a country's
heritage, as its commons. If controlled by foreign corporations, they
can also be symbols of continued subservience. Unequal power comes
into play, as core countries partially live off the carrying capacities
of the semi-periphery by continually claiming portions of the latter's
non-renewable heritage.

Long before the present wave of globalism subjected most core
countries to similar pressures, our four countries were exposed to
intensive global integration pressures. All have sought, at various
points, to define and defend their national identities and institutions
in the face of imperial and globalizing forces. Other common threads
run through the changing relationships these four countries have had
with the core and the periphery. As semi-peripheral countries, each
has had less economic and political autonomy than core countries
in the recent past, yet are sometimes able to adopt positions on
international and domestic issues that are distinct. Currently, these
four countries are integrated with the US and Northern powers in
their economic institutions and frequently in their military relations
with the global South. During the 2003 invasion of Iraq, the US
and its allies sought support from the semi-periphery for legitimacy.
Australia signed on as US 'deputy sheriff', as Prime Minister Howard
put it. However, despite Washington's pressure, the US's NAFTA
partners, Mexico and Canada, refused. Norway, a NATO member,
also rebuffed the call to arms. Each also had pasts as colonies. But
in gaining formal independence, they did not, unlike core countries,
occupy other countries. (Australia is a partial exception to this.[3])
All, however, have had internal colonial relations with indigenous
peoples and continue to attempt to remove aboriginal title over

valuable resources. All four countries also remain subject to much influence from one or more core country, partly because they rely on exporting strategic resources like oil, natural gas, minerals, and food, and importing finished goods from the core. Also, they had high levels of foreign ownership before the current globalism era. Yet none of the four countries is home base to any of the world's hundred largest transnational corporations.[4] This includes Canada, despite its G7 membership. In contrast, each of the other G7 countries houses the home office of at least three of the world's top one hundred transnationals.

In response to unequal power relations in the 1900s, our four semi-peripheral countries broke from Anglo-American laissez-faire orthodoxies and used state-centred strategies, at various times, to win more autonomy and reverse high levels of foreign ownership control. They also promoted economic diversification away from exporting raw materials and, due to popular pressures, redistributed incomes. But, beginning with the debt crisis in Mexico in 1981, such autonomy strategies came under extreme pressure as neo-liberalism gained force, and all four countries abandoned many long-held economic nationalist policies, while still retaining considerable autonomy and capacity to change direction. In our volumes, readers will discover why such developments took place, the national specificities pertaining to each, and the intellectual currents that emerged.

Empire and the semi-periphery

This series is being written while debates occur everywhere about globalism and whether the US is a hegemon or an empire. Thomas Risse (2003: 3) defines hegemonic power as resting on the superpower sustaining an international order, on smaller states' acceptance of that order, and on their willingness to obey the rules of that order. In contrast, the imperial power plays only by the rules when it suits its interests, but insists that smaller states obey them.

Although the United States dominated the neo-liberal project before September 11, it has significantly moved along the continuum from hegemon to empire in its aftermath. As a result, many now question previously held assumptions about global integration, the inevitability of a borderless world, the eclipse of nations and states, and the emergence of a global civil society.[5] Walden Bello (2003), founding director of Focus on the Global South and a leader of today's anti-corporate globalization movement, argues that the shift in US policies is not the aberrant turn of a particular regime, but reflects deeper structural crises in the globalism project. He argues that the 'consensus' side of the Washington consensus is undermined when neo-liberal policies are imposed through force. The greater use of coercion signals imperial weakness. When 'security trumps trade' and borders tighten, is the present historical conjuncture best characterized as one of globalism and generic corporate rule, or as a neo-liberal US empire in which corporations tied to the imperial cause receive advantages over those based in countries not party to 'coalitions of the willing'? Or is it a combination of the two? A neo-liberal, neo-imperial model implies a complex interaction and contestation amongst three agencies: corporations, states, and citizens. In such a model, a crucial focus becomes contestations over whether the state will be corporate-oriented or citizen-oriented.

As well as the struggles over the state, struggles over resources, land, and nature are central to the economic, cultural, and political contestations around globalism and empire. They are also central to semi-peripheral national identities. Globalists advocate turning most things in the commons into commodities so corporations can profit from them. When implemented, such strategies contribute to unsustainable development and the exploitation of workers, who are treated as factors of production, not citizens. Privatizing the commons reduces the scope of public life and the possibilities for bottom-up democracy. Current trade patterns and the vertical control over resources by TNCs based in the US and other core countries allow them to maintain their profligate lifestyles by living off the carrying capacities of countries in the periphery and the semi-periphery. These patterns transfer massive ecological costs to resource-based economies, while reducing the costs of energy-intensive use and hyper-consumerism in the core.

Such semi-peripheral countries as Australia, Canada, Mexico, and Norway occupy contradictory positions. They live off the carrying capacities of the periphery and internal indigenous lands, while at the same time they are locked into depleting and commodifying their own commons as part of their resource-exporting dependence on the US and the rest of the globe's core countries. This contradiction is recognized in debates about *sustainability*, the *commons* and attempts to *decommodify* public life and nature. The prevalent use of the term *sustainability* has been co-opted to mean sustainable growth, sustainable profits, and sustainable capitalism. Some authors in this series are trying to reclaim sustainability to mean removing capitalism's predations on nature and restructuring society so that no person, country, class or gender dispossesses others or claims a disproportionate share of the earth's carrying capacity.

Still other writers are developing the concept of the eco-social commons. The commons is a compelling tradition and vision of sharing and participation, which provided the basis for popular democracy, the provision of public services, the cohesion of social and national citizenship, and the transgenerational stewardship of public or crown lands and resources. The idea of the commons dates back to at least fourteenth-century England and carries multiple connotations – ecological, democratic, non-elite, social cohesion, and popular culture. In *The Great Transformation*, Karl Polanyi outlined the dynamic of market expansion which generated counter-movements to protect society from the insecurities created by turning nature into commodified resources, people into factors of production, and money into prices, exchange rates and debts that can imperil productive organizations. Today's ecological and civil commons face near annihilation under neo-liberal pressures to commodify fresh water, the sea, the air, crown land, the ejido system in Mexico, public life, public services, non-commercial cultures, genetic material, shared knowledge, and the right to earn a decent living.

There are competing conceptions of governing future civil commons as a single global commons or as many commons. Those who hold a global conception of the commons tend to come from the core. In the neo-liberal version, the global commons is a space to be managed by international institutions and global elites, and may be restricted to spheres like the air and oceans that cannot be divided into profit-seeking, private property rights (Goldman 1997; Vogler 2000: 3). A more radical version demands the decommodification of the global commons, to be governed by a bottom-up global democracy. On the other hand, advocates of popular-democratic and national sovereignties over the many commons tend to come from indigenous peoples and those in the periphery, who think of globalism as recolonization. If it is recolonization, contentions against globalism may be mainly around national political communities gaining a great deal of autonomy from imperial influences, so there can be popular-democratic control over their own commons. Indigenous peoples are unlikely to give up their lands for an abstraction called the 'global commons', however benignly conceived.

Reflecting the contradictory, in-between positions of observers from the semi-periphery, views in this series range from those who support the global commons and global citizenship to those who support the popular-democratic and national sovereignty of real communities grounded in their own commons. Others attempt a synthesis, holding both views in creative tension, developing a multi-scaled model of the civil commons, which links struggles for democracy across local, national, and transnational settings.

Books in this series

What can be learned from the semi-periphery? Living in the semi-periphery distances actors and observers from taken-for-granted assumptions of the core, while still being close enough to have insider understandings of those assumptions and the state capacity to do something about them. Clearly, the very resources which give our countries strategic importance to the US and other core countries can have ambiguous consequences. If the semi-periphery countries use their resources as bargaining chips, it may lead to greater independence. Or they may fall into dependencies, begging for access to core markets and for foreign investment in exchange for loyalty to the US. In short, the semi-periphery is a provocative environment in which to live and study the dynamics of global integration and its opposition.

Our studies try to analyse stress points in the neo-liberal model within semi-periphery countries. The latter are conscious of their subordination to core powers, but have cultures, resources, and the will to carve out distinct areas of action. It is critical for social scientists, in this age when both national and international societies are rapidly changing, to understand why some countries rapidly fall into step, while others do not, at least not all the time. The authors in this series focus on both those external pressures that force these countries to conform, and the internal and external factors that allow them to dissent. Understanding some of these mechanisms within semi-peripheral countries – the countries best able to shape their destinies according to the desires of their people in an age of globalism – will give some sense of whether alternatives to a neo-liberal globalization are possible.

The Globalization and Semi-periphery series grew out of a five-year project funded by the Social Sciences and Humanities Research Council of Canada – The Neoliberal Globalism and Its Challengers Project (www.ualberta.ca/globalism). It involves about thirty researchers in Canada, Australia, Mexico, and Norway. Future books in this series cover a range of themes. *Mexico in Transition: Neoliberal Globalism, the State, and Civil Society*, edited by Gerardo Otero, explores how Mexico has fared since it abandoned inward-looking development and adopted neo-liberal reforms. How have peasants adapted to globalization pressures while Mexico lost its food and labour sovereignty? What has been the impact of neo-liberalism on wages, trade unions, and women workers; and of the emergence of new social movements like El Barzón and the Zapatistas?

Reclaiming Sustainability: The Commons, Market Forces and Scales of Resistance, edited by Josée Johnston, Mike Gismondi, and James Goodman, investigates ecological exhaustion, the idea of the eco-social commons, and how citizens' movements work across local, national, and global scales to counterpose public power against private interests.

Not for Sale: Decommodifying Public Life, edited by Gordon Laxer and Dennis Soron, critically develops the twin notions of commodifying and decommodifying as unique means to understand current struggles over what should and should not be for sale. What are the implications for bottom-up democracy of putting water, genetically modified organisms, knowledge, people's labour power, and nature up for sale?

Further down the road, look for books on the following themes. *Changing Semiperipheries: The Political Economy of Change in Australia, Canada, Mexico and Norway*, co-authored by Stephen McBride, Paul Bowles, Ray Broomhill, Lars Mjøset, and Teresa Gutiérrez-Haces, will provide an analysis of the unique historical development of the four semi-peripheral countries and a framework for understanding possibilities for future progressive change.

Nationalism and Globalism: Resistance on the Semiperiphery; Australia, Canada, Mexico and Norway, written by Gordon Laxer, James Goodman, Teresa Gutiérrez-Haces, and Øyvind Østerud, will explore how three main currents of nationalist discourse, an elite version, a right populist version and a progressive, internationalist nationalism, compete for supremacy in each of the four countries.

In *Endangered Species: National Currencies in the Semi-periphery*, Paul Bowles will explore the future of independent currencies for countries with intermediate-sized economies. Debates include the implications for democracy and sovereignty of US dollarization in the western hemisphere, and Norway adopting the euro.

In *Electricity Deregulation on the Semi-periphery: Australia, Canada, Mexico and Norway*, Marjorie Griffin Cohen will examine pressures for electricity deregulation, privatization, and 'public/private partnerships' in electricity production and distribution.

Reconfiguring Gender on the Semi-periphery, edited by Marjorie Griffin Cohen and Habiba Zaman, will focus on gendered experiences with globalism in semi-periphery countries, on experiences unique to each country, and on gender-based activism on globalization issues.

In *Deglobalizing the Transnationals: The Case for Re-nationalizing Citizen Control over the Economy*, Gordon Laxer will argue that the drive to global integration has ebbed and flowed and that there may be opportunities for national experimentations in social transformation along new, societal democratic lines.

In *Somewhat Less than Meets the Eye: The Governance of North America*, Stephen Clarkson will examine the complex relations of the United States' dominance of its two continental neighbours.

We are very pleased to start the series with *Governing under Stress: Middle Powers and the Challenge of Globalization*, which focuses on the loss of autonomy and control by states, in what the editors call a 'semi-periphery of power'. By analysing recent experiences of our four non-core countries, readers will gain a more profound understanding about the commonalities and the uniquenesses of contemporary changes under globalism in ways which have resonance with many other parts of the world. Also, they will learn about circumstances and chances for challenging those forces. In *Governing under Stress* Cohen and Clarkson have put together writing from some of the best contemporary political economists in each of the countries and set the stage for the provocative series on Globalization and the Semi-periphery.

Notes

Thanks to Marjorie Cohen and Stephen Clarkson for extensive editorial suggestions and to Josée Johnston and Gerardo Otero for very thorough critiques. Thanks, too, to Paul Bowles, Janine Brodie, and James Goodman for excellent suggestions.

1. For a discussion of the intellectual and political origins of the idea of 'in-between' countries, see my preface to *Mexico in Transition*, edited by Gerardo Otero. This is the second book in the Globalization in the Semi-periphery series.

2. Writers outside the series, such as Stephen Gill, have also developed formulations on the new constitutionalism.

3. Australia has had imperial outreach in the South Pacific.

4. Australia comes closest, with Telstra at number 108. The four countries do better in the top 500 TNCs. Canada is home base to 18, Australia has 9, Mexico 6, and Norway 2. *Financial Times*, Special Report, 11/12 May 2001. Calculations by Ineke Lock.

5. See Ulrich Beck: however globalisation is understood, it 'implies the weakening of state sovereignty and state structures' (2000: 86).

References

Beck, Ulrich (2000) 'The Cosmopolitan Perspective: Sociology of the Second Age of Modernity', *British Journal of Sociology*, vol. 51, no. 1.

Bello, Walden (2003) 'The Crisis of the Globalist Project and the New Economics of George W. Bush', FOP Newsletter #33, fopnewsletter-owner@yahoogroups.com.

Goldman, Michael (1997) 'Customs in Common: The Epistemic World of the Commons Scholars', *Theory and Society* 26.

Polanyi, Karl (1957) *The Great Transformation* [1944], Boston: Beacon Press.

Risse, Thomas (2003) *Beyond Iraq: Challenges to the Transatlantic Security Community*, AICGA/German–American Dialogue Working Paper Series.

Vogler, John (2000) *The Global Commons: Environmental and Technological Governance*, 2nd edn, Chichester: John Wiley.

I

Introduction:
States under Siege

Marjorie Griffin Cohen
and Stephen Clarkson

This book is about how countries in the middle of the global power hierarchy confront the loss of control over their own futures through their experiences with globalization. It is about how people are governed within nations at a time when external forces have rendered existing institutions and practices inadequate and about how nations have accommodated new international powers in distinct ways. But it is also about the choices still to be made and what these choices will mean for democratic government as a global regulatory regime unfolds.

Globalization, globalism, and global governance

No word is currently more overworked than 'globalization'. It can describe many kinds of changes in the world, such as the inter-continental movements of peoples, the increasing interdependence of economies, the international transmission of diseases, or the trans-national mobilization of criminal or terrorist organizations. But mostly the term has economic, ideological, and political meanings. Among political economists, *globalization* refers mainly to economic trans-formations that link together formerly separate national economies; a linking that is increasingly shaped by international mechanisms of governing. Its driving force is generally thought, by conven-tional economic analysis, to be integrally related to the trajectory of capitalism itself, although twentieth-century technological advances in computerization have accelerated the trend by enabling capital markets, production processes, and distribution systems to link the world in hundreds of nearly seamless corporate systems.

Neo-liberal globalism, the ideas that have conceptualized and rationalized these economic movements, has become a paradigm preaching a specific liberal doctrine of transformation. Often referred to as the 'Washington consensus', its notions of constraining governments in order to liberate markets is based on the American model of development and became a monolithic system of thought prescribing one formula for how the world's economic systems should work. It is also backed up by American military might that has been used on occasion to eradicate rival models. Enforced by such multilateral financial institutions as the International Monetary Fund and the World Bank, over which the US government exerts considerable influence, the Washington consensus became the template for economic and political deregulation in nation-states throughout the world, as though it would equally benefit all countries – from the richest state in the core to the poorest nation on the periphery.

Building on the framework of international financial institutions established after World War II to assure currency stability, regulate capital flows, and promote international trade, neo-liberal globalism has become codified, albeit so far in a fairly primitive form, in international economic law in order to establish new modes of transnational regulation to meet the needs of international capital. The primary objective of the new regulatory regimes is to create markets, and in doing this the focus for regulation is on the actions, or regulatory powers, of the state.

The European Community, which had evolved as a continental system of governance dedicated to preserving and promoting its members' traditions of socially responsible capitalism, moved in the 1980s towards a more market-centred, less regulated European Union (EU) to which was added a currency union. A truly continental governance regime was inaugurated for North America in 1994 when the bilateral Canada–United States Free Trade Agreement (CUFTA) was broadened to include Mexico in the North American Free Trade Agreement (NAFTA), which strengthened the rights of corporations operating across national boundaries. A year later almost a decade's worth of tortuous negotiations bore fruit with the creation, from the modest General Agreement on Tariffs and Trade (GATT), of the powerful World Trade Organization (WTO). The EU, NAFTA, and the WTO are the leading institutions comprising the *global governance* that, in turn, constitutes the political face of economic globalization and its ideology, neo-liberal globalism.

Global governance and the semi-periphery[1]

This book shows how Australia, Canada, Mexico, and Norway are affected by neo-liberal globalism and its counterpart institutions of global governance. Diverse though they are, these four countries share the characteristic of being closely integrated into the global economic order in a largely subordinate but partly autonomous position. While considerable analytical efforts have been expended to understand the effects of globalism on both the most and the least powerful nations in the world, the medium-sized powers, which are the focus of this book, have not been the subject of extensive scholarly efforts to conceptualize their position in the world order. They have, to be sure, been studied individually, and have often been described as junior partners, middle powers, hinterlands, dependencies, go-between nations, satellites, or staple-based economies – to list some of their monikers. Researchers trying to pinpoint their special status have noted they enjoy less autonomy than countries at the metropolitan centres of the power system, but have more political muscle and have achieved more economic 'development' than the most destitute states. Suspended somewhere between the very strong and the very weak, they act both as objects and as subjects. They have responded – as objects of influence – to international stimuli generated by metropolitan countries. As subjects, they have also exploited for their own benefit economic or political relationships with weaker countries and with their own indigenous people.

The conventional understanding of semi-peripheral states is based on notions developed in analyses of dependency (Wallerstein 1985). While identifying states in the core and periphery was fairly easy – the former being rich and the latter being poor – the distinguishing economic features of each varied considerably. One criterion related them to a range of commodities, with core countries producing industrial goods and peripheral countries exporting primary products. In this optic, semi-peripheral countries were those that had a balance of both types of production (Chase-Dunn 1990). However, this distinction does not capture the changes that have occurred as service industries and, more specifically, high-technology sectors have begun to determine the direction of the world economy. This and the spectacular rise of large transnational corporations made the economic distinctions between resource-based and industrial-based nations less clear-cut, particularly in an age where corporate ability to shift production between nations also shifts the power structures between nations.

The notion of semi-periphery focuses attention not just on the situation of dependency but also on how to overcome it. It affirms that some countries enjoy a certain measure of power that allows them a more autonomous relationship with the core. Dependency theorists tended to concentrate on how forms of subordination and exploitation changed as the world's capitalist economies became more integrated (Arrighi 1985). This approach was crucial for understanding the dynamics of power in an international context (Packenham 1992), although it seemed to condemn poor countries to perpetual poverty without offering them a means (other than revolution) to bring about substantial change.

Semi-periphery is a more dynamic concept because it suggests the possibility of movement – for instance from the periphery to the semi-periphery, as occurred at least with Mexico and with the Asian economies in the last quarter of the twentieth century. Our question in this book is whether such upward movement characterizes the current trajectory of globalization. As Satoshi Ikeda shows in Chapter 14, the overwhelming change in the position of countries throughout the world in the past twenty years, as measured by per capita national income, has been *from* the semi-periphery *to* the periphery. More countries are poor and more countries have less power than ever.

Since the concept of the semi-periphery is not as easily quantifiable as 'core' and 'periphery', it is more helpful to locate the economic and political power of semi-peripheral countries on a continuum. The four countries that are the subject of this book are very different in appearance but they share, in varying degrees, a history of being subjected to the influences of powerful core countries. In response, they developed policies aimed at achieving more political autonomy, a more diversified economy, and a more socially equitable distribution of incomes. However their semi-peripherality is seen – whether in social, cultural, economic, or spatial terms – Australia, Canada, Mexico, and Norway have generated both the consciousness of their subordination and the means of resisting it. In this way they are differentiated from the core, which may lack the consciousness that anything should be different, and the periphery, which may lack the required means to resist what is happening.

The new generation of international institutions – the WTO, EU, and NAFTA – have changed the conditions under which states must govern themselves. Usually these shifts in national power are examined either from the perspective of core countries in the 'North' or from that of the periphery in the 'South'. By studying globalization from the perspective of countries on the semi-periphery, we hope to generate insights on the political economy of governance under the conditions of globalization that cannot be obtained from the existing literature.

One theme is to explain what the new institutional contexts created by globalization mean as conditioning frameworks for countries in the semi-periphery. Arising from this, the second theme explores what opportunities for influence and change are available in the semi-periphery. While neither Australia nor Canada, nor Mexico nor Norway is a major force constructing the world order under globalism, each country is experiencing a process of reconstruction. Since the construction of a global society is just beginning, this process's tensions create a fluid situation that provides these countries with scope for some influence over the centre and some autonomy within their own frontiers. So while our authors focus on what has happened and the constraints imposed on states in the semi-periphery, they also indicate the possibilities for the future as new and different kinds of political spaces are created through global change. Both individually and collectively, our four cases could, with political will, pursue policies unique to their own needs and goals.

The contents

The four countries in this study have very different relations to the centres of power: Canada and Mexico are intimately tied to the United States of America. Norway is both more closely integrated with the EU and maintains considerably more autonomy in its relationship with its centre than do Canada and Mexico. Australia, while nominally more autonomous than the other three, has a precarious relationship with the centre and tends to be marginalized in unique ways.

The book begins with neither markets nor states, but people. In 'Globalization and the Social Question' (Chapter 2), Janine Brodie sets the context for examining national responses to global governance by raising the question of *globality*. Globality is the transnational social space that has been created by the failure of the neo-liberal state to resolve the problems of solidarity and cohesion. The social dislocations that arise from globalization make it imperative for governance to focus on human security. Establishing goals for social well-being must transcend the current fixation on short-term objectives of economic efficiency, capital mobility, and the creation of greater markets.

The next eight chapters provide paired discussions of a number of issues in our four semi-peripheral countries. Given the broad range of issues raised by our problematic, we have not attempted a parallel discussion of exactly the same issue in each country. Rather, each chapter, even when dealing with one country, also examines a specific problem. For instance, Øyvind Østerud (Chapter 3, 'Globalization in Norwegian: Peculiarities at the European Fringe') concentrates on how Norway, as a rich, semi-peripheral country, is affected by globalization and how decision-makers and political factions are responding to its major challenges. The relatively recent debate about globalization in Norway is set in the context of the constraints that globalization has imposed on this country's foreign policy, an issue not analysed elsewhere in the book. Østerud's assessment is that Norway under globalism will be shaped both by its affluence and by the dilemmas and ambiguities that have long been inherent in Norway's relations to the outside world. Ultimately the issue of access to resource rents will determine Norway's future under globalism.

Dag Harald Claes and John Erik Fossum in Chapter 4 ('Norway, the EEA, and Neo-liberal Globalism') examine the deeply intrusive nature of their country's ongoing relationship with the European Union by documenting the functional policy areas where the Scandinavian outrider has been most influenced. While some EU decisions are not legally binding on Norway, they still influence the path Oslo has consistently chosen to follow. Many other regulations made in Brussels automatically take effect in Norway, thus compromising long-practised democratic traditions. The resulting slide towards neo-liberal policies demonstrates the power of the centre even over a wealthy semi-peripheral country like Norway, despite its having governments that were never committed to this ideology.

Mexico is by far the least affluent of our four states (see Ikeda, Chapter 14), but it has much in common with Canada in its close and subordinate relationship with the US. Teresa Gutiérrez-Haces in Chapter 5 ('The Rise and Fall of an "Organized Fantasy": The Negotiation of Status as Periphery and Semi-periphery by Mexico and Latin America') places Mexico's encounter with neo-liberalism and continental free trade in the broader geographical and historical context of the fundamentally different import substitution strategy developed throughout Latin America following World War II. She details the consequences of rejecting an approach which enabled countries in Latin America to pursue autonomous political directions in favour of the neo-liberal policies that accompanied the open, export-dependent economy that was shaped by NAFTA.

Within this framework, Alejandro Alvarez in Chapter 6 ('Mexico: Relocating the State within a New Global Regime') argues that the international projection of Mexico as a successful model of neo-liberal restructuring leading to true democracy is based on deliberate misinterpretations that need clarification. He shows how the 'structural adjustment programmes' initiated in the 1980s became locked in with NAFTA and deepened with the democratic transition. Alvarez analyses the nature and scope of the new democracy but stresses its inability to change the economic model that has been imposed on Mexico. He explains the recurrence of financial crises, addresses the costs paid by Mexicans for 'free trade' and export-oriented industrialization, and concludes with an analysis of the perverse dynamic of a de-statization strategy that is championed by the Mexican state itself.

Australia has a decidedly different relationship with the centre than do the other countries in this volume. Dick Bryan in Chapter 7 ('Australia: Asian Outpost or Big-time Financial Dealer?') shows how the Australian economy's integration within the global economy can be presented through two distinct and contrasting sets of characteristics. One image situates Australia on the edge of Asia, focusing on the volume of trade and industrial composition that results from this. The other optic emphasizes Australia's financial and investment links to Europe and North America. Bryan characterizes Australia as a state in search of its own economy. Unlike the other semi-peripheral countries in this study, which are highly conditioned by governance frameworks established by the centre, Australia's state agenda none-theless facilitates corporate agendas, rather than steering them.

Assuming the path of least resistance to globalization seems to permeate Australia's governance structure. Ray Broomhill in Chapter 8 ('Australia: Neo-liberal Globalism and the Local State') explores how laissez-faire ideology has affected government and society at the sub-national level of the South Australian state. He shows that the most common political response to powerful global economic and political forces restructuring the local level is to adopt neo-liberal policies, which he sees as a temporary 'institutional fix' that will be unable to provide a stable framework for the future.

Although Canada is considerably wealthier than Mexico, it shares with Mexico export-oriented development strategies and a decidedly subordinate relationship with its main trading partner, the US. The economic and public policy decisions of both countries are highly conditioned by the trading agreements between the countries. While ostensibly these international agreements provide a neutral, rules-based system that all must follow, the tremendous disparity between the political and economic power of the US makes these agreements highly asymmetrical in practice. Stephen Clarkson in Chapter 9 ('Global Governance and the Semi-peripheral State: The WTO and NAFTA as Canada's External Constitution') shows how the WTO and NAFTA institutionalize constraints for Canada. He examines the state as 'rule-taker' by showing the way that international trade rules and the decisions made by their dispute settlement processes affect the Canadian state's capacity to exercise regulatory power over its national market. But he also examines Canada's role as 'rule-maker' in its avid participation in international bodies that ultimately establish the rules that constrain its own governments.

In Chapter 10 ('International Forces Driving Electricity Deregulation in the Semi-periphery: The Case of Canada') Marjorie Griffin Cohen examines a specific case of Canadian public policy – the privatization of electricity – to show how regulatory changes in the major power (the US) are a very powerful force for change in Canada. She argues that the relatively small but lucrative export market coupled with US regulatory pressure and NAFTA's rules provide the impetus for shifting from a public system of electricity production that served the country well to an unstable regime of deregulation.

The next section of the book, 'Dealing with the Centre', presents three chapters that explore how the semi-periphery deals with the core. Paul Bowles in Chapter 11 ('Money on the (Continental)

Margins: Dollarization Pressures in Canada and Mexico') assesses how Canada and Mexico confront the pressure coming from certain business sectors to enter into a currency union with the United States. Increasing trade with the US and the low value of the Canadian dollar bolster those who argue that Canada's real income would soar and the large gap between the two countries would shrink. But others in both countries' business sectors see a flexible exchange rate as a useful mechanism for resource-based economies to adjust to the external shocks of commodity markets. Ultimately, Bowles argues, dollarization would further entrench the power of the US in continental decision-making.

David Schneiderman in Chapter 12 ('Taking Investments Too Far: Expropriations in the Semi-periphery') focuses on the extraordinary provisions in NAFTA's Chapter 11, which empowers American corporations to attack as 'expropriation' Canadian or Mexican govern-ment regulations that impinge on their profitability. The ability of foreign corporations to sue states for damages is unique in inter-national trade law and has been a powerful tool constraining the ability of both Canadian and Mexican governments to uphold a wide variety of legitimate environmental protection policies. This chapter shows not only how all levels of government have been challenged but also how they have tried to contest the new power of the corporate sector.

Stephen McBride and John Erik Fossum in Chapter 13 ('The Rule of Rules: International Agreements and the Semi-periphery') compare the European Union and NAFTA as alternative models, the former more progressive, and the latter more regressive, for the economic integration of the semi-periphery. In North America the disempowerment of states in the semi-periphery has been more severe than it has been through the EU. This chapter argues that the EU, while initially launched as an economic-type organization, did not have a neo-liberal agenda and did not propound neo-liberalism as its ideology. While this may change in the future, the EU has the capacity to develop market-correcting features and the power to deal with social issues.

The book focuses on relative state power as the common defining feature of the semi-periphery. But this is not to deny the significance of economic performance itself for determining where countries stand in relationship to each other and in relationship to power. Our last section, 'Comparing Economic Performance', presents a synthesis of the main economic indicators of the four countries. In Chapter 14 ('Zonal Structure and the Trajectories of Canada, Mexico, Australia, and Norway under Neo-liberal Globalization') Satoshi Ikeda places the four countries in the context of all national economies' results over the two decades driven by neo-liberal globalism. With their gross domestic product per capita measured in relationship to the American standard, only Norway improved its position, moving up to status as a central economy because of its vast oil-generated wealth. But measured by the criterion of purchasing power parity, we find that the four economies under review in this book have had trouble holding their own – even Norway. Norway's astonishing prosperity aside, it becomes clear that, by either standard, neo-liberal globalism has not proven to be the panacea that its proponents promised would raise the semi-periphery to new levels of well-being.

In this way, the impersonal data provided by the International Monetary Fund's statisticians support the general theme developed by the previous twelve chapters. Their message says loud and clear that the crusade started in 1979 for the United Kingdom by Margaret Thatcher, brought to Washington in 1980 by Ronald Reagan, universalized in the supraconstitutional legal orders established by the WTO and NAFTA, and championed to a greater or lesser extent by economic and political elites in our four semi-peripheral states, has failed to deliver notable improvements in economic welfare, social cohesion, or political democracy.

But our story does not end with failure. It ends with the need for scholars and for citizens to consider how to construct alternatives to a dogma that, for all its manifest deficiencies, is still deeply entrenched as the paradigm guiding both supranational governance and national governments. All of the authors stress that neo-liberal globalism is still being constructed, with crucial decisions about future institutions and the power of the state still to be made.

Ideationally a social-democratic post-globalist intellectual system would call for a rebalancing of global governance to give at least equal weight to environmental, labour, and human rights as the WTO gives to investment and commercial priorities. While nostalgia for a nationally based Keynesianism is understandable, it is not viable when capital has already freed itself to a considerable extent from national regulatory control. A global regulatory regime is another matter, particularly if it is one that is accompanied by a redistributive policy. Should global elites be pushed by their publics to support enforceable norms that mandate efforts to pull nations up to high standards, then a race to the bottom characterized by social and environmental dumping could be brought to an end by international cooperation. Optimism about the future lies in our individual hands, in our national choices, and in our solidarity across frontiers with those in all countries who are determined to repair the damage wrought for a quarter of a century in the name of unfettered markets.

Note

1. Much of the information for this section is from an unpublished research paper prepared for the globalism project by Karine Peschard, 'Rethinking the Semi-Periphery: Some Conceptual Issues'.

References

Arrighi, G. (ed.) (1985) *Semiperipheral Development: The Politics of Southern Europe in the Twentieth Century*, Beverly Hills: Sage.

Chase-Dunn, C. (1990) 'Resistance to Imperialism: Semiperipheral Actors', *Review*, vol. 13, no. 1: 1–31.

Packenham, R.A. (1992) *The Dependency Movement*, Cambridge, MA: Harvard University Press.

Wallerstein, I. (1985) 'The Relevance of the Concept of Semi-periphery to Southern Europe', in G. Arrighi (ed.) *Semiperipheral Development*, Beverly Hills: Sage: 31–9.

2

Globalization and the Social Question

Janine Brodie

In January 1998, Joseph Stiglitz, then Senior Vice President and Chief Economist of the World Bank, gave a speech in which he roundly condemned the fundamentals of neo-liberal globalism as being misguided, misleading, and antithetical to equitable economic development and human well-being. In language that must have sent a chill through the ranks of neo-classical economists, international capitalists, and the bureaucracies of international financial institutions, Stiglitz methodically dissected the foundational neo-liberal principle that markets are superior to governments in generating development, welfare, and freedom. This claim was misguided, he argued, because markets systematically fail to develop human capital and increase inequalities both within and between countries. The obvious ineffectiveness of the policies of the World Bank and International Monetary Fund (IMF) to achieve human security challenged global decision-makers to exercise some humility, recognize their policy failures, and begin to contemplate the contours of a socially responsible 'post-Washington consensus' (Stiglitz 1998, 2002). Although governmental and non-governmental actors have only begun to explore what such a consensus might involve, the growing popularity of the term signals widespread acknowledgement that the neo-liberal project is rife with contradictions and that defining a new social settlement is the fundamental challenge for governance in the early twenty-first century.

The Chief Economist's speech signalled an apparent crack in the global elite's consensus on economic governance, coincided with a growing and diverse tide of popular resistance to economic globalization, and opened new space for debate about alternative governing strategies that promise to foster social well-being and social cohesion. Most importantly, it gave substance to one of the most glaring paradoxes of our time. Although there has been almost universal consensus for more than two decades among the global policy elite about the economic preconditions for growth and prosperity, these outcomes are more elusive than ever for the vast majority of the world's population (Friedman 2002: 13). Neo-liberal orthodoxy has intensified economic globalization and the generation of wealth but it has not solved the social problems associated with the old economy – for example, un- and under-employment and poverty – and has created new social tensions, such as extreme income polarization, written on a global scale (Emmerji 2001: 56). As a consequence, the politics of globalization are increasingly being fought on the terrains of social policy and, more broadly, human security and well-being (Yeates 2001: 1).

The social question raises a series of basic issues about the parameters and scale of politics in a globalizing era. This chapter addresses four of the critical issues that complicate the development of a new social settlement within the context of intensifying globalization. The first section describes how, in recent years, there has been growing elite anxiety about the societal consequences of neo-liberal globalism, not the least because global inequalities and political instability threaten the continuing viability of this experiment in governance. The second section traces the historical development of the social, as a governing strategy, which enabled modern states to build social solidarity and maintain social control within the context of unstable and inequitable capitalist markets (Perez Baltodano 1999: 20). The third section explains how the social question in a globalizing era revolves around the continued autonomy and capacity of national states to implement strategies of societal protection in the face of diminished sovereignty and the growing power of the institutions of global capitalism. The final section identifies the strong globalization and the race-to-the-bottom theses as metaphors of decline that do not adequately describe either the capacities of the national state or the contradictions of neo-liberal globalism. The contemporary national state has been rolled back in selected policy fields and rolled forward in others, thus eroding familiar political institutions and practices as well as constituting new ones. This experiment in governance, however, has yet to resolve a paradox of its own making – the paradox of the social.

The erosion of a myth

For almost a generation, the proponents of neo-liberalism have maintained that there is no alternative to governance through markets, and that the global triumph of liberalism and capitalism marked the end of the modern struggle between individualism and collectivism (Fukuyama 1989). Neo-liberal globalism is a philosophy of governance, an updated version of the nineteenth-century doctrine of laissez-faire. Although realized through different policy instruments than those employed during the first era of liberalism, neo-liberal globalism seeks to create markets where they did not exist previously and to construct an unfettered global political economy that transcends national boundaries and state regulations and enables the spontaneous flow of capital to every corner of the world.

Neo-liberalism is also a philosophy of minimum government, of 'rolling back' the state, especially with respect to economic regulation and to the provision of social welfare. From its conception, neo-liberal theorists advanced a series of substantive claims, some now woven into conventional wisdom, about the apparent defects of the welfare state and post-war social policies. Among other things, the welfare state was indicted for being wasteful, unproductive, and ineffective as well as for limiting consumer choice and for generating a cross-generational cycle of dependency on the state (Pierson 1998: 45–6). In place of the welfare state, neo-liberals recommended the freeing up of old markets and the creation of new ones, deregulation, privatization, lowering the cost of government, and fostering self-reliance, entrepreneurship, and competition. The resulting economic growth would see jobs and income trickle down to the poor. The rising economic tide, so the metaphor went, would raise all the boats in the harbour, from the luxury liner to the humble rowboat. Neo-liberalism thus prescribed a subtle but fundamental cultural shift that enables the values and rules of the market to reform and transform virtually every sphere of social organization (Dean 1999: 161).

After almost two decades of neo-liberal governance, however, there is an obvious and yawning gap between its promises and its

lived realities, among them an absolute growth of poverty world-
wide, the deterioration of social capital, a growing polarization
between the rich and the poor both within and between countries,
increased human insecurity grounded in economic, social, and political instability, and the rapid destruction of the environment (UNDP
1999). As neo-liberalism appears increasingly unable to contain the
contradictions of its own making, there has been a pronounced shift
in the policy discourses of international financial institutions and
of influential Western think-tanks away from a celebration of the
miracles of the market to increasing concern about an imminent
crisis in national and global governance and about the absence of
effective institutions capable of reversing deteriorating social cohesion on a global scale. The growing consensus among the winners
in the globalization game is that, if these tensions 'are not managed
intelligently and creatively', the very survival of the global neo-liberal
project itself is threatened by a political backlash against free trade,
a resurgence of protectionism, and widespread social and political
disintegration (Rodrik 1997: 2, 6).

Elite anxiety about political stability, social control, and the sustainability of the neo-liberal experiment clearly intensified after the
events of 11 September 2001. In a World Bank study published in
the immediate aftermath of the terrorist attack, senior economist
Branko Milanovic speculated about the future of a world that is
marked by ever-deeper inequalities and ever-closer interconnections.
Opulent Western lifestyles displayed on television and in the movies
raise 'expectations and often breed resentment among the poor', he
warned, and 'resentment breeds terrorism' (CCPA *Monitor* 2002: 7). In
February 2002, the World Economic Forum focused on the themes
of security, vulnerability, poverty, and inequality. The global policy-
makers, international capitalists, and opinion shapers attending the
meeting also attributed terrorism and the growing political tensions
between the North and the South to unprecedented global economic
inequity and to abject poverty in the developing world.

Meeting at the same time, more than fifty thousand, primarily
non-governmental, activists, representing a wide spectrum of policy
sectors and political postures, gathered at the 2002 World Social
Forum to shift strategies from simply protesting globalization to
proposing alternatives to the unsustainable social imprint of neo-liberal governance. The International Forum on Globalization issued a
report proposing a Third Way between what Walden Bello described

as the two 'blueprint disasters in the past fifty years – centralized socialism and corporate capitalism'. Among other things, the Report called for a process of de-globalization, involving the reorientation of local economies toward domestic rather than foreign markets, significant land and income distribution, policies de-emphasizing growth and maximizing equity, and the subordination of markets to social justice (Cooper 2002: 12–13).

Like its predecessor, the welfare state, neo-liberal globalism is an experiment in governance that is neither a necessary governing strategy in a globalizing world nor capable of reproducing itself. Similar to previous experiments with hyper-liberalism, the social question has resurfaced both in the form of popular demands for societal protection against the deleterious effects of unfettered global markets and as a governance strategy aimed at rebuilding political consensus and social cohesion. Nevertheless, the parameters of a new social contract and the path to its realization are far from obvious. As the next section of this chapter explains, the very idea of the social – that is, collective intervention in the private sector in the name of societal protection and social solidarity – is a relatively recent invention of modern governance.

Locating the social

Nicola Yeates argues that, despite the current erosion of the social state, 'there is no reason to believe that the political pendulum could not in future swing in favour of forces emphasizing redistribution and comprehensive public provision' (Yeates 2001: 168). This metaphor of a pendulum of modern governance swinging between the dominance of markets and the necessity of public regulation and provision owes a great deal to the arguments advanced by Karl Polanyi, who contended that modern capitalist societies embodied an ongoing and inherent tension between the principles of economic liberalism and of societal protection (Polanyi 1957: 136). The ascendancy of market logics over a century ago was necessarily followed by a breakdown in the social fabric, the rise of civil society counter-movements, and, ultimately, a movement back to the prioritization of social protection in public policy.

Polanyi stressed that the first great era of laissez-faire was a deliberate act of governance, a historical encounter with a pre-existing field of social problems as well as the embodiment of a particular political rationality and (im)balance of social forces. Collective responses to the negative social impacts of this grand experiment in economic liberalism were neither anticipated nor prescribed. 'While laissez-faire was the product of deliberate state action', Polanyi argued, 'subsequent restrictions on laissez-faire started in a spontaneous way' (Polanyi 1957: 141). A unique political construct, never before encountered in the productive organization of human societies, the idea of a self-regulating market as a governing system was destined to be short-lived. When the market mechanism was the unrivalled principle of governance, societies, especially their cultural institutions and values, imploded (Polanyi 1957: 69). As Polanyi explained: 'Robbed of the protective covering of cultural institutions, human beings would perish from the effects of social exposure, they would die as victims of acute social dislocation through vice, perversion, crime and starvation' (Polanyi 1957: 73).

Following in Polanyi's path, contemporary theorists have explained the emergence of the social and social policies as technologies of liberal governance designed both to reduce the social contingencies of capitalist economies and to secure social order (Perez Baltodano 1999: 21). Religious, philanthropic, and charitable organizations initially engaged with the grim realities of early industrialization, but these interventions were sporadic, uneven, and inadequate in the face of the scope of the social dislocations. Liberal governments were soon required to intervene in the spheres of the market and private relations, redefining such things as pauperism from religious–moral questions to social questions and so problems for liberal governance. During the past century, public power was increasingly deployed in the name of social rights and the solidarity principle of government 'wherever the head of the family or a business [seemed] inadequate ... to the smooth running of society' (Donzelot 1988: 395). The subsequent elaboration of social rights under the rubric of the post-war welfare state reflected both the contradictions of liberal governance and the progressive democratization of liberal polities that prompted tangible accommodations to reduce poverty and social insecurity among the working classes. Social policies were part of the prevailing theories and instruments of governance, whose express purpose was the 'smoothing out' of the jagged social and political edges of modern capitalist development (Donzelot 1988: 169–80).

Grounded in a fundamental contradiction between the rights of citizens and the rights of property, liberal democracies have not collapsed under its weight because historically they have evoked the social as a set of solutions to the problems of modern governance (Dean 1999: 53). The idea of the social, according to Dean, is neither lodged in liberal theory nor antithetical to liberal government. Instead, liberal social formations have historically given rise to particular discontinuities which come to be identified and acted upon as the social question, social problems, and social issues in order to secure social order and continuity. 'The social does not arise from the implementation of a theoretical model of society', Dean writes; 'rather, it is the condition of such a model' (Dean 1999: 54). The social field of liberal democracies expanded during the past century as ever more solutions were offered for an ever-wider range of problems thrown up by industrial capitalism and by modern social formations.

This discussion highlights two dimensions of the social that should inform our thinking about a new social settlement in the contemporary era. First, the social represents a victory neither of the state over the market nor of the public over the private, but, instead, is a governing instrument emerging from a specific historical configuration of states and markets. The development of social policies to ameliorate the worst abuses of capitalism and as a response to democratization has been profoundly inductive and conjunctural, reflecting the dual role of the liberal state to underwrite material production and social cohesion. Second, the consolidation of national sovereignty allowed states largely to contain, within their formal boundaries, the main determinants of their political evolution and to regulate and condition social relations. The social question was a national question: 'the emergence of "a social state" and of social policy resulted from the intersection of national societies, national economies, and national states operating within the legal and territorial boundaries of sovereign national territories' (Perez Baltodano 1999: 28–9; Brodie 2003). The social thus emerged within and has been analysed through the lens of what Beck terms 'methodological nationalism' – a container theory which assumes, theoretically and politically, that the contours of society coincide with the formal boundaries of the national state and that the state controls this space (Beck 2000: 23).

The contours and constraints of governance in the contemporary era of intensifying globalization challenge both of these assumptions. Globalization, it is now widely argued, has prompted epochal shifts in modern social organization, not the least because it has progressively shifted power away from the national state – modernity's pre-eminent political institution and societal organizing principle. Extreme versions of this view represent national states as being reduced to a zombie-like existence, living yet dead (Beck and Beck-Gernsheim 2002: 27), or to 'unnatural, even impossible business units in a global economy' (Ohmae 1995: 5). Others contend that globalization has not erased the state as much as it has driven all states, regardless of their social and political history, institutional configuration, or place in the global economy, to abandon social policies in favour of market-friendly (neo-liberal) governing structures and policies. Ulrich Beck, for example, asserts flatly that 'all the premises of the welfare state ... melt under the withering sun of globalization' (Beck 2000: 1). As the next section explains, the contemporary erosion of the social as well as the ascendancy of neo-liberal globalism as the prevailing logic of governance is linked both to the new institutional regime governing the global economy and to the power and logic of global capital.

The new constitutionalism and the power of global capital

It is widely argued that state sovereignty was one of the first casualties of the ascendancy of neo-liberal globalism in the late decades of the twentieth century. Sovereignty is generally taken to mean that a national state has both the legal authority to act on behalf of its citizens in the international system and the autonomy to realize policy outcomes within its territorial boundaries (Krasner 2000: 126). One of the difficulties in assessing whether globalization has compromised the territoriality and the formal autonomy of the national state is that there is no obvious point from which to measure the alleged decline. As the chapters in this volume repeatedly underline, different national states, both now and historically, have exercised varying levels of autonomy from external actors or of capacity to realize home-grown solutions to social problems. State sovereignty has been regularly compromised in past centuries through conventions, coercion, contracts, and imposition (Krasner 2000: 127–9). Indeed, few states, especially those in the South, have exercised the levels of autonomy and regulatory capacity commonly ascribed to the prototype of the modern sovereign state. Claims to sovereignty have been systematically denied to colonial states, weak states, peripheral states, and, indeed, often to semi-peripheral states. As Clarkson argues in Chapter 9, semi-peripheral states such as Canada are both rule-makers and rule-takers. Semi-peripheries are also significant in terms of their susceptibility to centripetal forces. In the contemporary era, the exercise of sovereignty presents a paradox. Many national states now exercise their external sovereignty – that is, their exclusive right to act as legal entities in international fora – in order to undermine the scope of their internal sovereignty and policy autonomy. Through membership in the World Trade Organization (WTO) or as signatories of regional agreements such as NAFTA, rulers agree to narrow the terrain of state competency by complying with externally derived and binding rules that almost exclusively relate to the (de)regulation of capital within their jurisdictions (Krasner 2000: 127). This denationalization of economic governance is simultaneously outside of the state and yet embedded within national institutions (Sassen 1996: 23).

This sovereignty paradox has been variously described as the 'new constitutionalism' (Gill 1995), 'transconstitutionalism' (Schneiderman, Chapter 12) and 'supraconstitutionalism' (Clarkson, Chapter 9). As these studies demonstrate, the 'new' in the new constitutionalism relates to how control over designated policy fields has been eclipsed by constitution-like agreements which regulate global and regional capitalism, trump the decisions of national democratic bodies, are binding for an indefinite future, are difficult to amend, and define a new set of negative freedoms from democratic interventions for global capital operating in national spaces (Schneiderman 2000). This new constitutionalism also has generated new non-democratic institutions and juridical processes for dispute resolution. For example, participation in the WTO and NAFTA effectively attaches extra institutional tiers (global and regional) onto Canada's national legal order (Clarkson, Chapter 9).

These trade and investment rules thus shield global capital from the levelling impulses of democracy and relieve the national state from orchestrating a popular consensus about the parameters of politics and the conditions under which economic activity is socially acceptable or politically legitimate (Beck 2000: 9). Although these agreements make some provision for a small number of enumerated social policies, the terrain of public regulation and provision is clearly delineated by precise prohibitions against state interventions in the market through the regulation of capitalist enterprises, markets, and workplaces, through public ownership and the provision of public goods and infrastructure, and through a partial redistribution of income, opportunity, and security. As important, these agreements have the effect of inhibiting developing countries from constructing a collective social infrastructure. Indeed, the conditions imposed on these countries by international financial institutions in order to receive aid often demand decreased social expenditures and the privatization of public services.

If national states themselves authored this shift in governing practices (McBride 2001: 16), then, at least in theory, states retain the ultimate power to abrogate binding trade agreements and the autonomy to pursue national development strategies. States can choose not to participate, but the costs of withdrawing from or being excluded by these agreements are prohibitive. But perhaps a more relevant question is: where would dissenting states withdraw to? The global economy and national economies do not exist in opposition to one another as distinct social spaces. Many elements of the national and the local are now saturated with the global, if not constituted by the manner of their (non-)integration into the global political economy. Nostalgic notions about turning back the clock to the ideas of closed spaces, territorial boundaries, and a national template of governance are largely illusory. As Hardt and Negri argue quite bluntly, the decline of the national state is not 'the result of an ideological position that might be reversed as an act of political will'. Rather, economic globalization and the new constitutionalism are 'structural and irreversible', superseding the 'effectiveness of national juridical structures' (Hardt and Negri 2000: 336).

At the same time as the autonomy of the national state is threatened by the new constitutionalism, the race-to-the-bottom thesis proposes that the de facto capacity of states to regulate and redistribute in the name of societal protection is being eroded by the growing power and scope of global capitalism. The convergence of national states around neo-liberal governing practices, in other words, owes as much to domestic institutions reacting to the perceived demands of transnational corporations and international financial institutions as to compliance with the new constitutionalism (Cox 1991; Yeates 2001: 9).

The extraordinary growth of transnational corporations is a defining mark of the contemporary era that has effected a lateral shift in the sites of economic decision-making from national states to corporate boardrooms. In varying degrees, all national states are forced to adapt to corporate accumulation strategies that are formulated to maximize global rather than national outcomes. Transnational corporations may still be headquartered in one country but their operations are increasingly deterritorialized. They can demand subsidies and expensive infrastructure in one country, elect to pay taxes in another, and dump the human and environmental costs of production on yet another jurisdiction. It is this deterritorialized logic of capitalist accumulation rather than the nationality of corporate entities that drives the global economy as well as national public policy-making.

To the extent that the globalization of production and finance accounts for policy convergence around the lowest common denominator with respect to public provision, regulation and redistribution, states find themselves locked into a permanent referendum – being continuously monitored by international financial institutions, transnational corporations, and bond rating agencies as to their desirability as sites for global capital (Pierson 1998: 68). In their turn, states judge themselves according to whether they have got 'the fundamentals right', a metaphor for a host of potentially 'anti-social' policies, including fiscal austerity, balanced budgets, low taxation, privatization, minimum regulation of health, labour, and environmental standards, and, at best, residual social welfare regimes. These and other policy reforms launch all states into a competitive race to the bottom. State capacity to pursue citizenship rights and environmental sustainability is forfeited under the threat of capital mobility or on pain of crippling disinvestments.

The consequences of policy convergence around neo-liberal governing instruments are the erosion of social welfare and other policies promoting human security as well as the social and fiscal dumping that shifts the burden of human security to lower levels of government, to philanthropic and voluntary organizations, and, ultimately, to families and individuals. The degree to which states have engaged in this competitive race to the bottom varies according to their place within the global economy, national histories, institutional, and political power structures, and previous development of social security infrastructures (Yeates 2001: 3, Perez Baltodano 1999: 20). Obviously, the erosion of social welfare policies has been most pronounced in advanced capitalist as opposed to developing countries that have not had the resources to build elaborate social safety nets.

Pressure to engage in tax competition and social dumping is also more pronounced in countries that are highly exposed to global markets and/or are more dependent on foreign direct investment and external capital (Drezner 2001: 58). Finally, the erosion of social welfare regimes has been more pronounced in Anglo-American than continental European liberal democracies that have a longer and stronger tradition and institutionalization of class-based politics (Esping-Anderson 1996).

Metaphors of decline

Both the new constitutionalism and the power of global capital theses point to transformations in the institutions and practices of modern liberal-democratic governance through a shared discourse of rupture, erosion, and dispossession. Globalization is represented as a stark, if not irreversible, break from the past, a divorce from progress, which strips from the national state its defining power – sovereignty – and diminishes its unchallenged capacity to legislate, regulate, and distribute within territorial boundaries. This discourse of decline rests on different metaphors than are generally associated with neo-liberalism's celebration of 'the end of history' (for example, Fukuyama 1989) or predictions of global anarchy (Kaplan 1994), but each of these visions conveys the message that democratic politics and the political realm have been exhausted and superseded by neo-liberal globalism (Gamble 2000: 2).

There is a growing debate, however, about whether metaphors of decline accurately represent the status of most contemporary states or the contradictions of governance in a globalizing era. Clearly there has been some loss of state capacity, but this erosion has occurred unevenly – horizontally – across the traditional domains of liberal-democratic polities. Advanced capitalist states have been 'rolled back' on the terrain of the social, specifically with respect to the battery of post-war social programmes and social citizenship rights that embodied the 'embedded liberal compromise' of the post-World War II years (Ruggie 1997: 1). Public initiatives with respect to social planning, social regulation, income redistribution, and, in some cases, economic nationalism have given way to an almost singular preoccupation with the creation of markets and international competitiveness. In the process, the view of the state as 'protector'

or 'insulator' is rapidly being erased from popular political discourse
and from historical memory (Sbragia 2000).

At the same time, state autonomy and capacity have been 'rolled
forward' in other areas such as policing, surveillance, border and
immigration controls, and, especially, the national implementation
of the requisites of neo-liberal globalism. National states are critical actors in the creation, expansion, and regulation of markets. As
Polanyi emphasized, all markets, even deregulated ones, depend
on the exercise of public authority. What some call a race to the
bottom is for others offensive interventionism where 'states themselves become global competitors by vying to provide within their
respective territories the most attractive economic geography for
corporations' (Reinicke 1998: 8). States that actively participate in the
creation of transnational rule-structures to govern national practices,
often in the face of widespread public protest, are far from being
entities in atrophy. Echoing Polanyi, the implementation of neo-
liberal globalism has required an abundant measure of both state
sovereignty and capacity.

This said, there are few other parallels between the golden era
of laissez-faire at the beginning of the twentieth century and contemporary neo-liberal globalism. It involves more than a shift in
emphasis in governing practices between the principle of societal
protection and the promotion of the markets. Rather, neo-liberal
globalism represents a transformative experiment in the scales of economic and political governance, the disarticulation of policy sectors at
the level of the national and local, the creation of authoritative transnational institutions, and the reconstitution of the public sphere and
of the legitimate terrain of politics. These changes are accompanied
by severe social dislocations, the national and global undermining
of human security, and with calls for a new social settlement. They
also give rise to a series of paradoxes and contradictions that suggest
that the pursuit of a socially buffered global capitalism must occur
outside the timeworn boundaries of the national state.

Paradoxes of the social

Put simply, the first paradox of the social is that the same strategies
deployed to implement the contemporary regime of neo-liberal
globalism also deny national states the capacity to build social co-

hesion and, ultimately, to sustain that regime. The current experiment in global governance limits the capacity of liberal states to react to social and political dislocations by limiting the field of governing instruments that national states can deploy to regulate capital and to lessen its divisive imprints on the social fabric. At the same time as the new economic order has widened the gulf between the rich and the poor, national states are constrained from reverting to proven strategies of societal protection, among them public ownership, interventionist industrial policies, the provision of a family wage, and social security programmes (Bensaid 1998).

In effect, economic and social governance, strongly linked by the welfare state, are detached both horizontally within territorial borders, and vertically from the national, where the capacity to manoeuvre is frozen by constitution-like rule structures, to the global, where these rules are created and adjudicated. This inflexibility applies both to rehabilitation of markets, which never have been self-governing, and to the promotion of social well-being. The erosion of public authority, however, is ultimately counterproductive. Without a public sphere, there can be neither conflict management nor security, and without forums and forms of regulation, both nationally and globally, there is no economy whatsoever (Beck and Beck-Gernsheim 2002: 5).

The second paradox of the social is closely related to the first but is more strongly rooted in the foundational assumptions of neo-liberalism. This paradox states simply that neo-liberal globalism simultaneously minimizes spaces for social intervention and maximizes the need for it. Even the laissez-faire state recognized that the provision of certain goods was incompatible with market principles (police, defence) while other goods and services were deemed so vital to national development that the ever-present possibility of market failure could not be risked (education, power) (Brodie 2002). Neo-liberalism, assuming that corporations and countries can be run in the same way, is antagonistic to the public sector and to the idea of collective responsibility and provision. It seeks to replace the public sphere, for example, through privatization, curtailing public programmes and services in order to create new markets, and downloading risk onto individuals and families. In the extreme, this governing philosophy rejects the very idea of society and thus of the need for societal protection. Instead, the governance of society is devolved to the market and to the progressive transformation of social citizens into self-sustaining individuals (Brodie 1997).

At the same time, certain forms of state intervention and regulation are now vetoed by the new constitutionalism. All of these factors
clearly minimize the space for both the articulation of collective
demands and the implementation of social policies. However, the expansion of deregulated markets, the de-socialization of public goods,
and the commodification of social needs produce deeper inequalities
and insecurities, which, in turn, generate popular demands for more,
not less, state intervention. This is especially the case considering that
prosperity has not trickled down to the poor or to poorer countries
and that the voluntary sector has not filled the gap created by the
erosion of the welfare state (Mishra 1999).

The third social paradox – the deterritorialization of the social
– suggests that while the ideas of society, the social, and social policy
have been framed almost exclusively in relation to national space,
they are increasingly influenced, if not superseded, by the dynamics of
globality (Yeates 2001). Globality refers to the transformative changes
in social organization brought about by the deepening global integration of national economies and societies and represents a unique
and irreversible foundation for a global society with 'shared values,
processes, and structures' (Perlmutter 1991: 898). Globality challenges
the idea that society is a discrete and governable entity contained
within territorial boundaries and suggests that closed national spaces
no longer capture the most relevant factors influencing human security and social cohesion. In a globalizing era, society is constituted
by a complex of forces, identities, hierarchies, and movements that
integrate individual members of national polities in different ways
and, at different scales of governance, into 'overlapping communities
of fate' (Held et al. 1999: 442). Localities are often more directly
linked to distant forces and actors than to the state, whose capacity to
shield national social formations is further diminished by a growing
number of political issues that are largely immune from the policy
interventions of any single state.

Social questions escape national boundaries when their causes
and solutions are not confined to national institutions and structures.
Economic and environmental migration, un- and under-employment,
refugees, geo-economic inequalities, and peoples' health and life
chances are increasingly determined by decisions made in transnational institutions (Yeates 2001: 17–19). International financial
institutions such as the WB and the IMF as well as instruments
of the new constitutionalism such as NAFTA and the WTO not

only dominate economic and social policy but also engage in trans-national redistribution, supranational regulation, and global provision (Deacon et al. 1997). This redistribution has increasingly benefited countries in the North at the expense of those in the South. Thus, while social policies once served to contain tensions generated by capitalism within countries, globality raises the challenge of lessening inequalities both within and between countries.

Conclusion

Eras of dramatic change, almost by definition, are accompanied by equally dramatic social dislocations that aggravate ongoing tensions and inequalities and create new ones. Such eras also demand the invention of new collective interventions and governing formulae in the name of social stability and of societal protection. The dust-bins of history are filled with blueprints of governance that either ignored or failed to respond to growing inequalities and suffocat-ing impoverishment. Contrary to the pronouncements of the most fervent merchants of contemporary neo-liberal globalism, 'there is no alternative' but to respond to the social and political vulgarities wrought by this strategy of governance.

As this chapter describes, the social, understood as a field of col-lective intervention and of governance, was initially introduced as a response to the insecurities and instabilities generated by industrial capitalism and modern social formations. In *The Idea of Poverty* (1984), Gertrude Himmelfarb described how these social problems eventually gave rise to new ways of thinking about society, to concepts such as poverty and unemployment, and, most important, to a change in the 'moral imagination' of government. Writing about the same period, Polanyi argued that space for social thinking came only after naming the pauperism that 'fixed attention on the incomprehensible fact that poverty seemed to go with plenty'. Polanyi observed that this 'was only the first of the baffling paradoxes with which industrial society was to confront modern man' (Polanyi 1957: 85). The contemporary period obviously invites a revival of our moral imagination, one which demands that the goals of governance stretch beyond the short-term calculations of economic efficiency, quarterly profits, and capital mobility to embrace the meaning of human well-being and security in a globalizing era.

This exploration of globalization and the social question has paid scant attention to the important differences among states of the centre, semi-periphery, and periphery, although clearly these locations have direct relevance to the capacity of states to respond to the social needs of national populations. These geopolitical designations of relationships among states in the international political economy also have been complicated by the multiple processes of globalization. They have simultaneously reinforced the dominance of some centres, such as the United States, and constituted new sets of power relations both within and between states. The periphery and the peripheral are increasingly identified not by their relationship with a dominant state or set of states but, instead, by the degree of their marginalization in or exclusion from the global economy. Moreover, to the extent that this economy grows ever more transnational and virtual, the very idea of a geo-political centre loses its coherence.

From this perspective, countries categorized as semi-peripheries increasingly find themselves challenged by a series of ambiguities and contradictions. Semi-peripheries exist both inside and outside the global economy, exploit and are exploited, and mediate, both nationally and internationally, between the few winners and many losers created by the contemporary global economy. Yet perhaps it is precisely this contradictory location that lends itself to a revived moral imagination and to struggles for more socially sustainable alternatives to neo-liberal globalism. As the chorus 'Another World is Possible' rings ever louder in the South, on the streets of our cities, and among non-governmental actors, the moral and political choices of the citizens of the semi-periphery, as well as the alliances they form, will have inordinate weight in determining the social contours of that alternative world.

References

Beck, U. (2000) *What is Globalization?*, trans. Patrick Camiller, Cambridge: Polity Press.

Beck, U. and E. Beck-Gernsheim (2002) *Individualization*, London: Sage.

Bensaid, D. (1998) 'New Centre, Third Way: How Left is Left in Europe?' *Le Monde Diplomatique*, December.

Brodie, J. (1997) 'Meso-Discourses, State Forms and the Gendering of Liberal-Democratic Citizenship', *Citizenship Studies*, vol. 2, no. 1.

Brodie, J. (2002) 'In Search of Community: Globalization and the Canadian Identity', *Review of Constitutional Studies* 7.

Brodie, J. (2003) 'Citizenship and Solidarity: Reflections on the Canadian Way', *Citizenship Studies*.

CCPA (Canadian Centre for Policy Alternatives) (2002) *Monitor*.

Cooper, M. (2002) 'From Protest to Politics: A Report from Porto Alegre', *The Nation*, 11 March.

Cox, R. (1991) 'The Global Economy and Social Choice', in D. Drache and M. Gerler (eds) *The New Era of Global Competition: State Policy and Market Power*, Montreal: McGill-Queens.

Deacon, R., M. Hulse, and P. Stubbs (1997) *Global Social Policy: International Organizations and the Future of Welfare*, London: Sage.

Dean, M. (1999) *Governmentality: Power and Rule in Modern Society*, London: Sage.

Donzelot, J. (1988) 'The Promotion of the Social', *Economy and Society*, vol. 17, no. 3, August.

Drezner, D. (2001) 'Globalization and Policy Convergence', *International Studies Review*, vol. 3, no. 1.

Emmerji, L. (2001) 'World Economic Changes at the Threshold of the Twenty-First Century', in J. Nederveen Pieterse (ed.) *Global Futures: Shaping Globalization*, London: Zed Books.

Esping-Anderson, G. (ed.) (1996) *Welfare States in Transition: National Adaptations in Global Economies*, London: Sage.

Friedman, S. (2002) 'Democracy, Inequality, and the Reconstitution of Politics', in J. Tulchin (ed.) *Democratic Governance and Social Inequality*, Boulder, CO: Lynne Rienner.

Fukuyama, F. (1989) 'The End of History', *The National Interest* 16.

Gamble, A. (2000) *Politics and Fate*, Oxford: Blackwell.

Gill, S. (1995) 'Globalization, Market Civilization, and Disciplinary Neo-liberalism', *Millennium: Journal of International Studies* 24.

Hardt, M. and A. Negri (2000) *Empire*, Cambridge, MA: Harvard University Press.

Held, D., A. McGrew, D. Goldblatt, and J. Perraton (1999) *Global Transformations: Politics, Economics and Culture*, Stanford, CA: Stanford University Press.

Himmelfarb, G. (1984) *The Idea of Poverty: England in an Industrial Age*, New York: Alfred A. Knopf.

Kaplan, R. (1994) 'The Coming of Anarchy', *The Atlantic Monthly*, vol. 273, no. 2.

Krasner, S. (2000) 'Compromising Westphalia', in D. Held and A. McGrew (eds) *The Global Transformation Reader: An Introduction to the Globalization Debate*, Cambridge: Polity Press.

McBride, S. (2001) *Paradigm Shift: Globalization and the Canadian State*, Halifax: Fernwood.

Mishra, R. (1999) *Globalization and the Welfare State*, Toronto: Edward Elgar.

Ohmae, K. (1995) *The End of the Nation State*, London: Collins.

Perez Baltodano, A. (1999) 'Social Policy and Social Order in Transnational Societies', in D. Morales Gomez (ed.) *Transnational Social Policies: The New Development Challenges of Globalization*, London: Earthscan.

Perlmutter, H. (1991) 'On the Rocky Road to the First Global Civilization', *Human Relations*, vol. 44, no. 9.

Pierson, C. (1998) *Beyond the Welfare State: The New Political Economy of Welfare* (2nd edn), University Park, PA: Pennsylvania State University Press.

Polanyi, K. (1957) *The Great Transformation: The Political and Economic Origins of Our Time*, Boston: Beacon Hill Press (originally published in 1944).

Reinicke, W. (1998) *Global Public Policy*, Washington DC: Brookings Institution.

Rodrik, D. (1997) *Has Globalization Gone Too Far?* Washington, DC: Overseas Development Council.

Ruggie, J. (1997) 'Globalization and the Embedded Liberal Compromise: The End of an Era?', Max Planck Institute for the Study of Societies, Cologne.

Sassen, S. (1996) *Losing Control? Sovereignty in an Age of Globalization*, New York: Columbia University Press.

Sbragia, A. (2000) 'Governance, the State, and the Market: What is Going On?' *Governance: An International Journal of Policy and Administration*, vol. 13, no. 2.

Schneiderman, D. (2000) 'Investment Rules and the New Constitutionalism', *Law and Social Inquiry*, vol. 25, no. 3.

Stiglitz, J. (1998) 'More Instruments and Broader Goals: Toward the Post-Washington Consensus', 1998 WIDER Annual Lecture, Helsinki, Finland, 7 January.

Stiglitz, J. (2002) *Globalization and Its Discontents*, New York: W.W. Norton.

UNDP (United Nations Development Program) (1999) *Human Development Report – 1999*, New York: Oxford University Press.

Yeates, N. (2001) *Globalization and Social Policy*, London: Sage.

PART I

Semi-peripheral Countries:
Norway, Mexico, Australia, Canada

3

Globalization in Norwegian: Peculiarities at the European Fringe

Øyvind Østerud

The Norwegian variety of capitalism has moulded the impact of globalization in peculiar ways. The debate about globalization arrived relatively late, and in a muted fashion. This was due to a variety of factors, including national prosperity, a strong public sector with the state as the major capitalist owner, robust public institutions, strong social welfare policies, and a social distribution of the resource rents. Social-democratic governance controlled the open economy with a high import–export component for several decades after World War II. The legacy of the Nordic Model – based on a strong state and labour–capital cooperation – had an impact when economic globalization increased with deregulation of capital flows from the mid-1980s.

During the 1990s, globalization emerged as the Grand Narrative of our time. The full-fledged story said that economies, cultures, and social formations were disconnected from their territorial frameworks, and that the world now was woven together in a network of new kinds of contact, collective agents, dependency relationships, and self-constructions (Castells 1996–98; Held et al. 1999; Beck 2000).

This epochal diagnosis has rather dramatic implications. National and parliamentarian democracy becomes impotent and irrelevant within the new power relations of globalized networks. Representative democracy is tied up with a political system that is narrower than the supranational structures that permeate social life – economically, politically, culturally, and even linguistically. Thus the nation-state and its political institutions recede as remnants from bygone times.

Democracy, traditionally conceived, becomes an illusion that is veiling the new, borderless modernity. Still, the globalization debate has not arrived in such a neat packet. There is a plethora of globalization debates both within and across political boundaries. Globalization – economically and culturally – is an uneven process of development, with winners and losers. The debate about globalization, accordingly, is a reflection of this uneven process as well as a formative element within it. Furthermore, there are, paradoxically, national specifics to the debate; it comes in versions emerging from the national scenes and discursive traditions in various countries. The debate about globalization, then, is not really a global debate, even if some features of the general theme have diffused globally.

The topic here is the specifics of the globalization debate in Norway as it has emerged over the last few years. Some basic characteristics of the debate will be explained against a double backdrop: the peculiarities of Norway's foreign policy debate prior to globalization; and the peculiarities of Norway's structural conditions – economically and politically – in relation to the transforming forces. First, however, some more general features of the debate on globalization will briefly be spelled out.

The coordinates of the globalization debate

'Globalization' is one word for a multifarious phenomenon – from financial transactions to the Internet, and from the power of the transnational firms to the network of personal encounters in multi-cultural societies. Even if we restrict the focus of the debate to economic affairs, which actually triggered the new diagnosis in most countries, there are vastly different ways of perceiving the situation both in the professional literature and in the general discussion.

Roughly, we might organize the terrain of the debate into two major camps. The so-called 'hyperglobalizers' argue, first, that global-ization implies a qualitatively new stage of development; second, that the development is driven by economic and technological factors; third, that neo-liberal modes of governance tend to emerge everywhere; and, fourth, that change is basically exogenous (Held et al. 1999; Tranøy and Østerud 2001).

There are variations between the hyperglobalizers, but their major positions are clear, although hotly contested. Their assertions have been met with empirical critiques from various angles, of which the following four are representative of the different arguments used by the sceptics.

First, it has been argued that the contemporary inter- and transnational market system is not unique in world history. It has, on the contrary, a predecessor in the liberal epoch lasting from the last quarter of the nineteenth century to the outbreak of World War I. International trade and foreign investments (as a percentage of GNP for the economically advanced countries) were equally high in 1913 as in the late 1990s, with a contraction during substantial parts of the twentieth century. Financial transactions now certainly move faster, and inter-firm transactions have an unparalleled scope, but for some major indicators the thesis of globalization as a qualitatively new stage is refuted. Similarly, the national home base is still vital to the competitiveness of most multinational firms (Hirst and Thompson 1996; Dicken 1998).

Second, the idea of a unilateral causal chain from changes in technology to changes in the economy has been contested. It is pointed out that deliberate policy-making was central to the re-emergence of a global financial market, and that legal rules of competition were designed to favour specific interests – national or private or both (Helleiner 1994). The centrality of the political dimension also implies that public policy does not necessarily break down between a state or market approach. They may be complementary institutional forms with state policies as important driving forces in the process of globalization. The evidence for this is that the public sector is now substantially bigger than it was during the liberal epoch pre-1914, with a wider range of methods to protect citizens from international market fluctuations. Often there seems to be a positive correlation between an open economy and a large public sector, with improved ways to compensate uncompetitive groups. This includes robust public institutions, such as legal institutions, a highly developed infrastructure, high levels of education, and extensive research and development, which make for a more efficient and competitive national economy (Evans 1995). The point of this argument is that it is the modes of state governance that may be changing, rather than there being a general obliteration of states (Weiss 1998).

Third, it has been argued that capitalism now comes in different models – a continental European type, an East or Southeast Asian type, a North American type, a Russian type – with various institutionally specific minor versions (Hall and Soskice 2001; Hollingsworth and Boyer 1997; Whitley 1999). Alfred Chandler, for example, made distinctions between the extremes of the competitive managerial capitalism of the United States and the cooperative managerial capitalism of Germany, with the personal capitalism of Britain somewhere between the two (Chandler 1990). Within this context, the Norwegian type has been characterized as 'democratic capitalism', tempered by small-scale enterprises and strong norms of popular legitimation (Sejersted 1993, 2000). The argument is that some of the dynamic features of capitalism are embedded in its non-standardized character, and that divergence may be reproduced in the comparative advantage of specific forms as attractive to different agents of investment. Multinational firms may invest in places that display comparative institutional advantages as they shape their location decisions. Educational standards, political-economic stability, and legal frameworks are among the likely attractions of a specific place. There are thus strong modifications and exceptions to the supposed globalizing trend of neo-liberal convergence.

The fourth main argument is that some of the recent developments in the OECD (Organization for Economic Cooperation and Development) area and elsewhere may be a result of parallel endogenous processes, rather than of exogenous pressure. Governments may be motivated to reduce public expenditure because of a structurally induced fall in productivity (such as a shrinking industrial base), a self-propelled increase in welfare demand, or the pressures of an ageing population. Learning from the mistakes of the 1980s – when the credit markets were liberalized – may also account for some of the convergence that occurred during the 1990s in monetary policies and the emergence of more autonomous central banks. Therefore the thesis of exogenous compulsion may be overstated, even if globalization may have increased some policy constraints.

While these were the major outlines of the different positions about globalism, they took a specifically Norwegian form, as will be seen in the next section.

The latency period

The immediate aftermath of the Cold War, and particularly the years from the referendum on European Union membership in the early 1990s until the consciousness of the implications of globalization in 1997–8, may be called the latency period in the Norwegian globalization debate. These years – with the foreign policy issues that were paramount – should be seen in historical context (Tamnes 1997; Heidar 2001; Riste 2001).

Norwegian foreign policy in the post-World War II era has consistently been a balancing act between internationalism and national self-assertion. In the early 1990s the balancing exercise was illustrated by the Oslo Peace Agreement between Israel and the PLO, on the one hand, and the insistence on limited commercial whaling, on the other. The dual image of Norway at the time was simultaneously the idealistic and harmless small power in engagement for the improvement of the world, and the self-righteous little country in defence of its national interests against world-wide moral indignation.

This balance of a dual image goes back to an earlier phase of Norwegian nation-building, with arctic and sea-faring interests combined with a drive to gain international support after the dissolution of the union with Sweden in 1905. In one lucky strike the nationalist and the internationalist strands coincided, when Norway extended its territorial borders with the Svalbard Treaty after World War I, as the harmlessness of a small country made Norwegian control of the Spitzbergen archipelago appealing as a compromise between contending Great Powers in the Arctic.

The peculiar compromises among the domestic elite were settled in the post-World War II period, first in security policy and later in economic affairs. In security policy the Norwegian consensus solution after 1945 was Nordic defence cooperation with an informal US guarantee, but this solution failed because of Swedish resistance. The North Atlantic Treaty Organization (NATO) was formed as the Cold War intensified after the Czechoslovakian coup in 1948. Norway joined with reluctance amid scepticism both from a fraction of the political centre-right, which feared an infringement on national sovereignty, and also – with outright resistance – from the left wing of the governing Labour Party, which saw NATO membership as a risky cementation of the Cold War. The outcome was an elite compromise on NATO that elevated security policy above partisan politics, although the radical left consistently opposed this position.

The compromise on NATO was designed to satisfy the needs for Western integration from a broad coalition of elites in business, politics, administration, organizational life, and military circles. In order to avoid endangering this policy through political opposition from the traditional centre and the moderate left, a solution was found that allowed NATO membership but included reservations designed to strike a balance between international integration and national shielding. The other side of this balance was a compromise between an American-led 'deterrence' position against the Soviet bloc, on the one hand, and a reassurance of peaceful and non-provocative intentions towards the Soviet Union, on the other. The shielding from the West and reassurance towards the East was worked out through specific reservations, such as a policy of having no military bases on Norwegian soil, no depots for nuclear weapons in times of peace, and no NATO exercises in eastern parts of Norway in the far north, towards the Soviet border.

The compromise on security policy worked quite well during the whole Cold War period, although the radical left gained some strength with the establishment of the anti-NATO Socialist People's Party in 1961. Since the Cold War, NATO as such has been next to non-controversial in Norway, although new discussions have erupted about operations in the Balkans and elsewhere. There are affinities between a posture favouring territorial defence as a paramount priority and a sceptical stance against erosion of sovereignty from globalization.

A compromise on the issue of the European Union was worked out after long and rather bitter strife. European Economic Community membership was first put on the political agenda in the early 1960s. The Labour government of the day decided to apply for membership, but the door was closed before a final decision was made when President de Gaulle excluded Britain, and by implication Denmark and Norway. In 1972, when Britain and Denmark obtained membership, the Norwegian government again chose to join, but the entry was blocked by defeat in a referendum on the issue. The referendum was formally considered advice to the National Assembly, since it was legally outside Norway's constitutional arrangements. But it was politically regarded as decisive because it was imperative for the governing Labour party to avoid a devastating split within its ranks. Through a referendum, the party eased some of the direct pressure on its representatives and made disagreement tolerable.

Still the campaign up to the referendum was a fairly bitter contest. Substantial parts of the elites in politics, the mass media, administration, and business were in favour of membership, while those against consisted of a broad popular coalition from trade unions, farming and fisheries organizations, peripheral regions, radical movements like student, peace, and women's organizations, academic institutions, and those representing cultural life. Labour Party leaders were out of step with substantial parts of their rank and file, while the Socialist People's Party and the agrarian Centre Party mobilized against membership and against the predominantly pro-European Conservative Party. It is probably fair to say that Norwegian elites generally favoured membership, with the notable exception of academic and cultural elites, while broad popular movements and peripheral regions were against it.

This pattern of support and opposition was amazingly stable during the new referendum on European Union (EU) membership in 1994. This stability persisted despite the fact that academic and cultural elites were now more divided on the issue, and the agrarian population had numerically declined. The peripheral regions, rural areas, and the public sector were consistently against membership, and their opposition was helped by the favourable economic position of oil-producing Norway outside the EU. The outcome of the new referendum duplicated the results from twenty-two years earlier, despite the fact that other Nordic countries, Sweden and Finland, this time had opted for membership.

But the remarkable feature of the European issue in Norwegian politics in the last decade of the century was a new political compromise: the treaty of the European Economic Area (EEA). The EEA was conceived by the Labour government in Norway in the early 1990s as an antechamber for European Free Trade Association (EFTA) members queuing for EU membership. After the renewed Norwegian No to the EU, the EEA became a more permanent solution to regulate EU relations for Norway, Iceland, and Liechtenstein. It secured a rather complete economic integration, while preserving some national autonomy in the regime for natural resources, fisheries, farming, and regional policies. Norwegian business accepted this solution, and so did substantial parts of the political spectrum on both sides of the issue. For the dominant party in the minority centre government from late 1997 to early 2000, the Christian People's Party, the compromise was its top priority, even preferable to full membership or a renegotiated trade agreement with the EU. Generally across political boundaries, the compromise was regarded as better than the prospect of consistent and unpredictable strife over Norway's links to Europe.

With both NATO and the EU, Norway has a unique position. In NATO, the country's reservations provide balance by shielding itself from integration with the West and, at the same time, giving reassurances over deterrence in the East. Its relationship with the EU is that of an integrated non-member eager to take part, but without abandoning all those aspects of sovereignty that were the subject of national debate. These political compromises are characteristics of Norwegian foreign policy and they betray the country's peculiarities: the political need to balance internationalism and nationalism – idealist as well as pragmatic participation, on the one hand, and the protection of sovereignty, on the other.

This ideological and political context is far more than a backdrop to the globalization debate from the late 1990s. It has framed the debate of globalization with political lines and mental maps. The privileged position of a robust welfare state rich in natural resources and the persistent prominence of the EU debates have established the framework for considering globalization.

'Globalization' hits Norway

The word 'globalization' (*globalisering* in Norwegian) was rarely used in Norway before 1997–8. A few trendy academics and journalists had picked it up from international sources, but it surfaced only occasionally in the mass media, and did not form part of either political or intellectual controversy. The themes which later were brought together under the domain of globalization – the implications of European integration, of the fall of the Berlin Wall, of deregulating capital export, of transnational mergers and acquisitions, of immigration, of the Internet, and of universal aspirations for human rights – had been parallel issues, with rather disconnected debates. The closest one could get to a common denominator to these themes was the idea of the obsolete nation-state, with post-national intellectuals criticizing the very idea of a national community, and with the contest about EU membership as the most focused issue. In this there was a very strong Norwegian resonance with the supranational wave of 'globalization' as it rolled towards the shores of Norway in the late 1990s.

Pro-EU commentators quickly adapted the new theme to the old cleavages of the EU debate, and argued for an emerging pro and con globalization pattern along the lines of the EU referendum, implying that denationalization – and thus the national issue – was the core of both globalization and Europeanization. The reception of 'globalization' appeared to echo the earlier Norwegian EU debate, with globalists and Europeanists painted in similar colours.

The real breakthrough in the public debate on globalization, however, was initiated with the media shock-wave that was produced by the publication in Norwegian of a German book – *Die Globalisierungsfalle* (*The Global Trap*) (Martin and Schumann 1996). It appeared in March 1998, and marked the beginning of a high profile for 'globalization' in Norwegian politics and the media. A major newspaper, *Aftenposten*, published a long series of articles on the topic throughout most of 1998.

The message of *Die Globalisierungsfalle* was rather incongruous with the subsequent Norwegian debate, and its importance was agenda-setting rather than the message itself. The message was concentrated in the subtitle, 'The Threat against Democracy and Welfare'. The globalization trap presented a sombre prospect: mass unemployment due to work-saving technologies; increasingly unequal welfare distribution even within wealthy countries; extreme vulnerability to global market fluctuations; gains in power for transnational firms at the expense of political institutions; and capital flight, causing a welfare crisis in rich countries. The way to avoid the globalization trap, according to the German authors, was to ensure supranational governance by closer EU integration. In principle, this was a consolation to EU protagonists in Norway, but membership was now beyond the horizon, and the point did not loom large in the Norwegian reception of the message. The message was significant, however, because it confirmed economic scepticism about the blessings of a post-national world, without deterring those inter- and supranationalists who greeted globalization in a positive way for its possibilities for cultural encounters, communication, and enhancing rights across national borders. Two basic questions from this book were translated into Norwegian and played out in a peculiar setting: (1) Is globalization real or a myth? (2) Is it good or bad?

Globalization in Norwegian

To the socialist left, in Norway as elsewhere, globalization was real, and it was basically bad. To the liberalist right, it was real and it was good. The intellectual debate, however – in journals and news-papers – was not wholly consistent with this cleavage. Two aspects complicated the issue. One was the conceived difference between globalization in economic as opposed to cultural terms. The other was the shadow of the EU contest.

Academics tended to be split along the lines of their disciplines. Commentators from social anthropology and the history of ideas greeted globalization for its cultural border crossings, 'global' hybrid-ization, universalization of rights, and trendy modernization. Political scientists and economists were more concerned with nation-states as frameworks for representative democracy and the welfare state, and tended to be more sceptical about the consequences of globalization and the obliteration of borders. Some also argued that the open borders could lead to a backlash of neo-tribalism, renationalization, and political fragmentation, particularly because globalization present-ed a threat to stability, security, and the sense of belonging for broad sections of the unprivileged non-elite (Østerud 1999). Historians and historically oriented social scientists also placed globalization within a long-term context, arguing that some of its aspects had had an earlier heyday before World War I, and that national economies now were far more robust in welfare protection and stability measures than was the case in the liberalist epoch a hundred years earlier (Glimstedt and Lange 1998; Østerud 1999). While nobody disputed the novelty of the Internet or the radicalness of speedy financial transactions, other aspects of the thesis of hyperglobalization seemed exaggerated and were soon branded as myth-making.

In Norway it was particularly easy to see that economic globaliz-ation was not a natural force, but was brought about by politi-cal decision-making that was associated with the deregulation of capital controls. But the country's privileged position (its prosperity and strong public sector) gave support to the collective reassur-ance that it was less vulnerable to the 'globalization trap' than any other industrialized nation. The eschatological images of *Die Globalisierungsfalle*, though instrumental in triggering the Norwegian globalization debate, soon receded into the background, and came back to life only when some business consultant called for a radical, adaptive modernization of Norwegian industry and the entrepreneurial spirit. 'Globalization' was thus referred to as a call to action rather than as an irrevocable fate.

The other side of this coin, also due to Norway's undeniable prosperity, was that Norwegian politicians rarely, if at all, employed globalization for the purpose of blame avoidance, as was the case in many other countries. It was not generally regarded as credible that globalization was putting Norwegian prosperity and welfare in immediate danger. Still, Norway was transformed by forces of globalization: in the economy, with mergers and acquisitions across borders; in information and communications technology; in demographic terms, with increased immigration; and in the political legal field, in terms of loss of sovereignty. Some of these themes were subject to serious debate, while others were not.

Business mergers and acquisitions caused a great deal of uncertainty, particularly among politicians who did not have a clear perspective about the appropriate political position. While they wanted strong Norwegians actors and firms to meet intensified international competition, they were reluctant to increase business concentration because it would compromise domestic competition. It was, as always, difficult to square the circle. The new business debate was consistently foreshadowed by this dilemma each time a major merger or raid was on the agenda. The debate on new technology was primarily a debate about means and conditions for innovation and competitiveness; here the new world as such was taken for granted and above contestation. The radically transforming force of immigration was also shielded from serious public debate, because the hegemonic norms of political correctness trapped worried voices within a morally compromising corner.

Legal sovereignty was another matter. Here the implications of denationalization were increasingly obvious, and had resonance with the debates on the EU (Tranøy and Østerud 2001). Norway is now woven into a wide set of legal obligations which go beyond the interstate system and are regulated by international law. The most notable of these supranational obligations are the EEA agreement and the European human rights regime.

The EEA treaty implies that the parties are obliged to follow EU regulations, laws, and directives in areas that are not explicitly exempted from the treaty, like agriculture and offshore resources. The major EU regulations of economic competition thus also apply to Norway. The crux of the treaty, as far as legislative sovereignty is concerned, is the clause saying that EU regulations have priority over national law in case they conflict. The parties may veto certain decisions that are considered detrimental to their interests, but the political barriers against activating the potential veto are high.

Legal experts have criticized the EEA treaty for transferring nearly as much sovereignty as would have been the case with full EU membership, but without participation in legislative institutions. The Conservatives and the social-democratic leadership take this as an argument for full membership, while the Centre Party argues for terminating the treaty in favour of a renegotiated trade agreement with the EU. The interests of farmers in particular have been weakened, since they are now more commercially exposed.

Norway is exposed to another mode of supranational jurisdiction through the evolving regime of human rights. It is one of the signatories of the European Human Rights Convention, and in May 1999 this convention and two other human rights treaties were integrated by adoption into Norwegian law. The adoption was also referred to in a new clause in the Constitution, and the law itself stated that in case of conflict with other parts of Norwegian legislation – past or future – the Human Rights Law should prevail. The radical implication of this regime is that the supreme judiciary in these matters is not the Norwegian Supreme Court but the European Court of Human Rights. Thus the final, authoritative interpretation of what is Norwegian law resides in a supranational institution.

While there was some reluctance and scepticism within the bureaucracy and the legal profession about this radical transfer of sovereignty, the Norwegian Parliament enacted it without strong reservations. There was no widespread public debate, and the mass media were generally favourable to supranational harmonization in the field of rights. Here, globalization and Europeanization found Norway wide open to this new internationalization because of its double tradition as a legalistic 'small power' and as a champion for human rights.

The new internationalization

Within the terrain of the general globalization debate, there has been a tendency to oversimplify the normative solutions to contested problems. Those arguing for a return to Keynesian credit controls have been marginalized, due to the fact that the initial deregulation was far easier than any attempt at re-regulation. 'Keynesianism in one country' is not widely perceived as a realistic option. However, organized movements arguing for global governance are challenging the neo-liberal hegemony. For example, the Association pour taxation des transactions à l'aide des citoyens (Attac) is now the most well-organized movement in favour of control of financial transactions by taxing them, presumably to the benefit of distribution and social and environmental concerns. Originating in France, from the editors of *Le Monde Diplomatique*, in 1997–8, Attac spread to the Latin world, to Europe and to North America and Asia, focusing on the meetings and gatherings of the institutions of the international economy. It is a broad coalition ranging from socialists, agriculturalists, and trade unionists to mild versions of international social democrats and social liberals. It does, nevertheless, embody a new normative schism in the globalization debate, challenging the neo-liberal hegemony of the post-Cold War years.

In February 2001, there was a new turn to the globalization debate when Attac came to Norway. As in France and elsewhere, editors and journalists from intellectual journals played an active role in preparing the way for the establishment of Attac Norway. Also, as in France and elsewhere, both trade unionists and youth activists played a part. But there were Norwegian peculiarities. Attac was welcomed to Norway by a curious alliance between the Marxist, left socialist, daily publication *Klassekampen* and the intellectual late modernist weekly *Morgenbladet*. Post-national humanitarians joined forces with ecological movements, moderate social democrats, globally concerned conservatives, and the Marxist left. The Foreign Minister (Labour) expressed strong sympathies for the general idea of global governance and the specific idea of the 'Tobin tax' on financial transactions. A former prime minister (Conservative) also expressed clear sympathies for Attac, together with other Conservative notables. The Conservative Party leadership, however, was highly critical, and branded Attac a threat to the universal advantages of liberalized trade.

Attac certainly is an umbrella organization with a wide variety of motivations and concerns. In Norway its objectives seemed to be unusually wide. From the start, probably due to warnings against turning the organization into an anti-EU membership tool, its message emerged as an extremely broad plea for global governance, redistribution, ecological concern, and social stability. It succeeded in giving the various concerns about globalization an alternative to renationalization. It also succeeded in building a bridge across the EU divide in the Norwegian debate, at least in the interim period up to the formal foundation of Attac Norway in June 2001. It was principally the pro-EU faction that wanted the Norwegian branch to be silent on the EU issue. But the price for the broad appeal was a question mark on issues like the extent to which it would come out against free trade, or what constituted the 'plus' in 'Tobin tax plus'.[1] The legacies of the EU contest were heavy, because that cleavage was now something to avoid, despite the bipolar connotations, attachments, and attitudes that remained.

Attac as such went beyond the Norwegian EU debate, because the distant aim was some sort of repoliticization and governance at the global level. Factions from the pro and con EU camps tried to meet here, and they could do so provided the solutions were not too ambitious or specific. Thus the general dilemma of Attac was intensified in the Norwegian context.

State, business, and the politics of oil

The tacit, basic theme behind Norwegian responses to recent globalization is the characteristics of Norwegian capitalism. Norway is a rich country, with abundant natural resources; it has a historical business structure with small-scale enterprises and a tradition for social equalization; and the state is the biggest capitalist owner. The regime for the politics of oil has strengthened the backbone of public finance and of the state as owner and regulator in a leading economic sector. There are certainly pressures against the universal welfare system, but the political coalition behind the welfare services is rather robust, and public finance – with the public petroleum fund as a large back-up – signals no early demise of the welfare state. Economic globalization and intensified transnational competition will affect Norwegian conditions, but with much greater force when the revenues from petroleum resources level out some decades into the twenty-first century.

Norway as an oil producer has struck an uneasy balance between fellow-industrialized and oil-importing Western countries, on the one hand, and the oil-producing cartel OPEC (Organization of

Petroleum Exporting Countries), on the other. It has interests in common with OPEC, but has kept its distance because of other common interests with the oil-importing world. This ambivalence even affects Norwegian attitudes to the monetary union of the EU, since the peculiarities of oil-rich Norway, for instance, would favour a higher interest rate when the EU countries would like to lower the rate, and vice versa.

Norwegian authorities, based on a broad coalition in Parliament, have built up a huge fund from petroleum incomes in order to be able to provide welfare services and pensions in the future, when resources are diminishing. The fund is invested in scattered enterprises abroad, and by an amazing show of political restraint only interest on the investments is available for annual use domestically. These public investments are spread out as shares in a wide variety of businesses to avoid high risk, and by implication the Norwegian state is nowhere a dominant shareholder through these investments. Here, the Norwegian state, as a big capitalist, is a *passive* owner. Partially financed by Norwegian state capital, however, foreign shareholders may buy industrial and financial enterprises in Norway, as they increasingly have done. In this way, the offshore resources of the country itself stimulate globalization of the Norwegian mainland economy. The Norwegian economic-political scope of manoeuvre is becoming even more dependent upon oil revenues.

Economic globalization, then, tugs at the sleeves of the Norwegian business structure. Many firms and financial institutions have recently been fused with transnational companies; corporate managers have obtained salaries and benefits that are a provocation to the norms of equality and the moderation of Norwegian labour; and new IT enterprises have challenged the organized character of working relations and bargaining – that is, the basic prerequisite of the corporatist Nordic model.

The politics of the commons

There are many keys to the character of the Norwegian economy, but one necessary condition is the territorial expansion at sea from the 1960s. By clever legal manoeuvring, there was a domestication of the offshore commons with treaties of international law, whereby seaward countries partitioned the intermediate Atlantic Ocean between them.

Norway had a long tradition of pursuing territorial interests to the west and north, and through this legal manoeuvring gained exclusive access to substantial parts of the North Sea oil and gas. This dependence upon petroleum energy has, however, put constraints on another aspect of Norway's international policies – its ambitions as a vanguard environmentalist. The antinomies of these dual ambitions have been particularly acute in the regulation of CO_2 emissions, where Norwegian producer interests have counted heavily in the internal compromise behind the external environmental stand. It has been easier to keep a high profile in environmental matters that are less intrinsically mixed up with the backbone of the Norwegian economy. The contradictions between the country's environmental aspirations and its position as an oil-producing nation and its desire to maintain sovereignty over its oil resources have become increasingly acute in the oil-consuming environment of Europe. Norway is heavily dependent on the national regime of management of the offshore resources – fish, oil, and gas. But it has also gone a long way towards economic membership in the European Union through the EEA treaty. This has created complications, such as those associated with the fisheries regime, which was a stumbling block in the negotiations for full membership in the EU prior to the referendum in 1994. The EEA treaty also challenged the Norwegian management of oil and gas: the rules that are considered significant for the management of scarce resources by Norwegian authorities are considered restrictions on competition by the European Union. For example, the EU statutes on gas exploitation are structured to benefit consumer countries, a position that pressures Norway to abandon its national prerogatives on natural resources. The distinct trajectory of Norway is therefore under siege by globalizing forces – both in the present and in the future.

The peculiarities of the Norwegians: a summing-up

The globalization debate acquired distinct features in Norway. It was shaped by the dilemmas and ambiguities that were inherent in the country's relations to the outside world, and it was moulded by its structural characteristics and outstanding affluence. Globalization was not really, at least not widely, perceived as a dramatic process that would seriously threaten democratic institutions.

Two aspects had direct implications for the development of the globalization debate. One was the specifics of Norwegian capitalism, with the state as the leading capitalist owner, with the small-scale nature of private enterprises, and with a notable stability in political and economic affairs. These specifics were able to absorb some of the potential shocks of the globalizing trends. The second aspect was the long shadow of the EU contest, and the consistent balance of autonomy and internationalism that was built into the compromise solutions here. When an alternative to both renationalization and neo-liberal globalism was imported — in the shape of non-national, anti-globalist movements — it was mandatory to build bridges across the old schism. That bridge-building effort, however, did not solve the tensions of the movement; rather, it intensified them with a peculiar Norwegian flavour. The negotiated silence — or inclusiveness — on the EU issue in Norway meant that this issue was screaming in its absence because many aspects of the Norwegian globalization debate had EU connotations. At the heart of the debate about globalization are the peculiarities of Norwegian capitalism, social structure, and geopolitical features. The future battle of a globalizing Norway — a battle that is inevitable — will primarily be a struggle about access to and control of the resource rent from energy production and the fisheries.

Notes

Thanks to Ray Broomhill and other participants in the Globalism Project for apt and useful comments to an earlier draft.

1. The 'plus' dealt with radical measure for global redistribution.

References

Beck, U. (2000) *What is Globalisation?* trans. Patrick Camiller, Cambridge: Polity Press.
Castells, M. (1996–98) *The Information Age: Economy, Society and Culture*, vols I–III, Oxford: Blackwell.
Chandler, A.D. (1990) *Scale and Scope*, London: Belknap.
Dicken, P. (1998) *Global Shift*, London: Chapman.
Evans, P. (1995) *Embedded Autonomy*, Princeton: Princeton University Press.
Glimstedt, H. and E. Lange (eds) (1998) *Globalisering – drivkrefter og konsekvenser*, Bergen: Fagbokforlaget.

Hall, P.A. and D. Soskice (eds) (2001) *Varieties of Capitalism*, Oxford: Oxford University Press.

Heidar, K. (2001) *Norway: Elites on Trial*, Boulder, CO: Westview.

Held, D., A. McGrew, D. Goldblatt, and J. Perraton (1999) *Global Transformations: Politics, Economics and Culture*, Cambridge: Polity Press.

Helleiner, E. (1994) *States and the Re-emergence of Global Finance*, Ithaca, NY: Cornell University Press.

Hirst, P. and G. Thompson (1996) *Globalization in Question*, Cambridge: Polity Press.

Hollingsworth, J.R. and R. Boyer (eds) (1997) *Contemporary Capitalism*, Cambridge: Cambridge University Press.

Martin, H.P. and H. Schumann (1996) *Die Globalisierungsfalle*, Hamburg: Rowohlt. In English, *The Global Trap: Globalization and the Assault on Prosperity and Democracy*, trans. Patrick Camiller, London: Zed Books, 1997.

Østerud, Ø. (1999) *Globaliseringen og nasjonalstaten*, Oslo: Gyldendal.

Riste, O. (2001) *Norway's Foreign Relations – A History*, Oslo: Universitetsforlaget.

Sejersted, F. (1993) *Demokratisk kapiotalisme*, Oslo: Universitetsforlaget.

Sejersted, F. (2000) *Norsk idyll?* Oslo: Pax.

Tamnes, R. (1997) *Oljealder 1965–1995; Norsk Utenrikspolitikks Historie*, Vol. 6, Oslo: Universitetsforlaget.

Tranøy, B.S. and Ø. Østerud (eds) (2001) *Mot et globalisert Norge?* Oslo: Gyldendal.

Weiss, L. (1998) *The Myth of the Powerless State*, Cambridge: Polity Press.

Whitley, R. (1999) *Divergent Capitalisms*, Oxford: Oxford University Press.

4

Norway, the EEA, and Neo-liberal Globalism

Dag Harald Claes and John Erik Fossum

The purpose of this chapter is to analyse the contested relationship of Norway as a semi-peripheral power with the European Union (EU) as a core regional bloc. Our analytical challenge derives from the opposing perspectives that can be brought to bear on the problem. On the one hand the EU can be seen as either a promoter of or a bulwark against neo-liberal globalism. For its part, Norway's being party to the agreement on the European Economic Area (EEA) can be presented either as an arrangement that is necessary to retain or as an emasculation of national sovereignty (Andersen 2000).

We first present a historical outline of Norway's foreign economic relations since independence in 1905 in order to answer the question *why* Norway adapted to the EU. We then discuss two mechanisms of adjustment – that is, *how* Norway adapted to the EU's legal obligations and incentives for change – and address its normative, institutional, and policy consequences. Finally, we ask to what extent Norway's adaptation to the EU was consistent with or in opposition to its economy's and society's general pattern of globalization.

Norway and the world around it

Norway is no stranger to complex relations with the outside world. As Østerud has already noted in Chapter 3, its foreign policy has historically striven to strike a balance between internationalism and national self-assertion. Although united under a common king as early as 872, Norway lost its independence in the late Middle Ages, was ruled by Denmark from 1390 to 1814, and was then the possession of the Swedish king until obtaining independence in 1905. The country's national identity drew heavily on peasant folklore and traditions as well as on the European ideas with which Norwegian elites in Copenhagen were enamoured.

In his maiden speech to Parliament in 1905 the first Minister of Foreign Affairs, Jorgen Løvland, reflected on Norway's relationship with the rest of Europe. He distinguished between a commercial strategy of interaction and cooperation and a security policy stance of neutrality, which was maintained up to World War II. The government's foreign policy orientation was altered when it joined NATO in 1949 and became such an active participant in many international organizations that it was widely considered a 'humanitarian giant', despite its mere 4.5 million inhabitants.

The Norwegian economy has long been highly dependent on a limited range of resource exports, most important of which were timber and fish at the beginning of the twentieth century. At the end of the century the overwhelmingly dominant sector was petroleum. Owing to these sectors' dependence on international markets, Norwegian commercial interests have thus always been externally oriented.

In 1960 Norway joined the European Free Trade Association (EFTA), which included the UK, Finland, Sweden, Austria, and Liechtenstein. Oslo's applications to join the European Community in 1962 and 1967 were vetoed by France. After a small majority (53.5 per cent) of the population rejected adhesion by referendum in 1972 and Norway negotiated a trade agreement with the Community to ensure duty-free trade for manufactured goods, 'the European question' receded from its political agenda. Elite interest in Europe revived in the 1980s, when the prospect of the Single European Market triggered negotiations to link the EFTA states with the EU through the European Economic Area agreement (EEA). This implied de facto inclusion in the EU's internal market, although Norway obtained important exemptions in agriculture and fisheries.

Norway entered the EEA prior to submitting its next application for EU membership in 1994. As an intergovernmental agreement between the EU and the three remaining EFTA partners, Iceland, Liechtenstein, and Norway, the EEA became the backbone of Norway's economic relationship with the EU.[1] Taking this relationship well beyond the economic realm, Norway joined the Schengen agreement on police cooperation and border control and performs surveillance on the European perimeter as if it were another EU member state. It has also established close cooperation with the EU on its Common Foreign and Security Policy (CFSP).

Although Norway is an arctic country with a small proportion of arable land, its farmers have been important political actors. The population is unusually decentralized, in part because of the security requirement for maintaining a population in Northern Norway to bolster its border with Russia. The wide dispersal of people also has deep domestic roots.

Norwegian society demonstrates multidimensional cleavages with divisions between centre and periphery, rural and urban, producers and consumers, the secular and the religious, and among classes and linguistic groups (two official Norwegian languages, as well as Saami). Norwegian political culture has sought to deal with these tensions by entrenching consensus formation through institutions such as a multiparty system based on proportional representation.

Reconciling Norway's reliance on the world for exports with the protection of industrial and rural interests has also necessitated political bargaining. For instance, in the 1930s two deals laid the foundation for the Norwegian Labour government's subsequent handling of the country's external economic openness and internal political stability. In 1935 trade unions and employers' organizations signed the first general national agreement, initiating a long and strong tradition of consensual relations in the industrial sector. During the 1990s these consensual relations were exercised under the heading of the 'solidarity alternative', in which the government stimulated the competitiveness of the export sector by keeping the exchange rate in line with European trade partners (i.e. the EU/euro area). In return, the workers moderated their wage claims, contributing to a low inflation rate, while the employers accepted the principle of national regulation and a low degree of competition in the labour market. This trade-off constituted the core of the Norwegian version of what Peter Katzenstein has named 'democratic corporatism' (Katzenstein 1985).

In 1935 the Labour Party also made a budget agreement with agricultural interests in Parliament, which guaranteed subsidies for farmers. The government combined determining farmers' incomes and setting farm prices with strong import restrictions to protect against foreign competition in the food sector; as large exporters in the fishing sector called for free trade in order to expand. Norwegian food policy has thus always displayed a tension between an interest in free trade for fish and protectionism for farm products.

More recently, Norway's development has been profoundly shaped by its accumulating petroleum wealth. To start with, it has no public debt and no trade deficit. The economy was working at or near capacity throughout most of the 1990s, hence it could not absorb its petroleum riches. Recognizing this, a fund was established in 1990 to invest the public revenue from the oil sector abroad. The fund had reached about US$110 billion by the summer of 2003. Given the present oil price, the fund is set to increase substantially in the near future. Hence Norway is in the enviable position of having a great fiscal resource with which to face the future. The question is what such leverage entails in an increasingly globalized world to which the country is tied through a complex and multifaceted web of relations.

Adapting to what? The EU as a political system

Membership in an international organization generally reduces a country's decision-making autonomy. In the case of a tightly integrated entity such as the EU, which claims legal preponderance, the loss of independence extends from a formal to a de facto abdication of sovereignty. Given the EU's unprecedented depth and breadth of integration and its complex links to the outside world, such losses occur beyond its boundaries because its influence extends well outside its formal bounds, causing neighbouring states to gravitate far closer to it than they might want. In this chapter we explore Norway's characteristics as a semi-peripheral country so closely linked to the EU as to make it a halfway member. More specifically, we ask to what extent the EEA agreement imposes an institutional restructuring on its domestic political order and, if so, whether this constitutes a neo-liberal turn in Norwegian foreign and domestic economic policy.

As McBride and Fossum's Chapter 13 shows, the EU was not intended to be a neo-liberal project, although its approach to integration does bear a certain liberalizing imprint. That the process of integration has proceeded furthest within the economic realm is evident in the pillar structure of the Treaty of the European Union, in which the first economic pillar is both the most integrated and the one with the strongest supranational content.

In its present form, the EU is not a neo-liberal juggernaut that imposes itself upon the member states but a complex mixture of principles and governance arrangements (Schmitter 2000), its political system exhibiting a mixture of supranational, transnational, transgovernmental, and intergovernmental features. At present, the EU stands at a crossroads, having completed its economic project and launched a remarkably open debate with regard to its future development, including its possible enlargement to the East and South. Its very weak overall sanctioning ability, its consensus-based system, and its cumbersome decision-making procedures leave each member state considerable room for manoeuvre, subject to the constraints emanating from the legal system and the Common Market. Ironically, these constraints may emit stronger adaptive signals to non-members like Norway, which is less included in those aspects of the EU that may help undo some of the negative effects of the market.

Because Norway's relation to the EU is highly asymmetrical and because the EU is undergoing rapid and dramatic changes, it is not enough to understand the formal arrangement between the two entities. A more enlightening approach comes from examining the relationship as a process of *adaptation* (Sverdrup 2000), whose mechanisms we will now address.

Mechanisms: how Norway adapts

Two sets of adaptive mechanisms, each of which permits cross-sectoral analysis, are rooted in broader explanatory schemes in social science, and tell us about the extent of convergence between the EU and the nation. Each such mode of adaptation relates to a set of behavioural expectations, the first rule-oriented, the second incentive-based. The rule-based mode of *legal obligation* involves processes where national authorities abide by rules and regulations established at the EU level.[2] Norwegian authorities transpose EU directives and regulations into national law not only because of their beneficial effects, but also because of norm compliance; that is, from fear of sanctions or from internalizing the norms. Studies have shown that the EU suffers from a considerable implementation deficit (Olsen

2001; Schmitter 1996). Hence, the process generated by the logic of legal obligation is not sufficient to explain all aspects and cases of domestic adaptation to the EU. We thus also need to understand how the EU alters 'domestic opportunity structures, and hence the distribution of power and resources between domestic actors' (Knill and Lehmkul 1999).

The second mode of adaptation occurs when the EU causes changes in the *incentives* motivating domestic or national actors. Changing incentives influences actors' calculation of interest and can affect both societal agents and state actions. For instance, changed incentives can lead to policy change if the EU sets standards that national authorities consider necessary to provide a competitive business environment.

This sort of regulatory competition can occur without specific threats of exit from business. It is sufficient that governments believe they have to compete with other governments to remain attractive. Societal actors can obtain new incentives through Europeanization, because rules designed for the sake of the internal market can be used as levers against governments in fields which have so far been tightly regulated. One important source of such tensions is to be found at the intersection of social policy – largely the preserve of the nation-state – and competition rules at the core of the internal market. Pensions are a good example because they are at the heart of social policy and are integral to the financial services industry, a key component of the internal market. Let us now track these adaptation mechanisms in the Norwegian case.

Legal obligation: the nature of the formal ties – the EEA agreement

Under the EEA, Norway implemented the regulations pertaining to the free movement of goods, capital, labour, and services, thus providing its enterprises with opportunities equal to those of their EU competitors inside the internal market.

This economic agreement was never intended to allow the EFTA countries to participate in the internal EU decision-making process, although they are permitted to appoint experts to the European Commission's various preparatory committees. Lack of access to the EU's decision-making process underlines the one-sided nature of the relationship. In practice, Norway is obligated to include all relevant internal market regulations into national law, adapting its internal laws and regulations to those of the EU – regardless of political opposition – where the agreement and other binding agreements between Norway and the EU apply. Although the agreement provides EFTA partners with the option to reject EU legislation, Norway has so far never exercised this right of veto.

The case of the alcohol monopoly is a prominent example. The state monopoly for import, distribution, and sales of alcohol had strong political support as an important part of the Norwegian health and social policy. Through the EEA agreement and a few court rulings, however, all parts of the state monopoly were abolished except the retail monopoly (Bræin 1999). Likewise, Norway voiced strong opposition to the legislation liberalizing the gas market, but backed down after threats of legal action by the EU Commission. Moreover, when Norway supported the Netherlands in a court case opposing EU legislation regarding the legal protection of biotechnological inventions, this ended in failure.

The EEA agreement does not cover the total EU body of law, but where it applies it does not distinguish between member states and EEA members (with the important proviso that the member states are co-legislators and hence can make the rules). It might be thought that a non-member would be more relaxed in the implementation of EU law, but this is not borne out in practice since the EEA is more important to Oslo than Norway is to the EU. Because the EU can punish Norwegians for non-compliance, and because a single case might have wider implications, Norwegian authorities will do much to avoid a breakdown of the whole agreement. Legally, Norwegian law is presumed to be in conformity with international law in general and subsequently also EEA-relevant EU legislation. This so-called 'presumption principle' also implies that Norwegian courts will tend to interpret Norwegian laws as corresponding to relevant EU legislation.

Under the agreement, EFTA has set up a Brussels-based surveillance agency (ESA) which values its high standing with the Commission rather than with the ministries in the EEA countries (Martens 2001). Although this independent body has to cover Iceland and Liechtenstein, it is Norway that has by far the largest number of cases considered. Compared to the number of compliance cases concerning member states handled by the Commission, the ESA has a far higher staff-to-case ratio, but research has shown that there are no real differences in rule enforcement. In fact, in some periods EFTA countries have had a lower rate of transposition of legal rules than have EU members. However, the ESA has initiated fewer complaints than has the Commission against member countries (Graver and Sverdrup 2002).

A member state might more easily get away with a relaxed attitude to compliance with EU rules than would a non-member, because the latter has to prove itself all the time. As we see from the ESA's behaviour, this may have less to do with rule enforcement as such and more to do with the asymmetrical nature of Norway's relationship to the EU. Moreover, a non-member will have much greater difficulty than will a member state in using informal channels within EU institutions and during decision-making processes in order to increase its leeway.

Adaptation as changed incentives

External forces can influence the interests of political actors both at the state and at the societal level by either shrinking or expanding the scope of their options. The EU triggers actors at the societal level through changing existing policies of the nation-states and providing interest groups with new arguments and resources, which increase their influence on national policies. The EU can also change the balance of power among groups and so replace the key players who dominate the interest-representation or societal-corporate channels. This re-balancing can lead to subsequent changes in national policies.

Norwegian companies or organizations can initiate cases based on EU law against their public authorities. In such situations, EU law is not applied in Norway unless some actors have actually triggered the judicial process. In practice, this particular instance would thus not count as a rule-based adaptation because a domestic actor sets the process in motion. However, this can take place precisely because there is a system of laws in place that has already been injected into the nation-state. But this mode of adaptation is more voluntaristic than the first, in that it is triggered only when some actors find it worth pursuing.

Even without these rules, domestic actors or the Norwegian government might adapt to the EU's norms. EU decisions that the Norwegian government is not legally obliged to follow still influence its actions, as they set a standard that Oslo has consistently chosen to follow. For instance, for Norway to have weaker environmental protection than the EU would undermine its high profile in the international environmental community. Similarly, the Norwegian government decided to follow the EU's competition laws, in order to ensure that Norwegian businesses could compete on the same terms as their European competitors. Here concern with standards interacts with strong business pressure. In regulatory terms, such 'race-to-the-top' or 'race-to-the-bottom' pressures apply identically to members and non-members, as long as the actors whose interests are to be served interact with actors outside each state.

The Schengen agreement also illustrates this incentive mechanism. Norway was under no obligation to enter this agreement, but when Denmark and later Sweden decided to join, the existing Nordic Passport Union was threatened and it became impossible for Norway to preserve the status quo. Whilst theoretically possible, it was impossible in practice to reintroduce passport and full custom border controls between Norway and Sweden. Oslo's interest in retaining the rules regulating its relations with its Nordic neighbours led it to embrace a set of European rules and linked it more tightly to the EU.

The interaction of rules and incentives

Claes and Tranøy (1999) conducted a comparative study of eleven Norwegian policy sectors, identifying variations regarding the mechanisms of adaptation.[3] In two sectors, security and welfare, there was either minimal or non-existent EU law, so it is hard to determine the relative importance of rules and interest-based incentive change. The other two sectors where interest-based incentives prevailed over rules-based change are the two largest export sectors of Norway, energy and fisheries. These sectors are of major macroeconomic importance and contain strong lobby groups. In the EEA negotiations, the possible effects for the Norwegian energy sector were very high on Oslo's agenda. The fisheries sector was not part of the EEA agreement, although this issue traumatized Norwegian membership negotiations, both in the early 1970s and in the early 1990s.

Most of the remaining policy areas were characterized by various combinations of rules-based and interest-based adaptive change. Such combinations point to the way in which rules either create incentives for actors to act in certain ways or might structure the set of possible and perceived options for the actors. All legal texts are open to interpretation, and the spirit in which national governments interpret new texts from Brussels can run from the idealistic to the conspiratorial. This new supranational legal system ties Norway much closer to the EU than previously and than is the case with most other international organizations. This legal integration can take different forms. First, issues that used to be discussed in terms of what is desirable or possible from a political viewpoint, and decided through deliberations and negotiations, are turned into questions of legal compliance and are decided through legal settlements or in courts. Second, there are new procedures for political decision-making. Third, new actors, such as judges and attorneys, become more important in the decision-making process, at the expense of politicians and/or interest group representatives. Finally, political decisions that are still based on actors' interests to a large extent will have to be legitimized by normative arguments. This does not mean an abdication of politics. The law frames the political game and channels policies into new forms and frames, but it is still possible to identify political actors, their interests, and their strategies.

However, since EU integration relies to a large extent on regulation through law, the sheer volume of directives and regulations increases the possibility that the law becomes politicized. National laws have generally enjoyed a high degree of legitimacy, because they are subject to democratic procedures. In Norway, EU laws and regulations are politically contested, because their formation is not subject to these democratic procedures and controls. Further, the precision of laws and regulations varies considerably, so these are very often subject to dispute. For instance, there might be legitimate disagreement about whether a national regulation is in accordance with the EEA agreement. Concerning the internal market, national arrangements will come under attack from the ESA, which asks to what extent their political goals could be achieved by more competition-friendly alternatives. This forces national courts and especially the ESA to evaluate the relationship between political goals and the means adopted to reach them. Norwegian courts have traditionally regarded this means–ends issue as a political issue outside their field of operation. The possibility for individuals, companies, and others to take up cases against national authorities with reference to EU law increases the potential for law(s) to be part of political struggle.

With the EEA agreement, all government efforts to compensate particular groups for losses due to external changes have to be based on the EU's legal order. For small states like Norway, it is not new to assert that international regimes restructure their members' domestic legal orders by setting the rules of the political game, by establishing decision-making and law-making institutions, and by turning the national government into a rule-taker (see Clarkson, Chapter 9). Egeberg (1980) pointed to the international regional level as a 'fourth level of government' causing a multi-level standardization of public policy. The rule-based adaptation to the EU brings this tendency to an unprecedented level, diminishing in particular the ability of the Ministry of Foreign Affairs to coordinate the foreign relations of the other ministries (Claes 2001: 18–21; Trondal and Veggeland 1999).

The consequences of adaptation

The EEA agreement in general and Norway's adaptation to the EU in particular have had important effects on the role of the country's democratic institutions, and the substantive contents of its public policy.

The extent of the EEA agreement and the other arrangements favouring continental integration creates a challenge for the Norwegian government simply to keep track of ongoing policy processes in the EU. The implementation of EEA-relevant EU directives has become a demanding task for all the various ministries and government agencies involved. Norwegian authorities are often placed in the role of adapting to these policies, without their being subjected to domestic democratic procedures. In this regard the Norwegian experience is different in the areas covered by the EEA agreement from that of the EU member states, whose elected representatives (in the Council and in the European Parliament) are directly involved in most stages of the decision-making process.[4]

The oft-cited democratic deficit of the European Union – for instance the weak ability of the representative bodies at the EU and at the member state levels to hold the executives accountable – is exacerbated in Norway's relationship with the EU.

With new directives being constantly created, the EEA's dynamism only serves to heighten concerns about democratic representation and accountability. With no ceiling on the amount of EU legislation to be adopted by Norway, this situation can continue to increase indefinitely and affect an escalating number of issues. If Norway continues to commit itself to EU projects in the same manner as with the EEA, the Schengen agreement and the Common Foreign and Security Policy, this problem will spread. The democratic deficit aside, importing 'pre-packed' policies into the domestic realm can work only as long as the political elite and the most powerful interest groups are satisfied. Nothing guarantees that this will be the case indefinitely. If domestic political conflicts over EEA legislation increase, the whole agreement might be in jeopardy. Another source of uncertainty in Norway's relationship with Europe is the EU's commitment to it in the context of further enlargement to the East and South.

Direction of policy change

Whether adaptation has taken place through rules or incentives, we need to know how substantial are the contents of the changes that have occurred and to what extent they have gone in a neoliberal direction. Claes and Tranøy's (1999) study focused on the convergence of Norwegian policy with that of the EU and EU members states' policies in the same sectors by tracking the amount of substantive change in various policy areas. Seeking to distinguish the question of external pressure and of goodness of fit,[5] whilst also recognizing that adaptation is more than a one-way street, they started out with a wide definition. Norway–EU adaptation refers to Oslo's authorities doing something that they would not otherwise have done. They found few differences between Norwegian and EU policy in the issue areas they studied. In other words, the goodness of fit assumption was confirmed, not their assumption of divergence. They also found some differences across policy sectors regarding the importance of the two mechanisms of Europeanization.

In environmental policy, Norwegian regulations generally mandated a *higher* level of protection than did EU regulations prior to the EEA agreement. After the agreement was signed, the Norwegian level of protection fell *in relative terms* and is today to some extent lagging behind the EU protection level. The EU has thus raised its levels during this period more so than has Norway.

In the realm of foreign and security policy, Norway as a non-EU member has not been part of the transformation from one of territorial defence from invasion to a stress on intervention in non-EU areas. This has caused changes in the threat perception, in the organization of forces, weapons systems, and so on. In these policy areas there is not a good fit in that Norway is far behind the EU.

Of more direct interest to the question of neo-liberal globalism is the way adaptation to the EU has changed Norwegian economic policy, both on the macroeconomic level and in particular industrial sectors. Claes and Tranøy showed that adaptation in various economic sectors has increased liberalization and the use of market instruments in areas where the state previously held a strong regulatory position. The goals behind this change of instrument are the same for Norway as for the EU: increased economic growth through a freer movement of persons, goods, capital, and services. At the macroeconomic level three issue areas can be highlighted:

- *Monetary policy* Since the breakdown of the Bretton Woods system in the early 1970s, Norway, with varying intensity and within different regimes, has shadowed European monetary cooperation. Prior to 2001, the exchange rate of the Norwegian krone was tied to the ECU or the euro. In 2001, Norwegian monetary policy changed from stabilizing the exchange rate against the euro to maintaining low and stable inflation, defined as a 2.5 per cent increase in consumer prices. With the 2001 decision, Norway's ties to the EU here were *weakened*.

- *Fiscal policy* At the same time, fiscal policy guidelines were adjusted to allow for a modest and gradual increase in the use of petroleum revenues, which had come to dominate the Norwegian economy in general, and public budgets in particular. Combined with an unemployment rate of 3 per cent, the challenge for Norwegian fiscal policy had become whether and how to spend this increased revenue from the oil sector without increasing the pressure in the economy – and thus creating inflation.

- *Competitiveness* With the introduction of a common currency and a common monetary policy, the Economic and Monetary Union (EMU) does not resolve this fiscal challenge or change the premises upon which Norwegian monetary policy is based. The single currency will increase price transparency and reduce transaction costs among the participating member states, increasing their competitiveness and thus affecting Norwegian businesses inside the internal market. Most Norwegian export businesses will make expenditures in Norwegian kroner and receive income in euros, and will have to carry the risks of exchange rate changes. On the other hand, Denmark, Sweden, and the UK, which are major Norwegian trade partners, remain outside the EMU.

Claes and Tranøy (1999) also identified substantial changes in several sectors of the Norwegian economy, findings that have been corroborated by other studies. In sectors such as telecommunications, energy, alcohol, food, and transport, there has been a profound change from a high degree of state regulation to an increased use of the market as a key regulatory instrument. Public monopolies have been abandoned, and different forms of regulation of economic activities have been lifted. In sectors characterized by natural monopolies such as telecoms and electricity, new regulatory instruments were introduced to prevent the formation of private monopolies when the public monopolies were dismantled. These changes fit well with the pursuit of economic integration in the EU since the middle of the 1980s. Norway's decision to join the Schengen cooperation agreement also indicates a support for the idea of free movement – an idea that is intrinsic to the internal market process.

Conclusion: towards neo-liberal convergence

The EEA agreement has accelerated for Norway the breakdown of the traditional distinction between foreign and domestic policy. Many political issues which used to be handled by Norwegian authorities are now decided by the EU.

Roughly 70 per cent of Norwegian exports go to the EU and about 67 per cent of Norwegian imports come from it. Norway is thus in trade terms almost as dependent on the EU as Canada is on the USA. Being subject to the same set of laws and regulations is thus important to a very substantial part of the Norwegian economy. From this observation one can see the EEA arrangement as a workable national compromise that grants Norway's businesses (and, to a lesser degree, households) access to the EU market. At the same time it grants the 'No' majority of Norwegians a level of autonomy from Brussels that they would have lost if their country had become a full member. Autonomy to control fish and petroleum resources and to provide the agricultural sector with higher levels of subsidies than those which can be obtained within the Common Agricultural Policy were prime goals of the 'No' movement. In addition, the movement argued that Norway's democracy and welfare state, with its relatively high level of benefits and service, would be endangered by their further integration into the EU.

Supporters of Norwegian membership countered that the Norwegian economy would have responded to full membership by boosting rather than weakening the foundations for public welfare provision. Second, that the EU would have brought about congruence between the scope of expanding markets and the sphere of political authority, thus strengthening democracy through European political integration.

The fact that Norway has applied for membership four times underlines the importance that its political and economic elite, along with a significant portion of the populace, attach to the EU, in particular to the vital need for securing access to the European market. Popular resistance has precluded full membership through winning popular referenda but it has not prevented a tight integration into the Common Market. For all intents and purposes, Norway is a halfway member of the European Union, with secure access for the most vital economic sectors to the large internal market, albeit excluded from most of the EU's decision-making structures. In formal terms, this arrangement abdicates less sovereignty than would full-fledged membership, but in real terms the issue is more complex. Because EU membership is such a highly divisive issue, most parties are content to let it rest and not address the fundamental democratic and constitutional problems that the EEA agreement raises. Whether Norwegian adaptation to the EU would not have happened without Norway's formal ties through the EEA agreement is not entirely clear because other factors heavily influence both the internal market project itself and the liberalization of Norwegian economic sectors.

Globalization is an additional force whose influence is *independent of* and *different from* the EU. As a prominent example of globalization's independent effect, Norway deregulated the electricity market in 1990, *long before* the EU had developed any substantive deregulatory directives for the energy sector. The aim of Oslo's deregulation policy was to reap the societal benefits from integrating local electricity markets into one national market, an integration that was extended when the Norwegian market was joined with the Swedish market in 1996. Integration with the European market followed the adoption of the EU electricity directive in 1998, but even then the process of deregulation in the EU lagged behind the Norwegian.

The Norwegian telecommunications sector was partly liberalized in the first half of the 1980s, without any direct influence from the EU. The general idea behind this liberalization derived from the neo-liberal ideology associated with Thatcherism and Reaganomics prevailing at the time. Until 1994 Norwegian deregulation preceded similar deregulation at the EU level (Skogerbø and Storsul 1999: 200).

In both these cases of deregulation, there were also domestic forces involved, more so in the electricity sector than in the telecommunications one. The telecommunications sector experienced a dramatic technological change that made national borders virtually non-existent and vitiated the natural-monopoly rationale for its structure. The electricity sector remained a natural monopoly and could still be easily divided and controlled through its transmission networks. Thus, in the telecommunications sector the general approach was to abandon regulation, whereas competition in the electricity sector to a larger extent had to be created by public regulation. In both sectors, domestic and foreign private companies pushed for liberalization. But in the electricity sector several private companies were more concerned with protection of acquired rights and concessions than with the potential for increased market shares. The role of more general ideas of liberalization also played a part in both sectors, but more so in telecommunications, where the international trend had developed further. All in all this goes to show how the EU is both intensifying and constraining the forces of globalization. It follows that in some sectors Norway's adaptation will imply increased liberalization, and in other sectors the EU might increase public regulation and control. Such effects are not new for a country with a highly open economy. What is novel in the EEA agreement, however, is the fact that its processes are entirely defined by the EU and are to some extent non-negotiable. Thus the process of adaptation is taking place by the use of law and law enforcement, rather than political bargaining and compromises.

Given its petroleum-based wealth, which gives it more fiscal leverage than other states, why has Norway adapted to the EU and even pursued deregulation further than the EU in some fields? Although Norway has never had a government committed to neo-liberalism as an ideology, it has a general propensity to embrace the market as a problem-solving mechanism. This helps entrench it further, as more heads and hands are prone to pursue it uncritically. Policy-makers – private and public alike – copy and imitate and learn from each other and hence reinforce prevailing patterns and philosophies. This leads to a dearth of alternatives and also reinforces established political power relations. Policy-making is both a political act and an intellectual exercise. Reinvigorating the intellectual search for alternatives must go hand in hand with critical efforts to assess the effects of Norway's rather uncritical embrace of the market within the context of its overwhelming relationship with its European centre.

Notes

1. The EEA agreement was originally between twelve EU members and all the EFTA countries. Since the agreement was signed, Switzerland rejected participation and Finland, Sweden, and Austria joined the EU, leaving Iceland, Liechtenstein, and Norway as the three EFTA partners of the EEA agreement. The relationship between the two sides of the EEA agreement has become very asymmetric.

2. Institutional theory holds that humans will conform to rules when compelled to do so through sanctions (Scott's [1995] regulative school, or rational choice), or when the rules are somehow internalized (Scott's cognitive and normative school, variously sociological and political-historical institutionalism). Institutional theory – writ large – is a theory of action that emphasizes how institutions both condition and constrain human action – through providing meaning, setting constraints, and inducing actions.

3. The sectors were security, justice and home affairs, foreign exchange, social policy, environment, energy, transport, telecommunication, fisheries, food, and alcohol.

4. In formal terms they are not present at the initiative stage as the Commission, a non-elected body, is imbued with the power of initiative. They are, however, of course represented in the committees doing the preparatory work. Whilst the Commissioners are appointed by the member states, so that each member state has at least one commissioner, they are instructed not to take national considerations into account.

5. The essence of the 'goodness of fit' argument is spelled out by Cowles et al.:

'The degree of adaptational pressure ... depends on the "fit" or "misfit" between European institutions and domestic structures. The lower the compatibility (fit) between European institutions, on the one hand, and national institutions, on the other, the higher the adaptational pressures' (Cowles et al. 2001: 7).

References

Andersen, S.S. (2000) 'Utenforlandet i EU' [The Outside Country in the EU], *Nytt Norsk Tidsskrift*, vol. 16, no. 3: 263–75.

Bræin, S. (1999) 'Alkoholpolitikk: rettsliggjøring av norsk alkoholpolitikk' [Alcohol Policy: The Juridification of Norwegian Alcohol Policy], in D.H. Claes and B.S. Tranøy (eds) *Utenfor, Annerledes og Suveren? Norge under EØS-avtalen* [Outside, Different, and Sovereign? Norway under the EEA Agreement], Bergen: Fagbokforlaget.

Claes, D.H. (2001) 'EØS – demokrati eller diplomati?' [EEA – democracy or diplomacy?], ARENA Working Paper no. 10.

Claes, D.H. and B.S. Tranøy (eds) (1999) *Utenfor, Annerledes og Suveren? Norge under EØS-avtalen* [Outside, Different, and Sovereign? Norway under the EEA Agreement], Bergen: Fagbokforlaget.

Cowles, M.G., J. Caporaso and T. Risse (2001) *Transforming Europe: Europeanization and Domestic Change*, Ithaca, NY: Cornell University Press.

Egeberg, Morten (1980) 'The Fourth Level of Government: On the Standarization of Public Policy within International Regions', *Scandinavian Political Studies*, vol. 3, no. 3: 235–48.

Graver, H.P. and U. Sverdrup (2002) 'ESA – mer katolsk enn paven?' [ESA – More Catholic than the Pope?], ARENA Working Paper no. 11.

Katzenstein, P.J. (1985) *Small States in World Markets: Industrial Policy in Europe*, Ithaca, NY: Cornell University Press.

Knill, C. and D. Lehmkuhl (1999) 'How Europe Matters: Different Mechanisms of Europeanization', *European Integration Online Papers (EIoP)*, vol. 3, no. 7, http://eiop.or.at/eiop/eiop1-e.htm.

Martens, M. (2001) 'Europeisering gjennom overvåkning: en studie av ESAs opprettelse og virkemåte' [Europeanization through Surveillance: A Study of the Foundation and Operation of the ESA], ARENA Report no. 2.

Olsen, J.P. (2001) 'Organizing European Institutions of Governance: A Prelude to an Institutional Account of Political Integration', in H. Wallace (ed.), *Interlocking Dimensions of European Integration*, London: Palgrave: 323–53.

Schmitter, P. (1996) 'Imagining the Future of the Euro-Polity with the Help of New Concepts', in G. Marks, F.W. Scharpf, P.C. Schmitter, and W. Streeck (eds) *Governance in the European Union*, London: Sage: 121–50.

Schmitter, P. (2000) *How to Democratize the European Union – and Why Bother?* Oxford: Rowman & Littlefield.

Scott, W.R. (1995) *Institutions and Organizations*, London: Sage.

Skogerbø, E. and T. Storsul (1999) 'Telepolitikk: fra trendsetting til tilpasning' [The Policy of Telecommunications: From Trendsetting to Adaptation], in D.H. Claes and B.S. Tranøy (eds), *Utenfor, Annerledes og Suveren? Norge under*

EØS-avtalen [Outside, Different, and Sovereign? Norway under the EEA Agreement], Bergen: Fagbokforlaget.

Sverdrup, U.I. (1998) 'Norway: An Adaptive Non-Member' in K. Hanf and B. Soetendorp (eds) *Adapting to European Integration: Small States and the European Union*, London: Addison–Wesley Longman.

Sverdrup U. (2000) 'Ambiguity and Adaptation: Europeanization of Administrative Institutions as Loosely Coupled Processes', ARENA Report no. 8.

Trondal, J. and F. Veggeland (1999) 'Norske myndigheter og EØS: Mellom utenrikspolitikk og innerikspolitikk' [Norwegian authorities and EEA – between foreign and domestic politics], *Sosiologi i dag* 3: 57–78.

5

The Rise and Fall of an 'Organized Fantasy': The Negotiation of Status as Periphery and Semi-periphery by Mexico and Latin America

Teresa Gutiérrez-Haces

Latin America is a region where political life has overcome neither deeply entrenched social and economic polarization nor frequent outbreaks of violence arising from profound economic inequality. Owing to its proximity to the United States, Latin America has also been the ideal setting for the unrestrained expression of US interventionism over its periphery.

This chapter does not intend to analyse the events that have caused Latin America's structural polarization, a predicament already widely documented. Rather, its purpose is to examine the important processes that have taken place in Latin America at different times of its historical evolution, which should promote a better understanding of the challenges facing peripheral and semi-peripheral nations under the process of globalization. The central goal of this chapter is to detail the ways in which Latin America in general and Mexico in particular have pursued economic negotiations within an economic space dominated by central nations, specifically the United States.

The essay follows two analytical approaches: the first traces the strategies that Latin America and Mexico formulated during different periods as integral parts of the periphery; the second analyses two different ways in which these peripheral countries have inserted themselves within the world economy. The affirmative, reactive, and confrontational approach is that of the Economic Commission for Latin America (CEPAL: Comisión Económica Para América Latina), while the dependent, proactive approach that serves the interests of the centre is the strategy associated with NAFTA (North American Free Trade Agreement).

As a region traditionally considered peripheral within the world economy, Latin America had created, by the end of the 1940s, a clear strategy of resistance to US and European domination while at the same time it negotiated its own economic and political relationship with the great superpowers and institutions of the post-war period. The synergies that developed between the state, its institutions, and its citizenry, working on a regional economic project, were capable of launching an economic model distinct from the proposals of GATT, the International Money Fund (IMF), and the World Bank.

During the 1950s and throughout the 1960s, Latin America experienced a unique process in which most of its governments, together with a large part of its population and regional institutions, created varied policies and strategies directed toward protecting their economic identity and promoting self-determination as a region. This strategy sought, through diverse forms of expression, to build a model of economic and social development that was unique to Latin America.

The way in which Latin American nations defended and negotiated their economic asymmetry with the central nations – a bargaining stance that lasted from the 1940s to the beginning of the 1970s – showed the ability of government and institutions to negotiate peacefully their right to determine their own course of economic development. The common approach during this period was the firm belief among most governments, institutions, and people that all shared a Latin American as well as a national project that needed to be developed independently of the central nations. The project's proponents aimed, through regional economic integration and cooperation, to build a relationship that would renegotiate and reduce the area's economic dependence on the United States and other economic powers. Conceived principally within the Economic Commission for Latin America (CEPAL), the project was dubbed the 'Organized Fantasy' by Celso Furtado (1988).

However, the emergence during the 1960s of military governments in Latin America showed that this right to economic self-determination had limits and could be squashed by the interests of certain groups directly linked to the centre. At the end of World War II, while everything seemed to indicate that the region could return to the *status quo ante*, the reorganization of the world economy and the creation of international economic regimes, such as GATT, changed the framework under which negotiations took place. Latin America was forced to recast its role within the orbit of the central nations in order to secure the economic and commercial progress it had achieved during the war.

Latin America negotiates its position as a peripheral region

One of the distinctive features of the period after World War II was the way in which the international community began to perceive the economic differences between peripheral and central nations. Starting at the end of the 1940s, the concept of economic development replaced that of wealth, and the term 'poverty', which denoted the economic situation of peripheral nations, was replaced by 'under-development'.

This conceptual shift directly influenced the structures of such international institutions as the United Nations, the World Bank, and the IMF which where created at this time. These organizations took on the problematic of development and under-development as an institutional concern because, for the first time, low economic growth levels and income inequality were seen as obstacles to the establishment of free world trade.

During the Great Depression years (from 1929) Latin American countries were hit hard by the crisis in the centre nations, particularly that of the United States. They reacted with industrialization pro-grammes to substitute domestic production for a significant amount of goods usually imported from central nations. This is a process that became known as import substitution industrialization (ISI). World War II reinforced this tendency, with governments continuing to stimulate an industrialization that applied trade protection as its central principle to foster national industrial growth. The protection-ist strategy paid off. The post-war period brought a reawakening of world trade that had a definite and positive effect on Latin American economies, stimulating their rapid growth. All of these factors influenced the way in which governments began to see their performance in the region. No nation in the region was willing to give up ISI and go back to its original role as supplier of natural resources and raw materials. Neither governments nor the private sector was about to support a free trade project that would obviously nullify the progress made under the ISI. The process of ISI had unleashed a deep transformation in the social structure of the majority of Latin American nations by strengthening their working classes, creating a significant executive sector, and initiating the great urban migrations that changed the character of cities. All these trends consolidated a state that, based on Keynesian principles, became the promoter of economic modernization.

State intervention, particularly strategies of ISI, had been part of the economic ideas promoted by Raúl Prebisch and the Comisión Económica para América Latina of the United Nations beginning in 1948 (Prebisch 1967, 1970). CEPAL both created an explanation and a rationale for ISI mechanisms and openly influenced the governments of the region by encouraging them to build on their industrial development programmes established before the war. It thus resisted the plans that international economic institutions such as the General Agreement on Tariffs and Trade (GATT) had in mind for peripheral nations (Preston 1996: 219).

During the 1960s, CEPAL launched a strategy that combined pressure with persuasion. It aimed to raise the awareness of Latin American governments about the advantages of regional integration, and lobbied developed nations to adopt trade policies that accommodated the disadvantaged position of peripheral nations. The theory known as the 'Prebisch Thesis' stated that the global system was not a homogeneous market, with producers and suppliers that freely established mutually beneficial agreements, but was divided into powerful central economies and relatively weak peripheral economies (Preston 1996: 219).

One of CEPAL's most interesting arguments addressed the role the United States played in relation to the Latin American periphery. Prebisch asserted that one explanation for US hegemony was its relative economic autonomy, which allowed the US not to depend on export markets, as had the United Kingdom in the past. In this analysis, the advantages that the United States enjoyed after World War II would become the foundation for its later hegemony. CEPAL maintained that it was through the breaking down of the old hegemonic centre and its trade rules and the restructuring of the world's means of production that the new centre was able to obtain imports and place its exports in a variety of locations spread across the global periphery. Through this process it would be able to decide which markets and suppliers most favoured its interests at any given time. In this sense, the freedom of action of the centre weakened the position of the periphery in crucial trade relations (Preston 1996: 224).

As a result, Latin America developed a defensive strategy to face the world's geo-economic reorganization. CEPAL stressed structural dependence and inequality and offered as a solution a project of economic integration between Latin American countries, improved economic planning, and, of course, an economic policy based on ISI. This was the beginning of the multiple efforts towards Latin American economic integration, such as the Central American Common Market (1960), the Andean Pact (1969), the Latin American Association of Free Trade (1960), the Latin American Association of Integration (1980), and others. But, before trying to remedy conditions of under-development through regional economic integration, most Latin American governments struggled together to be heard in a very complex international context, in which the rules of the game were established entirely by countries from the centre.

Unlike today, in the post-war period Latin American countries put up a common front in face of the intentions of the more developed countries. For example, in the United Nations Conference on Trade and Employment in Cuba, when part of the proposals agreed to in the Havana Charter (1947–48) dealt with the creation of an International Trade Organization (ITO), Latin American delegates were united in their concern about the role that the United States would play in such an organization, and withheld their participation at that time. A short time later, Latin Americans once more took up their struggle within multilateral forums through the debate on the creation of GATT. Their negotiating perspective reflected their condition as peripheral countries and the flagrant economic asymmetry between them and central countries. While free trade for the central countries meant widening markets, for peripheral countries it was more urgent that their precarious level of development be recognized – and along with it the inherent asymmetry – than that they participate in a multilateral agreement to unify peripheral countries with the centre.

Latin American countries faced a contradictory challenge. On the one hand, they had to sustain an economy based on primary export activities, which obviously meant searching for external markets (usually located in countries of the centre); on the other hand, they had to protect the ISI project, which, to a large extent, required a customs barrier against merchandise coming from central countries. Therefore, during the discussion of the principles and the regulations that would constitute GATT, representatives of the peripheral countries (mainly Latin American) pressed for the legitimation of state intervention in the twentieth century's most important trade agreement (Gutiérrez-Haces 1992).

Beginning in 1950, GATT began seriously to consider the problem of the developing nations, partly because of the manifest distrust on the part of the peripheral countries, which viewed with great scepticism the free-trade proposals of central countries such as the United States and Canada. For this reason GATT modified Article XVIII so that peripheral countries could establish protectionist measures for the benefit of their economic development. From 1964 onwards, the United Nations Conference on Trade and Development (UNCTAD) became the forum of the peripheral countries, and their instrument of action at the international level. In 1965 they used it to pressure GATT member countries to introduce a special section (part IV) on commerce and development in the treaty. This modification to the original text established the philosophical and normative bases for relations between 'contract parties already developed, i.e. the industrialized nations, and contract parties with little development, represented by countries in development' (Malpica 1979: 29–49).

A focus on living standards and progressive economic development in 'developing countries' began to be accepted by industrialized nations of GATT as priority issues in the 1960s. According to Mexican sources at the time, 'contract parties may permit underdeveloped contract parties to apply special measures with the object of promoting commerce and development', and 'do not expect reciprocity for the obligations contracted by them in commercial negotiations to reduce or eliminate customs rights and other obstacles to trade by the underdeveloped contract parties' (Mora Ortis and Alvarez Uriarte 1967).

Another measure taken in the same vein was the creation within GATT in 1968 of the Committee of Trade Negotiations Between Developing Countries. The idea was to promote commerce between developing countries via reciprocal concessions that did not extend to other GATT members, and it insisted that non-GATT members such as Mexico, Brazil, Chile, Peru, Uruguay, and another ten non-Latin American countries take part in the negotiations.

It was a time of great importance for the purposes of this analysis, for it was during this period that Latin American nations developed their identity as peripheral countries and carried to a multitude of international forums their struggle to establish important principles for the negotiation of international trade relations, especially the role of the state as principal actor in the instrumentation of economic policies and its responsibility in the economic development of these countries.

The role of international organizations in the economic control of Latin America

Considering that there have always existed countries and institutions that have wielded a measure of dominance over others in international trade, many countries in Latin America have historically stood out from other disadvantaged regions because they were able to build an alternative economic model. Although this was challenged through various international institutions, like GATT, the IMF, and the World Bank, the responses of Latin American countries indicated both their autonomy and different notions of the ways development should be pursued.

This relative autonomy with regard to international institutions has changed considerably with the new international trade agreements. For example, some of the mechanisms established in NAFTA have allowed the United States to enact rules whose final objective is to discipline Mexico economically and politically. These are rules that affect in dramatic ways the actual governability of the country.

The new international governance mechanisms, like NAFTA, have required the active involvement and support of Latin American governments. This shift from resistance to compliance indicates a decisive change in the thinking of Latin American officials – in particular Mexican officials – whose job is to promote economic closeness through trade liberalization and integration in international forums. They belong to a group that could be referred to as 'like-minded'; that is, people who share the perspective of the dominant governments and who are prepared to act accordingly (Cooper 1997).

Implementing the so-called 'strategy of economic liberalization and export promotion' has, in practice, created a hybridization of both the ISI and the economic liberalization models. This outcome of economic synthesis has resulted in a lack of economic guarantees for Latin America, as the economic crisis in Argentina and Uruguay and the political chaos of Colombia and Venezuela have recently shown. Consequently, economic adjustment processes in Latin America can be viewed as part of a larger project that seeks to facilitate economic integration as led by the United States, which will in all probability be embodied in 2005 in the Free Trade Area of the Americas (FTAA).

However, in counterpoint to government acquiescence in favour of a project clearly leading to continentalization,[1] groups are emerging from civil society that question such a project and demonstrate a considerable capacity for organization. Latin America, in general, and Mexico, in particular, are far from reaching goals of economic growth and equitable income distribution as promised by economic liberalization. There are visible signs that social deterioration is beginning to undermine the political trust between governments and citizens, which will sooner or later have an impact on governability.

Most Latin American governments relied to varying extents on the assumption that if they applied the measures of structural adjustment and opened their economies, internal changes would follow automatically. However, globalization, both as a process and as a concept, is eroding Latin American rights to difference and with it the prerogative to demand correction of existing economic and social asymmetries between peripheral and central nations. Abandoning economic development projects of a nationalist nature in favour of strategies more in line with the interests of international institutions has produced confusion, and Latin American governments must sooner or later face a political and economic dilemma: they must either satisfy the demands of international organizations and powerful nations – whose policies are generally so drastic as to be unpopular and largely unviable – or they must respond to the needs of the populace, at the risk of facing ungovernability if they fail.

Even more worrying, Latin American countries really have few alternatives, since their degree of self-determination in economic policy already has been dramatically reduced by more than two decades of stabilization policies that have placed them in an economic dynamic they can barely control. Refusing to participate in trade or investment agreements such as the proposed FTAA would turn them into genuine international outcasts (Damián 2002).

Mexico and the shift to neo-liberalism

By the beginning of the 1990s, dictatorships and military regimes had all but disappeared from Latin America, with the exception of Mexico, which continued to be governed by the PRI (Institutional Revolutionary Party, *Partido Revolucionario Institucional*), and Cuba, where Fidel Castro continued to prolong his mandate indefinitely. In other Latin American countries, governments chosen by electoral process introduced a new orientation in their economic policies, one clearly inspired by the recipes offered by the IMF.

In the case of Mexico, the elimination of barriers to trade and the indiscriminate application of policies of adjustment were the result of the economic and political crisis that the country had been going through since 1982. The PRI endorsed a series of changes under three consecutive governments, sure that the innovations were far-reaching enough to bring a halt to the political deterioration being suffered both by the party and by the country as a whole.

From 1985 to 1990, the ISI economic model was questioned and finally officially rejected by the same political party that had first introduced it in the 1940s. Two factors helped the change in economic strategy: a prolonged period of economic deceleration and the weight of the external debt. The problems both of these created influenced public opinion, and the government was not criticized too deeply for its metamorphosis from the ISI economic model to one based upon trade liberalization.

Low resistance to liberalization was linked to the conviction that the economic relationship with the United States had been mismanaged and that Mexico's politicians and civil servants were inefficient. It was thought that a closer economic relationship with the United States through a free-trade agreement would heal the troubled economy, and, in passing, would perhaps discipline the civil service and bring an end to corruption.

Mexican nationalism had been sustained through emphasizing Mexico's self-determination vis-à-vis the United States and the sovereignty of an economic project based essentially on the exploitation of natural resources constitutionally belonging to the nation. To generate public support for the North American Free Trade Agreement required rejecting the country's existing ideological and constitutional make-up. Accordingly, the government developed a well-planned and articulated propaganda strategy to discredit the ISI model and win over Mexican society.

Evidently the reforms introduced by the government of Miguel de la Madrid beginning in 1986 – the year when Mexico finally joined GATT – and the proposal to negotiate a free-trade agreement with the United States and Canada put forward by Salinas de Gortari in 1990 represented such a sea change in economic policy that it was necessary to destroy the credibility of the ISI model in order to secure the support of economic groups that had enriched themselves under.

In an act of supreme political finesse, Salinas de Gortari introduced into the government a team of fresh-faced technocrats in order to distance himself from 'nationalist' PRI members who still supported the old economic model. This measure achieved the secondary objective of the reforms, which was to safeguard and prolong the life of the PRI as the party in power.

The plan was that NAFTA's trade opening would bring Mexico more economic growth through a more stable relationship with its principal trading partner, the United States, under more explicitly regulated terms and contracts than had been obtained previously. The radical economic changes required by the new economic model were implemented ahead of any political reform, which was deliberately postponed by PRI governments despite the discontent of a great majority of Mexicans.

Economic liberalization caused some dissatisfaction among certain sectors of the PRI rank and file, who nevertheless felt that the economic reforms would be eventually abandoned, as had already happened to a certain extent in the 1970s, when the government of Luis Echeverría attempted wider commercial diversification and with the administration of López Portillo, who in 1980 had cancelled Mexico's entry into GATT (Gutiérrez-Haces 2002).

To some extent the relative discontent in the bosom of the PRI served to sideline those militants high up in the hierarchy – and also at mid-level, especially those in the area of the economy who were categorized as 'nationalists' and replaced by a new generation of civil servants. These new officials had not necessarily worked in the official party, but were young enough, loyal enough to the monetarist creed, and had enough technocratic upbringing not to be nostalgic for any model of the past. Throughout the governments of Miguel de la Madrid, Carlos Salinas de Gortari, and Ernesto Zedillo, a considerable number of public servants who had previously served in the PRI were now abandoning its ranks. This was partly because they disagreed with the proposed new economic model, but above all because opportunities for political and personal gain had dried up to give room for the new generation of political technocrats. The internal decomposition of the PRI was hastened by the practice of the party's top brass of designating all candidates for public position from the national capital without resorting to internal democratic elections. This practice, known as 'party discipline', resulted in PRI members rebelling against party rule.

During all the years they spent openly attacking the old ISI economic model, the authorities took no initiative to evaluate critically the reigning *political* model – a model which in fact had emerged as an integral part of the ISI model and represented seventy years of electoral fraud, corruption, and party domination.

Governability and the North American Free Trade Agreement

During the negotiation of NAFTA, the Mexican government asserted that the main objective of the agreement was to achieve greater economic growth, employment, and, particularly, improved certainty and clarity in the economic relationship with its main trade partner, the United States.

Mexico's NAFTA negotiators had only three reliable points of reference in designing their own strategy: knowledge gained in the negotiation of Mexico's entrance to GATT in 1980 and 1986 and its participation in the subsequent Uruguay Round (1986–94); the experience accumulated during its participation in other processes of trade integration in Latin America, such as the Latin American Integration Association (ALADI, Asociación Latinoamericana de Integración) in 1980 and the Latin American Free Trade Association (ALALC, Asociación Latinoamericana de Libre Comercio) in 1960; and, last, the lessons that could be gathered from the negotiations and launching of the Free Trade Agreement between Canada and the US in 1988 (Gutiérrez-Haces 1997). (Of course some of these points of reference were of dubious value, since the agreements dated from prior decades when the economic model was protectionist, and Mexico's main partners were other Latin American countries – not the United States.)

Mexican officials gave priority to negotiating the elimination of customs duties and tried to keep their decisions from affecting key sectors of the economy, particularly those which were already liberalized and, to a greater degree, transnationalized. The broad scope of the negotiating agenda, which encompassed almost the entire Mexican economy, blinded the Mexicans to the 'small print' of the agreement, particularly the provisions that, because of their special characteristics, would affect governability not only from an economic standpoint but also from a political one.

During the negotiations, President Salinas de Gortari and his team were subjected to great pressure, especially from the US Congress and to a lesser extent from Canada's Conservative Prime Minister, Brian Mulroney, to show that the election process would be clean and that measures would be put in place to ensure greater democracy in the nation. From 1989 to 1994, the pressure for greater democratization threatened the signing of the agreement. In an effort to improve its image abroad, the government authorized international observers to monitor state and local elections and enabled a dialogue between the Mexican negotiators and those opposed to free trade. These measures improved the political climate, but the indigenous uprising in Chiapas on 1 January 1994 – the day NAFTA came into effect – showed that during the years of negotiations the measures taken in favour of greater democratization had only had a superficial effect. Not only NAFTA (1994) but also the Global Agreement of the European Union and Mexico (1998) were negotiated in an atmosphere that was deeply critical of Mexico's corruption, electoral fraud, and persistent human rights violations.

The climate of doubt about the lack of democracy in Mexico has presented a burden for the present government and its leader, Vicente Fox, who, since coming to power in July 2000, has had to deal with many problems inherited from previous administrations. In his first eighteen months in the presidency, Fox was able to free several persons unjustly imprisoned by the administrations of Salinas de Gortari and Zedillo. Outstanding among them was the case of Montiel and Cabrera, two peasants who opposed the logging activities of Boise Cascade, a US company protected by NAFTA's national treatment clause, whose liberation was due both to internal political pressure and to various international campaigns.[2]

Fox assumed the presidency handcuffed by a series of international economic commitments, foremost among them being NAFTA's, which has complicated his relationship with the legislature and with various local governments affected by NAFTA's regulations. The central problem is that NAFTA's implications have surpassed what was foreseen during its negotiation, so that it has become known as a 'treaty with teeth'. In any other situation, complaints arising from NAFTA would not be cause for much strife, but given the almost absolute dependence of Mexico on the US, any commercial dissent between the two becomes a serious problem. Such was the case of the 20 per cent duty placed on imports of US fruit in early 2002 by the Mexican legislature. Forced by pressure from the United States, which threatened to retaliate with similar measures on Mexican exports, Fox used his presidential authority unilaterally to reverse the measures.

In April 2002, the Mexican House of Representatives brought before the Supreme Court a constitutional complaint against the presidential decree because it felt that Fox had usurped a power reserved for Congress. In July, the Supreme Court declared unconstitutional the presidential decree that suspended for a period of six months the application of a tariff on high-grade fructose. Affirming the legislature's competence to establish the tariff levels, the highest court of the federation declared that the President had acted illegally when, on 5 March 2002, he eliminated the tariff on the sweetener, a US product in most cases. In the wake of the Supreme Court's decision, the US companies Arancia Corns Products and Almidones de México decided to sue the Mexican government under NAFTA's Chapter 11.

The Secretariat of Finance, for its part, anticipated collecting 1.374 billion pesos from the tariff, since high-grade fructose is one of the main raw ingredients used in the refreshment and agro-industrial transnational industries.[3] Mexico consumes 1.8 million tonnes of fructose yearly, of which 60 per cent is acquired by the non-alcoholic beverage industry. The fructose case illustrates the problems of governability in Mexico, since the initial decision of the Mexican legislators was closely linked with the problem of sugar exports to the US, which have been blocked since 1997 by the US quota system.[4] Cane sugar, grown in half of the states of Mexico, represents an important source of employment for more than three million people. In this sense, the tariff imposed by the legislators was aimed at protecting the Mexican cane growers, but President Fox's decree was also an effort to forestall possible US reprisals.

This long controversy, which complicated relations between the United States and Mexico as well as those between the legislative and local powers of each country, demonstrates the long reach of the new trade agreements, particularly when one partner dominates the economy of the other.

In a related case, the US company Metalclad used NAFTA's Chapter 11 to win a suit against Mexico for the closure of a toxic waste dump in the municipality of Guadalcazar in San Luis Potosí state. The local government's action was deemed an 'expropria-tion' and the plaintiff was awarded $15.2 million plus interest. (See Schneiderman, Chapter 12.) Also threatening to harm Mexican governability is the dispute over the distribution quotas of the waters of the Rio Bravo and its tributaries. Supported by a 1944 agreement between the US and Mexico, American farmers are threatening to apply to a NAFTA judicial board.

The application of sanctions generated under Chapter 11 has led the present government to take decisions that will provoke serious conflicts with the governors of certain federal entities as well as with members of the federal legislature. For instance, in 2002 the Secretariat of the Economy made each federal entity responsible for the cost of any legal action lost under the dispute settlement mechanism in NAFTA's Chapter 11. San Luis Potosí state and the municipality of Guadalcazar must therefore now pay the compensa-tion awarded to Metalclad by the NAFTA court.

Since the mid-1990s, panel investigations into anti-dumping duties, the application of countervailing duties, and violations of clauses of National Treatment, Most Favored Nation and the Rules of Origin demonstrate that commercial interactions between Mexico and the US have become complex, aggressive, and even treacherous. Thanks to NAFTA, Mexico has become one of the most frequent users of dispute settlement mechanisms both in NAFTA (Chapters 19 and 20) and in the World Trade Organization (WTO). Chapter 19 of NAFTA continues to have binational panels, even though the agreement is now trilateral. In each case, the adjudicators are nationals from the two countries involved. In most cases, the liti-gants are not the governments but individual businesses (Leycegui and Fernández de Castro 2000). In contrast, at the WTO, only the member states may participate in the dispute resolution. This means that a grieving business must have considerable clout to obtain its government's support. When a case in dispute involves several levels of government – federal, state, municipal – the situation becomes extremely complicated.

So far, the Mexican government has not defended any environmental or social case under NAFTA. This is because the federal and state governments have an explicit objective to attract foreign investment even against the interests of local communities. When COSTCO obtained permission from the local authorities in the city of Cuernavaca, Morelos, to build an enormous commercial complex on land that housed the historical hotel Casino de la Selva, a landmark with valuable mural paintings and several hectares of gardens, the organized protest of citizens and the imprisonment of several activists provoked conflict between federal and local powers and the citizenry. COSTCO may sue under NAFTA's Chapter 11. Environmental and labour disputes within NAFTA's side agreements have been resolved in terms unfavourable to the interests either of workers or of civil society at large.

The Mexican government's main priority in trade conflicts is to protect those businesses committed to the economic liberalization model, as was the case with the legal actions taken by the United States against Cementos de México (Cemex) or the state telephone company (Telmex).

Chapters 11, 14, 19, and 20 of NAFTA[5] have had a great influence on public policy in Mexico, especially those directly related to subnational economic sectors. NAFTA affects the relationship between the federation, the federal states, and the municipalities since both investment and trade concern the jurisdictions of all three levels of government. During the period of NAFTA's negotiation, the federal government excluded local governments from the NAFTA negotiations. A decade after the agreement's implementation it is impossible to centralize decisions affecting Canadian and US investments in Mexico, with the result that local governments can find themselves in conflict with federal policies on foreign investment. In some cases, as with Metalclad, the federal government was in open disagreement with the state government; in other cases, such as COSTCO, all three levels of government sided with the company against their citizenry. Notwithstanding his promises to reinforce the federal pact, President Fox was forced by trade and investment pressures from the United States, and to a lesser degree from Canada, to abandon regionally centred policies.

The culture of submission and alignment with the PRI government was modified by the advent first of the National Action Party (PAN) and then the Democratic Revolution Party (PRD) to municipal and state power. Whether it is in the hands of the PRI or the PAN, however, the federal government has been unable to overcome its highly centralizing tendency or its commitment to US interests.

Furthermore, trade and environmental legislation, which falls directly within federal power, sometimes goes against local legislation. In the last fifteen years, federal entities and municipalities have sustained an unending protest against the unilateral policies of the federation, which, until recently, decided practically everything in the economic and political life of the provinces through a fiscal policy which left little margin for autonomy to local governments. This situation became more critical when the presidency of Salinas de Gortari faced numerous 'declarations of disobedience' within the ranks of the PRI arising from the designation of state government candidates from PRI national headquarters.

NAFTA burdened the states and the municipalities with heavy responsibilities that they could scarcely bear with the scant funds allocated by the federation. The complaints of municipal and state governments focused on showing the burden that trade liberalization imposed on them. This problem was particularly acute in the northern border states (Gutiérrez-Haces and Hiernaux 1995: 233–44).

The administrations of both Salinas de Gortari and Zedillo expected that NAFTA would unleash an economic transformation process from the top, and did not take into account the tensions that would be created by the application of a model of integration insensitive to local considerations. In particular, local authorities on the northern frontier have not received sufficient resources from the federation to take on the burden of actions generated by NAFTA. Financial deprivation has had notable consequences for the quality of life in these areas, as well as for the competitiveness of their cities. Paradoxically, these federative states generate a gross internal product per capita much higher than that of some Latin American countries, such as Argentina, Brazil, Chile, or Peru.

The message sent by the federal government to the states was ambiguous. On the one hand, it encouraged each state to advertise its advantages and to give all types of assistance to direct foreign investments and, needless to say, to the *maquiladora* industry. On the other, it warned that labour and environmental conflicts could arise from NAFTA. As a result, when some foreign companies violated specific labour or environmental regulations, state governments reacted by protecting their citizens, not knowing that, under the legal concept of 'expropriation', companies could sue for infringement of NAFTA-given rights.

Perhaps the worst situation was that the government agency that negotiated and implemented NAFTA never gave the states – never mind the municipalities – the knowledge and tools needed to foresee possible trade conflicts with the companies, which under NAFTA would come to reside on Mexican soil. In an arrogant and thoughtless action, the Secretariat of Commerce and Industrial Support (SECOFI, Secretaría de Comercio and Fomento Industrial) considered that conflicts under NAFTA would be entirely handled by NAFTA itself, perhaps because its officials retained a centralized vision of public policies and did not remember that municipalities are granted autonomy by the Constitution and that states actually have a state congress.

In fact, SECOFI – today named the Secretariat of the Economy – has responsibility for the management of trade negotiations and the resolution of conflicts resulting from them, but this does not eliminate the possibility that local governments may act with sovereignty, as happened in the case against Metalclad in Guadalcazar. Local communities exercising their sovereignty are often in a better position than bureaucrats in the national capital to evaluate the environmental damage which foreign investment may cause.

Large corporations have successfully reinforced the legal mechanisms of international trade in order to protect themselves against any impediments to their plans for investment, production, and commercialization. The judicial provisions are backed by what we could call *global governability*, the coordinated action of those international institutions that control world trade and the economy and that are, in turn, supported by the governments of the nations of the centre. Global governability requires for its proper advancement that networks of subaltern nations be formed, including both peripheral and semi-peripheral countries, which impose domestically the same rules as institutions such as the WTO apply internationally. It seems paradoxical that in spite of the fact that most governments are aware of the detrimental effects that global governability has on their own sovereignty, they continue to negotiate trade agreements which reduce their autonomy.

Final considerations

The everyday use of power in Mexico has become more complicated since the PRI stepped down from the government and economic decisions became subject to an unprecedented degree of international intervention. Ungovernability in Mexico reveals the contradictions inherent in a political project that engendered change in its political, social, and legal structures through vertical economic reforms and electoral processes intended to convince the international community that Mexico is a safe place in which to invest.

Beginning in the 1990s, the Mexican government engineered a political and economic discourse aimed at offering up the nation. The signals it sent abroad announced a clearly permissive environment for those wishing to do business in Mexico. This discourse would have been worthless if it had not been largely backed by a legal framework that required important reforms and constitutional changes. In general terms, we could say that the priorities of the more recent governments in Mexico have been to satisfy a great number of the international business community's requirements.

During the years under NAFTA, central countries have taken advantage of their trade agreements with peripheral and semi-peripheral nations and have wielded what amounts to trade terrorism. These countries, of which Mexico is a good example, have been for decades the central subject of a carefully planned process to condition Latin American economies to play a specific role in the long-term interests of the United States and its transnational corporations. Since 1970 this process of meeting the interests of the centre can be divided into four main stages, with the first being the creation of the Trilateral Commission in 1973. Its purpose was to build and strengthen a partnership between the ruling classes of North America, Western Europe and Japan to safeguard the interests of western capitalism (Sklar 1980). The principles of trilateralism were rapidly adopted in US foreign policy and in turn became the philosophy of dominant business groups.

The second stage of meeting the long-term interests of the centre was initiated when the economic model of ISI stopped being useful to its interests in Latin America. This was when the IMF's programmes of stabilization and structural adjustment became part of the trilateral vision. Several Latin American countries, such as Mexico and Brazil, were classified by the Trilateral Commission as

'International Middle Class Countries' or 'New Influential Countries'. They were considered good candidates for being co-opted by being given an increased role that would split them from the ranks of other Third World countries (Sklar 1980). The US campaign in Latin America was supported by a campaign in favour of human rights and democratization with the slogan 'making the world safe for democracy'.

The third stage was launched at the time when the economies of the peripheral countries applied the measures that would lead to greater economic liberalization. In Mexico this was consolidated in a brutal way through NAFTA.

The fourth stage is the attempt to negotiate a Free Trade Area of the Americas (FTAA), which seeks to harmonize free trade and investment between Latin American, the USA, and Canada. While the centre's objective is to consolidate the gains made through NAFTA, applying them to the other countries in the South is proceeding slowly. The slowness of the process could allow the nations that form the FTAA zone to alter the course demanded by the US. At the very least they could become more familiar with the major flaws of NAFTA and MERCOSUR and negotiate better terms for the future.

The countries of Latin America are greatly affected by the economic framework established by globalization. But this does not mean that they could not build a sustainable response that would create another 'organized fantasy'.

Notes

This chapter was translated by María Vinós and Andrew Blake.

1. *Continentalization* is defined as a gradual process of economic, political, and to a certain extent territorial articulation with the United States, which has been in progress with Canada and, on a secondary plane, with Mexico.

2. Among the others released was General Gallardo, who had been imprisoned for proposing the establishment of a military ombudsman and talking about human rights violations and the death penalty in the army. (The Mexican Constitution outlaws capital punishment.) Also freed was Erika Zamora, a literacy activist in Chiapas who witnessed the massacre at the El Charco community.

3. *El Financiero*, 18 July 2002.

4. NAFTA stipulated that beginning by October 2002, Mexico could freely export its sugar surplus to the United States. It was only in September 2002 that the US agreed to increase the quota for Mexican sugar from 148,000 tonnes in

2001/2 to 300,000 tonnes in 2003 and thereafter allow a yearly, non-cumulative increase of 25 per cent.

5. Chapter 11 addresses foreign investment originating from a NAFTA nation; Chapter 14 deals with financial services; Chapter 19 is concerned with revisions of dispute resolution in dumping matters and compensation rights; and, finally, Chapter 20 addresses the institutional approaches and procedures for dispute resolution.

References

Cooper, A. (1997) *Canadian Foreign Policy: Old Habits and New Directions*, Scarborough, ON: Prentice Hall Canada.

Damián, A. (2002) *Cargando el ajuste: los pobres y el mercado de trabajo en México*, México: El Colegio de México.

Furtado, C. (1988) La Fantasía Organisada, Buenos Aires: EUDEBA.

Gutiérrez-Haces, T. (1992) 'Del GATT al Tratado de Libre Comercio: algunas consideraciones sobre el acuerdo trilateral Canadá–Estados Unidos–México', in B. Driscoll and M. Gambrill (eds) *El Tratado de Libre Comercio: entre el viejo y el nuevo orden*, Mexico: Centro de Investigaciones Sobre Estados Unidos de América, Universidad Nacional Autónoma de México.

Gutiérrez-Haces, T. (1997) 'L'ALENA: À travers de la crise économique de 1995', in H. Favre and M. Lapointe (eds) *Le Mexique de la réforme néoliberale á la contre-révolution*, Paris: L'Harmattan.

Gutiérrez-Haces, T. (2002) *Origen de los procesos de integración económica en México y Canadá: una perspectiva histórica comparada*, Mexico City: Instituto de Investigaciones Económicas, Miguel Ángel Porrúa.

Gutiérrez-Haces, T. and D. Hiernaux (1995) 'Reorganización territorial en el norte de México y pacto federal', Instituto de Investigaciones Económicas, *Problemas del desarrollo latinoamericano*, vol. 26, no. 100: 191–223.

Leycegui, B. and R. Fernández de Castro (2000) *Socios naturales: cinco años del Tratado de Libre Comercio de América del Norte*, Mexico City: ITAM and Miguel Ángel Porrúa.

Malpica, L. (1979) *Qué es el GATT?*, Mexico City: Editorial Grijalbo.

Mora Ortis, G. and M. Alvarez Uriarte (1967) 'México ante el GATT', *El Trimestre Económico*, vol. 34, no. 133: 52–82.

Prebisch, R. (1967) *Hacia una dinámica del desarrollo latinoamericano*, Montevideo: Ediciones de la Banda Oriental.

Prebisch, R. (1970) *Transformación y desarrollo: la gran tarea de América Latina*, Mexico City: Fondo de Cultura Económica.

Preston, W. (1996) *Development Theory: An Introduction*, Oxford: Blackwell.

Sklar H. (1980) *Trilateralism: The Trilateral Commission and Elite Planning for World Management*, Boston: South End Press.

6

Mexico: Relocating the State within a New Global Regime

Alejandro Alvarez

It is amply documented that the rich and complex experience of structural change in Mexico unfolded according to conditions imposed by the International Monetary Fund (IMF) and the World Bank during the 1980s. During the 1990s these conditions were maintained, and the pole star of the change was the North American Free Trade Agreement (NAFTA), which came into effect in 1994. These two pincers must be considered to understand the dynamics of political and economic change in Mexico. It is one of the 'emerging economies' with major global significance on the semiperiphery, but whose success has been deliberately founded on several equivocations.

This chapter will show that the remodelling of the relationship between the state and the market has been a reform rigidly and minutely managed by the state. The government has done this claiming that the previous institutional regulatory systems were obsolete; however, the new reforms put in place have provoked new institutional tensions and economic relapses.

There are two strategic orientations that dominate reform policies: one is to promote the rapid integration of the Mexican economy with that of the United States; the other is to dismantle the historically precarious institutions of the welfare state in order to put into place the famous 'minimal state' peddled by neo-liberal thinkers.

The costs paid by the country run from a mediocre economic growth rate amid recurring financial instability reflected in the various bank bail-outs, through collapses in production and the growing disintegration of the domestic production chains together with the pillage of natural resources such as oil, to the aggravation of economic polarity, social marginalization, and a wide institutional devastation. This institutional deterioration includes a singular crisis in the party system and new challenges posed by emerging political actors such as the indigenous communities.

The first part of this chapter will analyse the international environment of the 1980s and 1990s. The second part will examine the logic of electoral democratization and the main political challenges faced by Fox's regime in sustaining the neo-liberal orientation towards a 'second generation of structural reforms'. The third part will recount the dynamics of the first generation of structural reforms by bringing to light the causes of the recurring financial crises in Mexico. The fourth part will highlight the results of patterns of specialization and the costs paid by Mexicans for free trade and export-oriented industrialization. The chapter concludes with some reflections on the progress of the so-called 'second generation of reforms' in respect of the nature of the political transition.

The international economic environment during the 1980s and 1990s

It may be said that the 1980s were characterized internationally by the outbreak of two grave financial crises: the debt crisis in 1982 and the stock market 'crash' of 1987. These crises gave rise to an international environment of slow growth, scant liquidity, and major inflationary pressures which accompanied the long and complex negotiations involved in the restructuring of various countries' debt payment terms.

One effect emerging from the seriousness of these events, and lasting from the 1980s to the present day, has been the creation of large regional commercial blocs. Additionally, the international economic environment has been subjected to increased competition between the three core economies of Germany, Japan, and the United States of America, which are key players and the main reference points in the world economy.

If we want to characterize international conditions during the 1990s according to the dynamic of relations between the developed core and the under-developed periphery (second of the reference points of the world economy), another relevant issue is the confluence of new factors in the core economies and the semi-peripheral economies alike. These include a major shift in the shape and the direction of global and regional economies due to the exponential growth in the free movement of capital, the centralization of capital resulting from mergers and acquisitions, and an increase in the powers of persuasion of the central economies over the paths for reform in peripheral and semi-peripheral economies through international financial organizations such as the International Monetary Fund and the World Bank.

It should also be recognized that the international economic environment, and, of course, North America's regional environment, have been directly affected by the velocity of an economy that functions as its locomotive, namely the United States. The development and structural change of the international economic environment has been determined in general by monetary-fiscal behaviour, and also by the evolution of productivity and institutional changes in labour–capital relations (Frankel and Roubini 2001).

Among the developed economies, together with a low level of economic growth and tendencies for low inflation and low interest rates, general conditions changed to a 'liquidity abundance' – or of funds available for external use – during the 1990s, due to the appearance both of financial innovations and of new investors. It should be remembered that foreign portfolio investment in Latin America, which hovered in the region of $50 billion in the first half of the 1990s, reached $277 billion in 1997 and was still close to $200 billion two years later (IMF 2000).

On the side of emerging economies like Mexico, the culmination of the first generation of structural reforms permitted high returns to foreign (direct and portfolio) investment, while strict monetary policies kept inflation under control. Both forces resulted in Latin America's economies 'naturally' becoming important receptors of external funds (Vidal 2001b).

However, the hard facts that have contributed to international financial instability up to the present day are the generalization of speculative attacks on any currency seen as weak within the context of the configuration of a bipolar (dollar–euro) international monetary system, and the productive disasters resulting from the enormous oscillations in currency values, and the high fiscal cost of bank bail-outs. Financial instability is accentuated by the conditionality attached by financial organizations to their 'aid' requirements, which means the virtual death of the people's right to try out different strategies of national development, as the most recent Mexican political transition shows.

The Mexican democratic transition in 2000

The electoral victory of opposition candidate Vicente Fox made 2 July 2000 a date of great political significance for Mexicans, since it was the culmination of a long process of transition from an authoritarian regime with a state-party that had governed without interruption for almost three-quarters of a century.

With the advent of Vicente Fox, for the first time in seventy-one years a social group came to power with clearly entrepreneurial rather than populist perspectives. This group's ideological and programmatic positions were conservative: it intended to reduce the size of the government, it considered the private sector as the motor of the economy, and it raised private property to a crucial position of dominance over public property. In general it saw personal realization as a process that occurs through intermediate structures between the state and the individual – although still recognizing the legitimate role of government authority in the promotion of social justice as long as it occurs through subsidiary policies (Middlebrook 2001). Therefore policies were defined as temporary, transitional, and limited in scope, until those who could benefit were able to find their own means to solve their problems.

In calling it a positive by-product of the free-trade agreements, international financial organizations and the United States govern-ment have been quick to congratulate themselves for Mexican 'electoral democratization'. The project of democratization through bipartisan electoral alternation was carefully rehearsed during the 1980s. Beginning at municipal and state levels between the PRI (Partido Revolucionario Institucional) and the PAN (Partido Acción Nacional), it was finally accepted by the elite as the preferred option in the 1988 national elections, when official party presidential candi-date Carlos Salinas de Gortari suffered a landslide defeat at the hands of a surprise social coalition of the centre-left with Cuauhtémoc Cárdenas as candidate. This coalition, which later evolved into the Democratic Revolution Party (PRD: Partido de la Revolución

Democrática), sought alternatives to the merciless application of neo-liberal economic plans while challenging the bipartisan electoral scheme (Shirk 2001; Valencia 2001; Alvarez 2001a).

What is truly significant is that the depth and the frequency of the financial crises throughout the 1980s and 1990s prolonged the programmes of structural adjustment and precipitated negotiations for restructuring the electoral political system. This restructuring began a search for ways to redefine power relations between the executive authority and the legislative authority (today dominated by the PRI and PAN), between federal and state governments, and between voters and parties, and even to redefine the meaning of the vote itself.

The promise of deep economic changes stood in sharp contrast with the continuation of the same neo-liberal policies under Vicente Fox. This discrepancy between promise and reality caused Fox's legitimacy to crumble within a year of forming the government. The distance between his campaign promises and the reality of his economic programme has been revealed in the disillusion of even hardcore PAN supporters, not to mention the wide sector of society that voted for him only because of his strong anti-PRI discourse.

In his first year of government Fox had to face two important political challenges that clearly brought into question his ability to lead in a new direction. One was to lay the foundations for political negotiation with the national and Zapatista indigenous movements; the other was to deliver high economic growth and to pay special attention to social spending. In his second year, the challenge of providing an opening for private capital to enter into the Mexican energy sector was blown apart by a resolution of the Supreme Court of Justice, which declared that the Fox administration's actions were unconstitutional.

In the first year, Fox tried immediately to resume a dialogue with the Zapatistas, and placed before Congress the project of the 'Indigenous Rights and Culture' legal initiative originally formulated by the Concord and Pacification Commission (COCOPA, Comisión de Concordia and Pacificación) to legislate the so-called 'San Andrés Agreements'.

The original law was important because it contained five guiding principles from which to form a new relationship between indig-enous peoples, the Mexican state, and the rest of society: multi-culturalism, free determination, consultation and agreement, the strengthening of the federal system and democratic decentralization, and sustainability.

At the end of the complex legislative process set in motion by Fox, a law was passed which denied territorial rights to indigenous peoples, giving business free reign to exploit biodiversity and strategic natural resources without dealing with the possible harm to the territories of indigenous peoples. It was a heavy blow to Fox's legitimacy.

Almost simultaneously, Fox's government redoubled its environmental and developmentalist rhetoric by promoting the Puebla–Panama Plan, which, under the guise of an 'innovative strategy of regional development', aims to bring to the region stretching from Mexico's Southwest to Central America the same brew of neo-liberal policies as has been applied to the rest of the country. This occurred without the slightest consultation with or provision of information to the region's inhabitants, who – not coincidentally – form the majority of the country's indigenous population (Alvarez 2001b).

Fox's second political challenge has also ended in disaster; neither the promise of high economic growth (Mexico had zero growth in 2001) nor that of the priority of social spending in the federal budget has been met. In response to oscillations in international oil prices, the Fox regime even made three consecutive budget cuts in social spending in 2001, and announced three more in 2002 despite the spectacular rise in oil prices.

The plans for energy deregulation and the opening up of the country to private capital, presented by the Fox administration during his first year, clashed against the position of Congress and provoked a 'constitutional controversy' that was solved in April 2002 by the Supreme Court declaring the executive initiative 'unconstitutional'. In the near future the executive may be able to find some legal loophole that will allow it to push through an alternative road to privatization. Nevertheless, owing to the relationships of forces within the Congress and the timing of general elections, a chance for major legal reform cannot be sought until 2006.

Despite a democratic transition and electoral promises to attend to populist demands and redefine state–society relations, the Vicente Fox administration has, instead, attempted a rigid imposition of second-generation structural reforms that are oriented towards the complete dismantling of the pillars of the welfare state – the public services of education, health, and social security. Moreover, the next stage of this strategy will bring the deregulation of labour markets and a second attempt to open the door to national and international private capital in the energy sector.[1]

The unfolding of financial crises

From a macroeconomic point of view there is no doubt that the Mexican economy underwent a double process of structural change and adjustment during the 1980s and 1990s, amid declared stagnation (in the 1980s annual growth averaged 1.9 per cent) or slow growth (in the 1990s the average annual growth was 3.5 per cent), hyperinflation (averaging 65.1 per cent per year in the 1980s and 18.3 per cent per year in the 1990s), and a serious and recurrent financial instability (serious crises in 1982, 1987, and 1994–95). From 1980 to 2000 the gross national product (GNP) grew an average of only 2.7 per cent.

Throughout the period, the strategic direction of the Mexican economy was towards integration with the economy of the United States. In the end, the process was formally codified in NAFTA, which today objectively prevents the definition of a national strategy of Mexican-centred development. While it is true that under NAFTA there has been an explosion of commerce and investment flows (see Figure 6.1), there are also serious problems resulting from the high concentration of trade and capital: 85 per cent of foreign sales and purchases are made today in the United States, while 70 per cent of foreign direct investment (FDI) originates there.

FDI went from a yearly average of almost $4 billion before 1994 to a yearly average of $10.03 billion from that year to 2000. But only a small number of sectors, branches, regions, and companies have benefited in any real way from the export-oriented policy (Dussel 2000: 38).

A central aspect of the structural adjustment programmes in the 1980s and one advantage re-created by NAFTA in the 1990s was the amplified reproduction of the phenomenon of low wages. Rigid public policies have imposed a systematic deterioration both in the minimum wage and in wages in manufacturing industry. The figures (see Figure 6.2) cover the period from 1980 to 2000, and show this systematic deterioration in many areas. This is not just one more data sample: Figure 6.2 depicts the economic environment generated

Figure 6.1   Exchange rate and total exports in Mexico,
1981–2000 (annual growth rates, %)

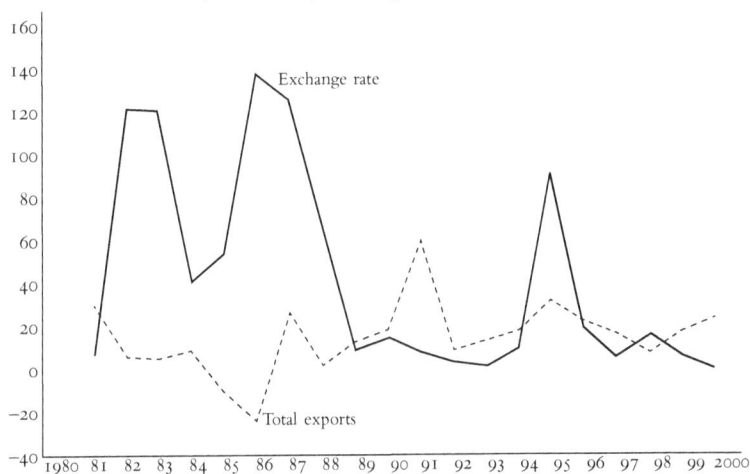

Source: Indicatores Económicos, Banco de México.

by neo-liberal policies and NAFTA and what this means for the Mexican wage earner. It also illustrates the big changes in the role of the state in regulating and managing labour markets through severe discipline and a centralized trade-union corporatism (Alvarez and Martínez 2001).

In the experimental phase of 'structural adjustment', Mexico objectively became the world's model of an emerging economy successfully reformed for one main, simple reason related to fiscal discipline (Lustig 1992: 98–103). Public finances were cleaned of productive and social expenses in order to concentrate on the needs of finance capital and bankers.

In 1982 the total financial requirements of the federal government (the economic deficit) had reached almost 11.2 per cent of the GDP. In 1989 this percentage had fallen to 4.7 per cent, in 1994 it was 0.3 per cent, in 1997 1.5 per cent, and in 2001 it reached a low of 0.2 per cent (see Figure 6.3).

At the same time, oil income was kept as a safety net for servicing the external debt and to reduce the fiscal burden on the private

Figure 6.2   Minimum wages, manufacturing industry average
remuneration and employment in Mexico, 1980–2000
(annual growth rates, %)

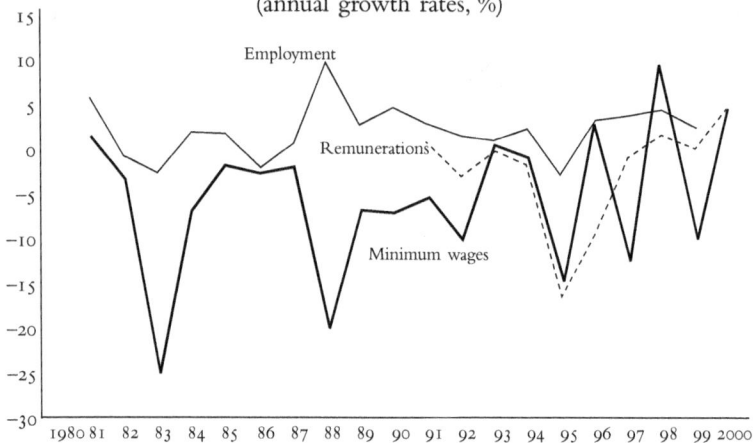

Source: Instituto Nacional de Estadística, Geografía e Informática.

sector. The policies of structural change imposed by the IMF and
the World Bank sought to modify developing economies in three
basic ways: to go from 'statist' schemes (that is, strong direct state
participation in the economy through public enterprises and subsidies
to local producers) to a 'small state' (through shut-downs or privatization of state enterprises); to abandon the wide and indiscriminate
use of protectionism – defined as 'closed economies' – by becoming
'open economies' operating under free-trade schemes; and, above all,
to abandon strategies of import substitute industrialization (ISI) for
export-oriented industrialization (EOI).

   The abandonment of the statist strategy was initially imposed in
Mexico with a rigid fiscal discipline, including a severe programme
of austerity in public finances. This had a long-term effect on the
kind of financing available and on the amount and structure of public
spending. Included also in this strategy was a rise in the prices of
goods and services provided by the state and a withdrawal of the
state from direct intervention through shut-downs or privatization
of public enterprises.

Figure 6.3 Economic deficit, service of external public debt, and health and education expenditure, 1980–2000 (as % of GDP)

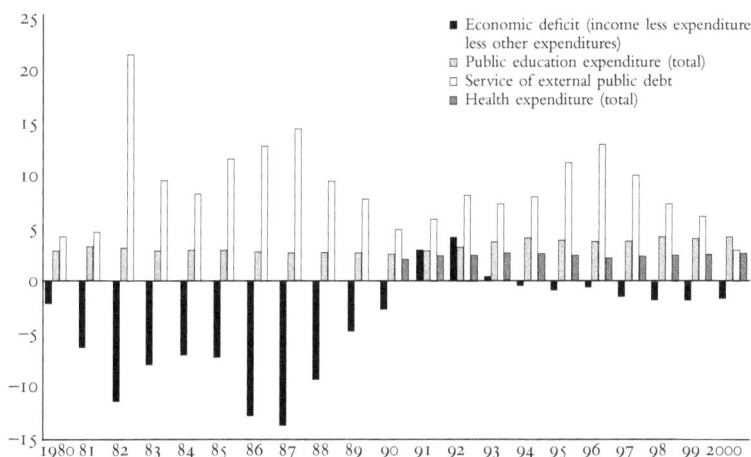

- ■ Economic deficit (income less expenditure less other expenditures)
- ▢ Public education expenditure (total)
- ☐ Service of external public debt
- ■ Health expenditure (total)

Sources: SHCP; INEGI.

The most significant results were a decrease in investment on high social-impact infrastructure, and the financial strangulation of already precarious welfare institutions, most particularly the public institutions of education, health, and social security (see Figure 6.3). It also caused a slow-down in employment growth (see Figure 6.2).

The structural changes, paradoxically, also implied the 'statification' of a financial system in deep crisis while, simultaneously, the state was retreating from direct economic intervention in agriculture, forestry, tourism, and important areas in the industrial sector.

The financial system, being privately and nationally owned, has, through its successive crises and restructurings, passed through recurring cycles of 'statification', 'reprivatization', 'covert statification', and again 'privatization with foreign domination'.

Between 1989 and 1994, financial reform was oriented towards deregulation, opening to foreign capital, and privatization, thereby indicating four key economic directions. First, banks could fix their own passive and active rates, and count on permission to register deposits in dollars. Second, there was a restructuring first of the external public debt, then of the internal debt. In 1990 foreign capital was authorized to buy bonds on the federal government's 'domestic debt'. Third, the stock market was deregulated and opened up, followed by bank privatization (Alvarez and Mendoza 1992: 32–7). Fourth, the financial system was further opened within the framework of NAFTA (Mendoza 1997).

Privatization was presented in international financial markets as an exemplary form of adopting market-oriented policies (Vidal 2001a: 122–30). But seeing its results, in terms of the cost of the bank bail-out – a sum of almost $80 billion – and the accelerated process of control by foreign capital, it would seem more exemplary of disaster.

This disaster is expressed also in an alarming increase in Mexco's non-performing loans. For example, in the 'boom' prior to NAFTA these loans rose by 450 per cent between 1990 and 1994. Over the flame of structural reform, financial intermediaries have been operating under permanent conditions of high interest rates with easy access to external debt and are focusing their operations on financing public spending – by buying government bonds, financing consumer credit (mortgages, car purchases, expensive credit cards), and by financing the operations of small groups of businesses and individuals closely associated with them. Together this explains bank and finance capital parasitism on public finances and the dramatic increase in banks' non-performing loans (Cypher 1996; Correa and Girón 1997).

The outbreak of an exchange crisis in December 1994 unleashed the third major financial crisis of recent years and led to a rescue operation that cost over $15 billion of national public funds. This was the beginning of the cycle of 'covert statification', where, so as not to act openly against the 'market-friendly model', massive use was made of public funds to rescue the banks while they maintained their 'private' nature. In short, the first cycle privatized the profits while the second socialized the private losses.

It is notable that the rescue package put together by the United States also made use of public funds to the amount of $18 billion, and an institution as formerly strict in developing countries' supervision as the IMF admitted that this was 668 per cent of Mexico's allowed quota, an open violation of its own rules.

The Mexican crisis of 1994, then, brought into question not only the theoretical validity of the IMF's stabilization programmes

– according to which crises could only occur through fiscal in-
discipline or by threats to the continuity of the structural reforms
– but also the IMF's own discipline (Krugman 1995; Ros 1995).
Moreover, that this kind of bail-out was supported essentially with
public funds clearly contradicts the model of which Mexico is said
to be an example. Worse still, it has reinforced bank and finance
capital parasitism on public finances.

To remedy the financial crisis it was decided to accelerate and
deepen the financial opening agreed to in NAFTA, paving the way
for foreign banks into Mexico via 'financial capitalizations' or strategic alliances. Before 1982, foreign banks had access to only 1 per
cent of Mexican financial assets; in 2001 they controlled 82 per cent
of them. Here we have privatization with foreign domination.

But none of these changes has brought any deep alteration in
the forms of operation of the financial system. Far from serving the
need for the articulation of a national project of development, it
continues to give segmented attention, favouring the largest companies and exporters, while the chronic depression of the internal
market persists and bankruptcies among small and medium-sized
companies worsen (Mendoza 1997).

Mexico is living through prolonged conditions of bank deterioration. High interest rates resulted in both an inability to encourage
productive projects and a fall in purchasing power for wide sectors of
the population. These were effects that ultimately restricted Mexico's
ability to pay its debts. The banks' weaknesses had a major impact
on the productive sector as is evidenced by the erratic behaviour
of the GDP: this fell by 7 per cent in 1995, but the following year
it experienced a spectacular recovery of 5.2 per cent. In 1997 it
rose surprisingly by 7 per cent, fell by 4.6 per cent in 1998, 3.5
per cent in 1999, and in 2000 surged by 7 per cent once more but
plummeted to zero per cent in 2001.

These oscillations reflect the persistence of banks' weaknesses due
to non-performing loans and their financially unhealthy position.
However, these weaknesses are objectively minimized by three main
factors: the positive effects of economic growth associated with the
largest US economic expansion in peacetime, a significant rise in
international oil prices, and the profitable business of financing the
state through the acquisition of domestic debt bonds.

In Mexico's chain of financial instabilities, the first and most
important link is the service payment of the external debt, since that

service payment weighs heavily on a significant portion of public expense and the income from oil exports.

Public and private external debt amounted to more than $170 billion in 1994, but, as noted above, this did not translate into high rates of growth. On the contrary, it seems to have contributed to the erosion of internal savings, which fell from 15.5 per cent of GNP in 1989 to 6.7 per cent in 1994 (Garrido and Peñaloza 1996). In the fifteen years between 1980 and 1995, Mexico paid an average of over $10 billion per year to service the external debt.

In interest and amortization payments alone, between 1980 and 2002 Mexico paid almost $300 billion while the consolidated debt was never over $100 billion. It is worth asking, then, if the external debt was not a partial problem but a generalized phenomenon which in Mexico, as in other Latin American countries, is now expanding on all sides.

It is expanding because there is a fundamental pressure on the rise in interest rates on government debt bonds – which in turn serves as a signal to attract the arrival *en masse* of foreign capital in order to meet in full the servicing of the debt and finance the current account deficit.

It is important to emphasize the problems at the heart of the 'market-oriented adjustment'. First, high interest rates lead to the permanent abuse of external savings (in Mexico predominantly coming from North America), sometimes charged to the public sector, sometimes to the private sector. For example, the total debt of the 124 companies listed in the Mexican stock market reached more than $96 billion in the second half of 2000. And a sample of the ten most important – including Telmex, Televisa, Grupo Carso, Cemex, and Vitro – revealed that their debt exceeded $80 billion, almost 40 per cent more than the internal public debt of the federal government which was then at $59 billion.

Another deeply rooted problem is the erosion of the productive base of the economy because of internal market exposure to massive waves of imports, not all of them necessary but nevertheless entering due to 'trade openings'. Both high interest rates and massive imports are problems that not only lead to recurrent financial crises, but also deepen and prolong the costs of adjustment that are charged to public finances (Rosales 1995).

Trade openings: winners and losers

To change from a 'closed' to an 'open' economy, imports were liberalized, and the doctrine of 'free trade' was taken up as a guide to strategic commercial policy. The opening was rapid, profound, and carried out in several stages. The first (1983–85) included reductions in import tariffs followed by the partial elimination of import licences and the relaxing of export controls.

The second (1985–88) began with a round of macroeconomic stabilization measures, such as the depreciation of the exchange rate combined with the reduction of quota restrictions. The reform of the tariff system and Mexico's entry into GATT in 1986 were followed by major tariff reductions leaving only autos, auto parts, and pharmaceuticals still protected.

The third stage (1988–92) included the freeing of those remaining internal prices that were still controlled, and the deregulation of requirements over FDI flows. The fourth stage (1994–2001) is essentially related to NAFTA, which has brought in new protectionist instruments such as the 'regional rules of origin' and the loss of 'domestic content requirements' for foreign investment, plus uneven periods of tariff reduction for industrial, agricultural, and service industry branches.

Since 2001, Mexico has silently moved in the direction of creating a Customs Union in North America by unilaterally lowering external tariffs, something that has had devastating effects for the domestic market (Alvarez and Dussel 2001). Trade liberalization was a central component in the determination of real competitive currency exchange rates in order to facilitate the abandonment of import substitution industrialization and to shift to export-oriented industrialization. As mentioned above, this was the third line of structural change.

Export booms in Mexico have corresponded, point for point, to periods of strong under-valuation in the exchange rate, with two very clear and cyclical stages – one of under-valuation from 1982 to 1988, and another of over-valuation from 1989 to 1994, then under-valuation again from 1995 to 1997, and finally another period of over-valuation between 1998 and 2001 (see Figure 6.1). In the end, the shift to EOI resulted, paradoxically, in 'import-oriented growth'. Between 1988 and 1996 the average annual rate of growth was 14.1 per cent in exports and 15.3 per cent in imports.

In industry, there is ample evidence to suggest that Mexico has been converted into an export platform with few significant linkages to the interior of the country through the creation of production chains, which was the main goal under the ISI model. The success of manufacturing exports is debatable. It has reinforced an industrial structure dominated by transnational and national big business and resulted in the destruction of small and medium-sized companies, making the economy an 'addict' of imports. It leads Mexico to concentrate its external commerce even more on only one country, the United States. These exports originate in fewer sectors with fewer products and fewer and larger companies. The rise in manufactured exports has been accompanied by a larger rise in imports of capital goods and intermediate inputs (Dussell 2000).

The winners in this model have been, not unexpectedly, modern capital-intensive transnational industries and producers of consumer durables such as autos and consumer electronics, in which intra-industry trade is the foundation of their success. Also doing well is manufacturing based on natural resources or intensive energy consumption such as petrochemicals, non-metallic minerals, and wood and steel products (Borja 2001). Losers have been the traditional, labour-intensive industries such as shoes and furniture. Unsurprisingly, we must also include here the strategic branches of the capital goods sector, and those industries with higher technological complexities, such as machinery and equipment production (Velasco 1994).

The growth in imports was not confined to industrial and consumer goods. Agriculture suffered devastating waves of imports of basic grains, while exports changed towards a greater orientation of fruits and horticulture. These structural changes mean that Mexican agriculture has undergone overwhelming pressure to accommodate itself to the logic and interests of two powerful depredating forces: national banks searching for a way to enter into these activities, and the complementary regional role assigned by North American agriculture to support the rise of a regime of global food production.

The forms of operation of both forces accentuate polarization, a structural feature of Mexican agriculture. They also accentuate unemployment and extreme poverty, which are the principal calamities of a country with a high percentage of youth and three million people who work for much less than the minimum wage. The agricultural sector in Mexico employs the core of the extremely poor.

The classical theory of international commerce that is used to vindicate free trade asserts that countries trade abroad to take advantage of the benefits of specialization in developing 'comparative or competitive advantages'. Without doubt, in terms of theoretical explanations, the Mexican patterns of specialization are, at the very least, contradictory in industry and agriculture.

Rather than 'comparative or competitive advantages', it seems that 'relative degrees of asymmetry' are operating within Mexico. The imposed reforms have denied, until very recently, the importance of having an industrial policy and the strategic significance of stimulating endogenous technological change.

'Relative degrees of asymmetry' refers to the size and diversity of an economy, its backwardness, the capacity of its physical infrastructure, the treatment of intellectual property rights, the level of human development, the systems of certification and norms validation, and the solidity and complexity of its institutional development (Ayala 2002).

It is important to draw attention to the fact that the lines of structural change in the industrial sector have not affected its historical weakness in the generation of employment or in the concentration of income – two long-standing problems.

Policies of structural change and adjustment had very grave effects on manufacturing in the general sense of a loss of salaried positions and a growth in non-salaried positions. Slow economic growth, trade liberalization, technological change, and polarization between large and small businesses explain this pattern of behaviour.

Another significant outcome of the structural change has been the tertiarization of the economy, in the sense that the service sector has become the principal generator of non-salaried positions. The erosion of wages in the productive sector, the increasing inequality in income distribution, trade liberalization, the ease of access to self-employment mechanisms, the feminization of the workforce, and the proliferation of part-time activities explain this last trend (Velasco 1994).

In Mexico the existence of a 'social debt' is often seen as a by-product of the prolonged policies of adjustment. This relates to the fact that according to figures of the last General Population and Housing Census (INEGI 2000), 70 per cent of the economically active population earn three times the minimum wage or less. In contrast, the 10 per cent of the population with highest incomes enjoy the larger part of total income and private consumption.

Between 15 and 20 per cent of the population live in conditions of extreme poverty – that is, with incomes insufficient to ensure basic nutrition. And, depending upon the methodology employed by the experts, between 50 per cent and 80 per cent of the population live at some level of relative poverty, having incomes that are not sufficient to cover the basic costs of food, clothing, shelter, health, education and transport.

More than ever, the Mexico of the twenty-first century faces the difficult challenge of finding a way to convert a growing market into an opportunity that will promote the growth of the country around a well-defined programme of long-term national development. What is happening instead is an uncritical sanctioning of a process of regional integration, centred basically on the production and decentralization strategies of American transnational companies, which emphasize a continuation of the 'second generation of reforms', such as energy privatization, financial deregulation, labour market deregulation, and the merchandizing of public health and education. This path to global integration will eventually lead to the destruction of key Mexican cultural and national institutions (Alvarez and Martínez 2001).

Conclusions

The main conclusions to this chapter highlight the ways that the Mexican government has used the instruments presented to it through globalization to strengthen neo-liberal policies. Through the acceptance of free-trade agreements, specifically NAFTA, the state has entrenched patterns of specialization that are unsustainable in the long run because they tend to deepen and widen the relative degrees of asymmetry that have been persistent problems in Mexico.

The new role of the state in this global regime has deepened the parasitic relationship between public finances and transnational and national finance capital. At the same time, the withdrawal of the state in any productive participation in the economy has only served to stress its operational rescue of bankrupted businesses. Through budgetary restrictions on public finances, Mexico has seen the dismantlement of historically precarious welfare institutions, and this has made the social environment more precarious and volatile.

Policies for imposing low wages have been a centrepiece for establishing a static comparative advantage at a time of rapid techno-logical change. These policies have been possible primarily because of the maintenance of a highly centralized and corrupt trade-union corporatism that has not been touched by 'electoral democratization'. Yet, despite low wages, economic problems persist. The predominance of restrictive fiscal and monetary policies, instituted as recommended by international organizations and finance capital, are responsible for slow growth, periodic currency overvaluation and devaluations, and permanent high interest rates.

While free trade is a cornerstone of the new economic regime, this opening up of the economy to trade has been financed with highly volatile capital flows. This makes economic growth extremely dependent on capital imports, something that makes the financial sector highly unstable.

Mexico is deeply reliant on state actions to construct its new global economic regime. The state has not stepped back from economic activity, but has shifted its actions to facilitate the internationaliza-tion of the Mexican economy. Its major activities have facilitated the organization of regional trade blocs, initiated the privatization of key sectors, and destroyed many of the most important welfare institutions of the country. In short, the Mexican state functions as the main facilitator for entrenching the second generation of neo-liberal structural reforms.

Notes

I am grateful to Sandra Martínez for the statistical information and the graphics on which many of the assertions of this chapter are based; also to Maria Vinós and Andrew Blake for the translation. However, any error or omission is my sole responsibility.

1. Energy is still state-owned, as mandated by the Constitution. The opening of the energy sector has been a very uneven process in Latin America, as demonstrated by Jesús Mora (1999).

References

Alvarez, A. (2001a) 'La izquierda y el PRD frente al neo-liberalismo', *Aportes* 16.
Alvarez, A. (2001b) 'El Plan Puebla Panamá: desarrollo regional o de un enclave trasnacional?', *Observatorio Social de América Latina* (CLACSO), vol. 2, no. 4.
Alvarez, A. and S. Martínez (2001) 'Significados del Tratado de Libre Comercio de América del Norte para México', *Información Comercial Española* 795.

Alvarez, A. and G. Mendoza (1992) *México 1988–1991: Un ajuste económico exitoso*, México: Facultad de Economía, UNAM.

Alvarez, J.L. and P.E. Dussell (2001) 'Causas y efectos de los programas de promoción sectorial en la economía mexicana', *Comercio Exterior*, vol. 51, no. 5.

Ayala, J.L. (2002) *Fundamentos institucionales del mercado*, México: Facultad de Economía, UNAM.

Borja, A. (2001) (coord) *Para evaluar el TLCAN*, México: Miguel Angel Porrúa-Tec de Monterrey.

Correa, M.E. and A. Girón (eds) (1997) *Crisis bancarias y carteras vencidas*, México: Desarrollo de Medios (Demos).

Cypher, J. (1996) 'Mexico: Financial Fragility or Structural Crisis?', *Journal of Economic Issues*, vol. 30, no. 2.

Dussell, P. E. (2000) *El Tratado de Libre Comercio de Norteamérica y el desempeño de la economía en México*, México: UN–CEPAL, LC/Mex/L.431.

Garrido, C. and W.T. Peñaloza (1996) *Ahorro y sistema financiero Mexicano (diagnóstico de la problemática actual)*, México: Ed. Grijalbo and UAM-A.

Frankel, J. and N. Roubini (2001) 'The Role of Industrial Country Policies in Emerging Market Crises', NBER Working Paper 8634.

IMF (International Monetary Fund) (2000) *World Economic Outlook*, Washington, DC.

INEGI (Information, Geography and Statistics National Institute) (2000), *Population and Housing Census*.

Krugman, P. (1995) 'Dutch Tulips and Emerging Markets', *Foreign Affairs*, vol. 74, no. 4.

Lustig, N. (1992) *Mexico, the Remaking of an Economy*, Washington, DC: The Brookings Institution.

Mendoza, G. (1997) 'Mexico: Economic Reform and Financial Crisis in the 1990s', paper to the Society for the Advancement of Socioeconomics, Annual Convention, mimeo.

Middlebrook, K. (ed.) (2001) *Party Politics and the Struggle for Democracy in Mexico*, San Diego: Center for US–Mexican Studies, University of California.

Mora, J. (1999) 'Reestructuración de la industria petrolera Latinoamericana: El contexto internacional', *Venezuela en Oxford*, Caracas: Banco Central de Venezuela.

Ros, J. (1995) 'Mercados financieros, flujos de capital y tipo de cambio en México', *Economía Mexicana*, vol. 4, no. 1.

Rosales, O. (1995) 'Algunas lecciones de la crisis mexicana', Santiago de Chile: CEPAL, mimeo.

Shirk, D. (2001) 'Mexico's Democratization and the Organizational Development of the National Action Party', in K. Middlebrook (ed.) *Party Politics and the Struggle for Democracy in Mexico*, San Diego: Center for US–Mexican Studies, University of California.

Valencia, G. (2001) 'The PAN in Guanajuato: Elections and Political Change in the 1990s', in K. Middlebrook (ed.) *Party Politics and the Struggle for Democracy in Mexico*, San Diego: Center for US–Mexican Studies, University of California.

Velasco, E. (1994) *Reestructuración neo-liberal y desarrollo industrial: competitividad y productividad de las manufacturas mexicanas*, México: Universidad Autónoma Metropolitana-A, mimeo.

Vidal, G. (2001a) *Privatizaciones, fusiones y adquisiciones*, México: Ed. Anthropos–UAM.

Vidal, G. (2001b) 'América Latina, flujos internacionales de capital y proceso de privatizaciones', in G. Mantey and N. Levy (eds) *Desorden monetario internacional y su impacto en el sistema financiero Mexicano*, México: DGAPA–UNAM, ENEP–Acatlán.

Yunes-Naude, A. (1996) 'El agro mexicano ante los procesos de apertura', paper presented at the Round table: *Apertura Económica, TLC y Economía Mexicana*, México: El Colegio de México.

Zepeda Miramontes, E. and D. Alarcón (1997) *Empleo y política social en el México de fin de siglo*, México: UAM–Azcapotzalco.

7

Australia: Asian Outpost or Big-time Financial Dealer?

Dick Bryan

Almost any map of the world will show Australia on the bottom right corner: a spatially somewhat isolated advanced capitalist country. With the exception of nearby New Zealand, it is surrounded by expansive oceans to the west, east, and south. To the immediate north are New Guinea, Indonesia, and a number of small Pacific Island nations. Australia's geography signals some important issues.

Between Europe and Asia

First, Australia is essentially Asian in location, yet its British colonial history and wealth, compared with most of Asia and the South Pacific, sees it gravitate towards Europe (Britain) and North America culturally and politically.

Second, physical isolation from advanced capitalist countries other than New Zealand has meant that Australia is not drawn into a spatially based economic bloc such as the North American Free Trade Agreement (NAFTA) or the European Union (EU). Australia is not sufficiently Asian in culture, politics or economy to be (or want to be) a credible member of the Association of Southeast Asian Nations (ASEAN). Australia's integration into the global economy is not significantly mediated by any supranational state.

These two characteristics signal some key distinctive issues that pervade 'the Australian story'. The first raises the tension within Australia between its economic ties to Europe and North America, on the one hand, and to Asia, on the other. The second raises the tension about whether economic activity in Australia should remain isolated and inward-looking, reflecting geography, or should be aggressively outward-looking, to 'compensate', as it were, for the absence of local advanced capitalist countries that would promote global integration by osmosis.

This chapter looks at each of these issues in turn. In combination, they depict a country that has, since the mid-1980s, been characterized by an internationalizing agenda by both the state and larger capitals, especially those in finance, and it is Europe and North America, rather than the Asian region, that have been the focus of this expansion.

But an Asian impact is also prevalent, especially via domestic responses to growing trade with Asia. In Australia, as in most other capitalist countries, the last twenty years have been characterized by a polarization of income. But the distinctive characteristic of Australia's development has been a focus on the intensification of labour as the source of competitive success. Reliance on an increasingly cheap, flexible, de-unionized labour force shows some of the basic characteristics of an Asian path to industrial competitiveness.

A popular work in Australian economic history written in 1966 depicted the plight of Australia as 'the tyranny of distance' (Blainey 1966). It argued, essentially, how the economic development of Australia had been dominated by its sheer distance from its colonial home in Britain. It had thereby developed as an agricultural economy, supplying Britain with wheat and wool, and in return importing British manufactures. But distance also creates distinctiveness.

The impact of mining

Almost from the time Blainey's book was published, circumstances changed rapidly, though the culture of 'the tyranny of distance' lived on. From the mid-1960s there were major mineral discoveries, leading to the development of large-scale mines of iron ore, bauxite, coal, gold, uranium, gas, and mineral sands. In each of these industries, Australia became a leading world producer. The development of these deposits had significant implications of long duration.

First, with few exceptions, the mines were located thousands of kilometres from population centres, developing outside the awareness and experience of city-living Australians. Moreover, they were on

Figure 7.1 Australian exports, major trading countries, 2000–2001

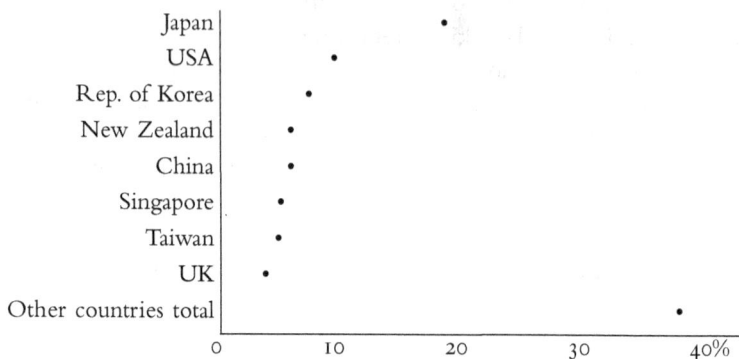

Source: ABS, 2002c.

land thought of as desert by city dwellers, but of profound cultural significance to the Aboriginal population of Australia. There arose both legal and political battles over Aboriginal land rights that have been defining events in Australian society and are a stark reminder of the impacts of colonialism (an issue beyond the scope of the current analysis).

Second, the mines opened up new and internationalized ways of funding investment. The mineral deposits warranted large-scale production, involving huge start-up costs, but there were no Australian-owned mining companies with the capacity to develop individual mines, let alone the industry generally. The issue of the role of foreign investment versus national ownership rose to prominence, as did the promotion of debt-funded investment as a means to keep massive investment projects under some degree of local ownership. Conflicts associated with these issues will be considered shortly.

Third, mining precipitated a profound change in the composition of industry in Australia, both by its own growth and by its impact on other sectors. Minerals took over from agriculture as Australia's major export earner, such that since the 1970s unprocessed minerals have consistently generated close to 40 per cent of Australia's export revenue, agriculture slightly less. It remains an open debate as to whether this was a progressive long-term development. On the one hand, the mines were, and generally remain, highly profitable investments, bringing in substantial export revenue. On the other hand, it is contended, this has been 'easy' export revenue, based on digging and shipping, but little mineral processing and no real manufacturing based on minerals. Hence, the argument goes, mining developments actually retarded the formation of an efficient, export-oriented manufacturing sector in Australia; the state had no need to plan future industrial development because mining provided a cornucopia of exportable products. Accordingly, manufacturing in Australia is very small compared with other Organization for Economic Cooperation and Development (OECD) countries, making up just 13.3 per cent of gross domestic product (GDP) in 2000.[1] As less than 16 per cent of manufactured output is exported, manufactured goods make up just one-fifth of all exports. If simply transformed primary products such as refined oil and sugar were excluded, the proportion of manufacturing in total exports would be tiny. Moreover, these manufactures go predominantly to Australia's near neighbours in New Zealand and the Pacific Islands and only minimally to the major markets of Europe and North America.

Fourth, mining developed a new Asian orientation in Australian industry. As these mines came on-line, demand for their output came from Asia, not Europe. In particular, the emerging Japanese steel and energy producers became the major purchasers of Australian-produced coal, iron ore, and gas. As other parts of Asia industrialized, this trend accentuated.

The third and fourth elements here have created a decisive Asian orientation in Australia's export trade in the last thirty years. Figure 7.1 shows the current direction of Australia's exports.

Japan remains the largest destination of exports (almost 20 per cent), but the predominant growth over the 1990s was in exports to other Asian countries, especially China and South Korea (370 per cent and 174 per cent growth over the decade, respectively). Most of the export growth has been in coal and crude petroleum, with China also having a large demand for wool (ABS 2002b).

Yet while this story of major mining developments is central to explaining the growing Asian orientation of that economy, it is important not to lose sight of the fact that the mining industry is a relatively small part of the Australian economy. Mining produces almost 40 per cent of exports, but only 4 per cent of GDP. The same is true of agriculture: almost 40 per cent of exports, but only 3 per cent of GDP. Indeed, Australia has for the past decade exported just over 20 per cent of its production – a figure low in comparison with other advanced capitalist countries.

Conversely there is a significant part of production oriented to the domestic market, with minimal export orientation. This production is in manufacturing and services. Basic manufacturing industries are not generally internationally oriented or competitive in international markets. For the last decade there has been much talk in government policy circles of the need to nurture high-technology, globally oriented manufacturing industries, but little government expenditure in this direction. There has been a small number of much-lauded, though isolated, export success stories, but no general momentum. High-technology products and capital goods remain dominant in imports. Services, which are over 70 per cent of GDP, now make up around 20 per cent of exports – mainly tourism and education – though these are always quirkish 'exports' because they involve tourists and students coming into Australia, not the international expansion of service production.

Protection of domestic industry

What is the background of this small, uncompetitive manufacturing sector? For most of the twentieth century, Australian manufacturing developed behind high tariff barriers – a history not significantly different from other smaller industrializing countries. As industrial technology developed rapidly over the last quarter of the twentieth century, the gap between global best practice and these domestic manufacturing operations widened considerably.

The standard political and economic pressures arose to reduce and eradicate tariff protection (inefficiency, high costs for other local producers, especially those competing in export markets, etc.). This pressure intensified with the floating of the Australian dollar in 1983 and the growth of the culture of 'international competitiveness' in national economic policy. Assistance to industry via the tariff and direct budget outlays fell in fits and starts, reflecting the inevitable political (and hence policy) tensions involved in the withdrawal of subsidies and consequent plant closures. With insignificant amounts of export-oriented manufacturing (which might potentially benefit from lower tariffs), manufacturing industries were the greatest losers from the tariff cuts.

Figure 7.2 Australian imports, major trading countries, 2000–2001

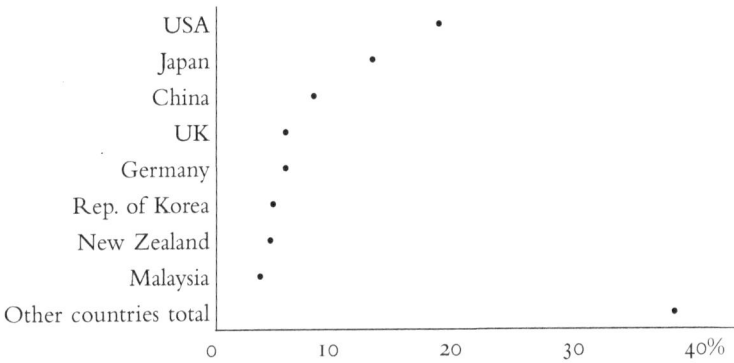

Source: ABS, 2002c.

Tariff cuts from the mid-1980s saw the effective rate of assistance[2] to Australian manufacturing industry falling, from 23 per cent in 1984 to 14 per cent in 1991 and 5 per cent in 2001, with motor vehicles and textiles remaining the primary recipients throughout. Manufacturing industries receive just over half of overall government budgetary support to industry, with both the level of support and manufacturing's share remaining relatively stable over the past decade (Productivity Commission 2001: 7, 53).

Accordingly, manufacturing's share of national production fell from a peak of 29 per cent in 1960 to 15 per cent in 1985 to 12 per cent in 2001, and employment in manufacturing fell from 20 per cent of total employment in 1974 to 12 per cent in 2001. Hence, to generalize across manufacturing, some part of manufacturing employment decline has been associated with labour-replacing technology, but most of the decline has been associated with the decline of the sector itself, especially the labour-intensive parts such as textiles and footwear.

The result, predictably, has been an increase in manufactured imports and the dominance of manufactures within the composition of Australia's imports. Here, too, Asian industrialization has proved critical, for a growing proportion of these imports are being sourced from Asian countries, as seen in Figure 7.2. The largest sources of imports are still the advanced capitalist countries (the United States, Japan, the United Kingdom, Germany), where the largest component of imports is machinery and transport equipment. But the fastest-growing proportion is from newly industrializing countries of Asia: China, the Republic of Korea, Malaysia, and, most recently, Thailand and Vietnam. From these countries come both machinery and transport equipment, but also basic manufactures, especially textiles and clothing.

It is important to note, however, that this is not a process of manufacturing industries such as textiles simply leaving Australia to become arm's-length imports. Internationalized Australian clothing brands such as Rip Curl and Billabong involve Chinese and Fijian clothing companies contracted to produce to Rip Curl and Billabong specifications and prices, and franchises in Europe and North and South America to retail the output.[3]

While cases such as Rip Curl and Billabong show a connection between tariff decline and the internationalization of capital, there is also a significant, and historically earlier, link between manufacturing protection and the inflow of investment to Australia. Tariff protection of the manufacturing industry saw international companies 'jump' the tariff wall from the 1940s to 1970s to produce for the domestic market. Industries like vehicles and pharmaceuticals have been dominated by international producers for a long time. Until the 1950s, this was predominantly British capital, though US capital became dominant in the 1960s and Japanese capital rose to prominence in the 1970s, especially in the vehicle industry.

A parallel process occurred in the mining industry. It was mentioned earlier that, with the opening of large-scale mines in the 1960s, the state developed strict protection of Australian ownership. However, the need for technology, expertise, and a capital base saw mines develop as joint ventures with 50 per cent local and 50 per cent foreign equity. As the restrictions on foreign ownership steadily lifted in the 1980s, the extent of foreign ownership rose, and here, as in manufacturing, there has been a shift from United States to Japanese ownership, including the Japanese steel and power companies that are end-users of the minerals. In the year 2000/1, the stock of direct investment in Australia (reflecting the history of investment) was dominated by the United States (29 per cent), the United Kingdom (25 per cent), and Japan (6 per cent). The annual flows for that year roughly reflect that same profile, but with a

Figure 7.3 Australia's current account deficit, 1985–2000 ($bn)

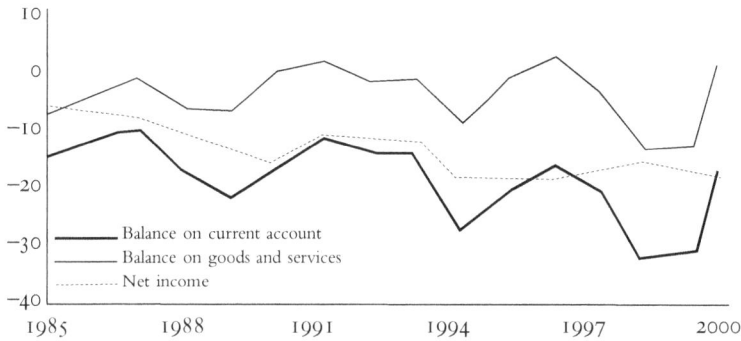

growth of investment from Asia, and especially Hong Kong (13 per cent of the annual inflow). As with trade, although to a lesser extent, foreign investment coming into Australia has an increasingly Asian origin (ABS 2001a).

Indeed, when trade and investment are considered in combination, it is apparent that the companies that do the most exporting from Australia are the Japanese trading houses attached to Japanese steel and energy companies. In the mid-1990s, these trading houses made up five of Australia's fifteen largest exporters (Thomas 1997). This is a process of global concentration of capital.

Overall, the depiction to this point is of Australia as a national economy dominated by primary industry, with a small and generally uncompetitive manufacturing sector, and with significant inward foreign investment. Such a depiction has seen the country characterized as a 'dependent' economy, locked into a role in the international division of labour of exporting raw materials and importing manufactures. In so far as this structure predictably results in international trade deficits, it is further argued that Australia is locked into a pattern of paying for its imports by accepting increased foreign investment and international loans. Consistent with this characterization, the current account of the balance of payments (see Figure 7.3) shows the consequences of an increased outflow of income (profits and interest), resulting in a mounting debt cycle. The figure shows that Australia's trade balance on goods and services has cycled somewhere between balance and a modest deficit. But the net income payable overseas has been steadily increasing over the period, so that the overall current account deficit (trade and income) is increasing, dominated by interest and profit payments.

In short, Australia has often been depicted as an economy with a third-world structure but first-world living standards, and that this is sustainable only so long as it sells more of its assets each year. This depiction is indeed consistent with the evidence, but it ignores a more complex story that comes from a detailed investigation of international finance and investment.

Globalization from one country

A consideration of international investment and finance not only poses a different interpretation of Australia's position in the global economy; it also challenges the very conception that the nation as a whole occupies a discrete 'position' in the global economy. International investment and finance have seen companies and capital expand in all directions, such that their relation to their nation of origin becomes tenuous. We see 'Australian' capital and 'Australian' companies circulating on a world stage in ways that cannot be reduced to their Australian origins, and that do not display a distinct national characteristic. Consider the following:

- The Australian dollar is the fifth most traded currency in the world (before European currencies combined under the euro, the Australian dollar was the eighth most traded) (HSBC 1998). Moreover, trade between the Australian and US dollars is the world's sixth most traded currency pair (RBA 2002: 16).
- The Australian foreign exchange market is the eighth largest in the world, larger than both France and Canada. Moreover, while foreign exchange markets globally contracted by 19 per cent in the three years to 2001, the Australian market grew by 11 per cent (RBA 2002).
- Australian dollar-denominated assets are held extensively outside Australia. There is significant issuance of bonds denominated in Australian dollars by companies and financial institutions with no apparent connection to Australia.

• In the early 1980s, under tight national capital controls, there was hardly any international direct investment of Australian origin. By 1987, however, Australia, with a three-year history of international investing, was the third largest international investing country in the world as a proportion of GDP; first and second were Britain and the Netherlands, countries with a three-*century* history of such investing (OECD 1992).

These are not the 'facts' of a third-world economy, and the story that lies behind them needs to be considered alongside the evidence of a 'dependent' economy. The investment and bond issues and the role of the dollar, while related, can be considered separately.

Internationalization of investment and finance

The story can again start with mining. It was mentioned earlier that the opening up of the large mines in the mid-1960s involved both foreign investment and local ownership, initially with protection of 50 per cent Australian equity. This process and policy initiated some decisive developments in Australia.

First, the privileging of Australian ownership in the opening of the mining industry meant that most large Australian-owned companies started to invest in mining. Foreign investors, desperate to find the Australian equity required for compliance with the ownership provisions, even offered incentives to Australian companies to invest in mining. As a result, a number of large Australian companies diversified out of manufacturing and into mining (and have sub-sequently themselves become international mining companies, such as BHP and CSR). They thereby diversified from the protected world of Australian manufacturing and entered the globally integrated world of Australian mining. While Australian manufacturing may have languished in the decades since the 1960s, many of those leading 1960s' manufacturing companies, now transformed into international mining companies, have flourished.

Second, the mining industry not only introduced global competi-tiveness to Australia, it also introduced debt financing. In those large-scale mining projects in the desert, no party, foreign or Australian, was going to (or needed to) develop their investments purely on the basis of equity alone. The growth of the mining industry was built upon debt, often using long-term mineral contracts with Japanese buyers as collateral. So even though Australia had tight international capital controls until the dollar was floated in 1983, international merchant banking was developing in Australia from the 1960s, largely (though not exclusively) to fund mining projects. In the late 1960s even the state and the trading banks developed merchant bank operations (the Australian Industrial Development Corporation and the Australian Resources Development Bank, respectively) to borrow internationally to fund mining projects.

There were also ramifications for the development of a domestic culture of borrowing, and by the early 1980s Australia's short-term commercial paper market was second in size to that in the United States. Companies such as Bond Corp, Quintex, and Elders that became (temporary) international-takeover high-flyers in the late 1980s had cut their teeth on takeovers in Australian domestic industry, funded by borrowings in the Australian commercial paper market. When the Australian state lifted capital controls in 1984, companies such as these gained direct access to Eurofinance markets, and they knew exactly how to operate. They replicated on a global scale what they had been doing successfully on a national scale and undertook large-scale international borrowing to fund large-scale international takeovers. In the absence of any substantial regional integration, such as provided by NAFTA or the EU, going international for these Australian-based companies meant going to the centres of international capitalism: Europe and North America.

These developments set the scene for the spectacular growth in the 1980s of both international bond issues and international investment by companies of Australian origin. These enterprises were part of the same process, where a handful of brash entrepreneurs were happy to take on the risk of converting debt into equity in the belief that the global stock market would keep rising faster than the rate of interest. So it was that Australia became the third largest investor as a proportion of GDP with, in 1988, just five companies doing 39 per cent and ten companies doing 52 per cent of the international investing (Bryan and Rafferty 1999: 161).

As that history unfolded, the stock market crash of 1987 left most of these companies insolvent. Others, such as NewsCorp., escaped this fate by a matter of a few days of liquidity (Shawcross 1993) and went on to global greatness. Australian international investment was, by the end of the 1980s, negative as a result of these crashes, though it grew rapidly again in the 1990s, especially through the internationalization of financial institutions of Australian origin.

A significant dimension of this international investment growth is that, as well as being volatile, it has been centred, in both its pre-crash and post-crash phases, on North America and Europe (especially Britain). Australian companies not only participated in the rush of international investment into US takeovers in the late 1980s, they also bought up banks and breweries in Britain. By 2001, the United States had attracted 43 per cent of the stock of Australian international investment, followed by the United Kingdom (14 per cent). In the local region and Asia, conversely, there has been little direct investment. New Zealand (5 per cent of total international direct investment) and Singapore (3 per cent) are the leading destinations (ABS 2001a).

So while trade goes *to* Asia and investment inflow comes increasingly *from* Asia, international investment by companies of Australian origin and the accessing of financial markets focus on the older, established centres of capitalism in Europe and the United States.

An international currency

The equivalent of US$75 billion in Australian dollars is turned over daily in Australian and international currency markets (HSBC 1998), making the Australian dollar the fifth most traded currency, albeit significantly behind the US dollar, the euro, the yen and the pound. It remains something of a riddle as to why it is so heavily traded.

The standard explanation goes back to mining. A large portion of Australian trade is tied up with minerals and Australia's export revenue is closely linked to mineral prices. The Australian dollar, it is argued, has had a reputation as a 'commodity currency'. Many of Australia's mineral exports (especially iron ore and coal) are traditionally sold on long-term contracts, not in spot markets (there is no iron ore or coal equivalent of the London Metal Exchange). Hence, a simple way to gamble or hedge on current mineral prices is via trading the Australian dollar. A high turnover on the Australian dollar is simply a reflection of this commodity hedge.

That was the standard explanation. The connection between the Australian dollar and mineral prices, however, was never as tight as that proposition would suggest. Moreover, in the last few years there has been no apparent connection between the value of the Australian dollar and mineral prices, and hence no reason to believe that the high level of trade in the Australian dollar was connected to mineral price speculation. Anyway, around 69 per cent of Australia's exports and over 90 per cent of mineral exports are contracted in United States dollars; only 29 per cent of exports (10 per cent of mineral exports) are contracted in Australian dollars (ABS 2001b), and derivatives markets now provide more sophisticated means to speculate/hedge on mineral prices than trading the Australian dollar.

A second explanation for the appeal of the Australian dollar is related to the perception of Australia as an Asian country. It is argued that financial market participants who want to hold exposure to Asia will often hold the Australian dollar as a safe alternative, reflecting a perception of Australia as Asian but with the stability of a Western economy. But there is little evidence for this explanation. If this were indeed the explanation, a close connection between the yen and the Australian dollar would be expected, and Australia would have been more caught up in the 1997 Asian financial crisis.[4] But neither of these has occurred.

Alternative explanations for the high rate of trade on the Australian dollar relate to the high level of international bond issues denominated in Australian dollars (*Journal of Australian Political Economy* 2000). Some of these bond issues are by or on behalf of Australian companies, and many are issued by third parties who then undertake currency swaps with Australian companies. But some are also issued by parties that have no apparent connection to Australia: they hold Australian dollar-denominated assets as part of their spread of currencies, perhaps because Australia's lack of a connection to a trading bloc gives its currency distinctive market status.

Whatever the reason, this high trade in the Australian dollar is not the sign of a third-world currency, though it is a currency that has extreme medium-term swings of value against the three major trading currencies. In current circumstances, with extensive facilities for hedging, large international companies are not seriously exposed to this volatility in the value of the Australian dollar, though the same cannot be said for smaller exporters, especially in agriculture or importers. The impact is also that domestic macroeconomic settings are driven conspicuously by potential inflationary impacts of exchange rate volatility − far more so than is required of larger countries.

Where does Australia stand?

The evidence just presented on international finance and investment suggests that Australia (or at least some part of capital of Australian origin) is an active player in the centres of international capitalism in Europe and the United States. The evidence presented in relation to patterns of trade and the composition of domestic industry suggests an Asian-oriented, peripheral country locked into low value-added industries and surviving by the sale of national assets. How can these two pictures be reconciled?

As posed, they cannot, so there is need to consider just how the question might be posed differently, so as to form a consistent picture. The 'problem' is that there is no single Australian story – international competition and the free movement of capital have seen different individual capitals go in different directions. Many of the medium-to-large firms are now truly international, and the extent to which these companies 'still call Australia home' is diminishing (Bryan and Rafferty 1997). Conversely, across a range of manufacturing industries that depended for decades upon tariff protection, the battle for survival still centres predominantly on political lobbying for isolation from international competition.

Australians individually have a corresponding fate. Some have joined the international labour market in vital, expanding industries such as finance, where North American executive remunerations set the benchmark for salary scales; others remain in near-defunct industries such as textiles, where Chinese and Indonesian wages set the benchmark. Under these sorts of pressures, Australia has seen a rapid polarization of wages and of income generally, though income inequality has not grown as rapidly as in the United States (Watson and Buchanan 2001)

But within this fractured experience of different facets of Australian industry and population, it is national economic policy that constructs the totalized image of a national economic identity.

The rise of competitiveness: implications for the labour market

From the mid-1980s, the state set about developing a raft of policies aimed at 'deregulation' and 'privatization', following broadly the trends of Thatcher's Britain and Reagan's United States. A distinctive characteristic of this transformation was that it occurred under four-teen years of Labour government, with the union movement locked into an 'Accord' with the government, giving peak union officials a voice in the detail, though not the direction, in which policy evolved. The effect was that some fundamental policy changes, with profound social ramifications, were introduced without significant opposition, except from the socialist left, which was already marginalized by its opposition to the Accord.

Concurrently, and perhaps discretely, the Australian dollar was floated at the end of 1983. There remains some debate as to whether this initiative was a matter of policy choice, or whether a managed exchange rate system had become unsustainable in the face of the growing global role of the Australian dollar. Either way, the float was associated with a discernible and decisive change in national economic policy arising out of 'the competitiveness agenda'. From that point on, a major driving force of (and rationale for) policy has been the pursuit of economic 'reform' to make industry in Australia 'internationally competitive'.

As well as the profound effects of tariff cuts that started from the mid-1980s, the most significant changes have been in the labour market. Australia began the twentieth century with a highly centralized system of wage determination and industrial dispute reso-lution. Indeed, tariffs and centralized wage fixation, along with the 'white Australia policy' that excluded non-European migration, were the three pillars of national policy from the formation of Australia as a discrete country in 1901 (Kelly 1994). But just as tariffs had survived throughout the twentieth century until the 1980s, so too did centralized wage fixation go into decline at roughly the same time.

The argument from the mid-1980s was that internationally com-petitive local industries are incompatible with centralized wage deter-mination. Companies, which now had to compete in internationally exposed markets, wanted the capacity individually to negotiate wages and conditions that reflected their particular circumstances, and not be burdened by national averages. Wages and working conditions had to be consistent with corporate profitability in internationally exposed markets. Hence there was, by government legislation, a progressive shift to enterprise-level determination of employment contracts, with the role of unions systematically reduced to workplace negotiators.

The consequences were dramatic, with some fundamental changes in the nature of the labour market. First, the dispersion of wages grew rapidly, as labour with bargaining power became unshackled by centralized wage determination and workers without bargaining power lost the protection of the centralized system. Real average earnings and real hourly labour costs remained in 1995 at the level they had been in 1982, while over the same period average labour productivity grew 15 per cent (Australian Treasury 2001). But the most dramatic change has come since the mid-1990s, associated with the state's strongest actions against the capacities of trade unions and the suppression of industrial conflict (Buchanan and Watson 2001).

Second, the casualization of employment grew dramatically, creating in Australia a highly insecure employment system. Casual employment, as a key measure of insecurity, grew by 70 per cent between 1989 and 1999 (compared with other employment growth of 9 per cent), so that, by 1999, 32 per cent of females and 26 per cent of males were in casual employment – the second highest rate among OECD countries (ABS 1999). This casualization has resulted in managers having tighter control over the way labour is deployed and the job done, so as to ensure that all hours worked are 'productive' (Burgess and Campbell 1998).

Third, working hours in Australia are getting longer. Australia has the fastest-growing working hours in the OECD, and it has the second longest working hours in the developed world – only South Koreans work longer average full-time hours, and in that country, unlike Australia, hours are decreasing. Further, Australia has the highest rate of unpaid overtime in the developed world. From 1985 to 2000, the proportion of employees working more than forty-five hours a week rose from 17.8 per cent to 26.1 per cent, with those working more than fifty hours jumping from 10.2 per cent to 17.4 per cent (Campbell 2001).

Fourth, unemployment has also stayed high across the cycle, at between 10.7 per cent in 1992/3 and 6.4 per cent in 2000/1 (ABS 2002a). Moreover, 20 per cent of part-time workers (equal to almost 6 per cent of employed people) are recorded as being under-employed (i.e. wanting full-time work) (ABS 2001c).

Not surprisingly, therefore, labour productivity in Australia grew in the 1990s at extraordinary rates. Indeed, for that decade, no OECD country exceeded Australia's productivity growth, and in the second half of the decade Australia was one of only two OECD countries to increase its productivity growth rate.[5] When we look to the reason for this growth, two related international comparisons of productivity growth by the OECD (Scarpetta et al. 2000) and the US Federal Reserve (Gust and Marquez 2000) are highly informative. Among the many factors that can cause labour productivity to grow (capital deepening, technological change, increased capital inputs, as well as the quality and intensity of labour), these reports associate Australia's record productivity growth predominantly with an increase in labour hours. This measure can be explained directly in terms of the changes in the employment contract system depicted above.

So it appears that Australian industry's 'competitiveness' is being sustained predominantly by the intensification of the labour process. Over the decade and a half that 'competitiveness' has been central to national economic policy, wages did not keep pace with increasing work effort. Working hours are getting longer, and employment is growing less secure. This represents the classic 'third world' response to globally competitive markets: in nations that have few industries at the frontiers of global levels of productivity (even if rates of productivity growth are high), the intensification of labour is being pursued to 'compensate', as it were, for less than leading absolute levels of productivity.

What has happened to wages and conditions of employment in Australia stands, in key respects, as the statement of the way in which Australia reconciles its dual attributes of a third-world industrial structure and its aggressive financial and corporate global integration. That is, some part of capital has become global in its production base, making conditions in Australia of diminishing importance. But that part of capital that remains in Australia, and is being attracted to Australia, is being drawn predominantly by low costs of production, not by exposure to a large and growing local market.

The Australian state (under both Labour and conservative governments) is complicit in the process. The sale of publicly owned industries and other assets, budgetary contractions and tax cuts, and a raft of policies to promote 'deregulation' of industry are rationalized as necessary in order to attain the higher goal of international competitiveness.

But perhaps there is a more generous interpretation of the role of the Australian state. This interpretation would focus on a severe problem of external balance, manifesting in mounting current account deficits (see Figure 7.3), and the need for a concerted policy response to this deficit. Here, the debate centres on those who see a need for fiscal austerity to rein in both private sector import demand and public sector debt, and those who are arguing that the state needed policies to initiate a manufacturing renaissance to generate export revenue and create jobs (see Bell 1997; Wiseman 1998; Sheil 2001).[6]

Alternatively, the state's policy strategy can be seen as an explicit class agenda, in which labour, as the immobile economic factor, has been systematically required to bear the burden of national economic adjustment. Wage increases less than productivity growth and the intensification of the labour process have substituted for the lack of a creative state industry policy initiative, and the failure of capital to innovate in local manufacturing industries.

In this scenario, which has become more explicit since the mid-1990s under a conservative government, we see that policy has not followed a simple path of 'privatization' and 'deregulation'. The driving force of policy is not laissez-faire but a systematic path of regulatory reform (sometimes deregulating, other times introducing new regulations and expenditures) which entrenches the power of capital in the name of having to make industry more profitable (Bryan 2001b).

Conclusion

Countries do not assume unique and consistent positions in a spectrum from periphery to centre. The world economy is structured by corporations and the relations between them, and we should not overstate the national characteristics of corporations. Hence the position occupied in the world economy by any locality or industry will be a reflection of the way corporations in that locality or industry are linked into global accumulation. A nation is too large a unit to be attributed an aggregated economic position in the world economy.

Nonetheless, there are national dimensions to accumulation, not least associated with the way in which nation-states invoke policies that construct national characteristics and rules. Perhaps there is something particular about the sorts of policy options perceived to be available to states in countries labelled 'semi-peripheral' that are established sites of accumulation, and where policies on accumulation within the country follow rather than set global trends. This depiction characterizes Australia over the past twenty years: accumulation has indeed globalized, and some leading global companies 'got their start' in Australia. But state policy has set the agenda of facilitating corporate initiatives and agendas rather than steering them.

For social democrats in Australia there has been a profound sense of disappointment in the last twenty years of economic policy choices. Policy-makers have taken the easy path of invoking 'market forces' as the unavoidable policy direction, and dressing it up in the language of competitiveness and national efficiency (e.g. Bell 1997; Capling et al. 1998). The social democrats will argue that there have been opportunities for hard choices to initiate state-driven programmes of nation-centred accumulation, and a focus on high technology, high productivity, and high growth sectors. Indeed, the models of Scandinavia and Asian industrialization are often invoked as the living alternatives for Australia to follow.

But the history of policy in Australia shows that capital had bolted – had internationalized – before the Australian state had systematically thought about reconfigured accumulation strategies. Industrial and financial corporations have headed for the centres of capitalism in Europe and North America, and the 'residual' capital in Australia is left in a lower league, relying on the physical attributes of land for mining and agriculture, or on extracting increased industrial productivity from labour intensification.

It is a story of accumulation that lacks a nation-centred dynamic, but where the global scale is intimidating. It is where successful capitals tend to leave their Australian origins behind, yet the Australian state and popular culture want to embrace those same companies as Australian ambassadors. It is a state in search of its own economy.

In practical, concrete policy, the Australian state has constructed its own economy not around capital (Australian industries, Australian innovation, and Australian-owned capital), but around labour. It has been labour in Australia that has taken on the mantle of securing national competitiveness via intensification and protraction of the working day, driven by increasingly casualized and insecure employment.

Labour is also defining Australian nationality on an international scale. Policies on 'free market' international openness in relation to trade, finance, and investment stand in stark contrast with policies on immigration that are highly restrictive and punitive. In recent years there has been a policy stand on refugees recognized internationally as inhumane and in breach of international law on refugees and on human rights. Here is a construction of national identity around labour ('us' and 'them') that sees the rest of the world as hostile. Indeed the refugee issue is recognized as having determined the outcome of Australia's 2001 general election.

This hostile attitude to migration feeds off the notion that Australia is alone, on the edge of the world, neither Asian nor European, neither a centre of capitalism nor a basket case, but looking to cut a distinctive international profile. In the absence of membership in a supranational bloc to make global integration 'safe', state social policies of xenophobia resonate deeply within the electorate. The tyranny of distance is transformed into a fear of proximity.

Notes

1. These and other basic data on Australian economic structure can be found (on-line) from the Australian Bureau of Statistics (ABS).

2. Effective rate of assistance is a measure of the support given to an industry by the state (through import tariffs and quotas and budgetary outlays, state marketing schemes, etc.) net of the costs imposed on that industry that come from assistance to other industries. For example, the effective rate of assistance to mining is made up predominantly of the tax concessions for mining investment less the costs imposed on the mining industry by having to pay tariffs on imported capital equipment. Half of this assistance goes to two industries: textiles, clothing, and footwear; and passenger motor vehicles.

3. See Cawthorne 2000, summarized in Kitching 2002: 35–6.

4. Australia escaped the Asian financial crisis largely unscathed for two key reasons: first, low levels of Australian-owned investment in Asia; and, second, trade (in contracts signed in US dollars) in basic commodities that could, unlike specialist manufactures, be readily diverted to markets in other regions.

5. The other was Switzerland.

6. My own view is that the construction of a balance-of-payments deficit was and is a product of the anachronistic structure of balance-of-payments accounting (Bryan 2001a), and that the way that Australia's current account deficit has been constructed is open to debate. In brief, the international borrowing for international investment by companies of Australian origin is recorded in Australia's balance of payments, and the interest payments on those loans are recorded as outflows from Australia. Yet these loans were in fact repaid from internationally earned income, not from Australia itself. Moreover, as private sector debt, this was never an 'Australian' liability, and when some of the big international investors became insolvent and liquidated after 1987, their 'foreign debt' was instantly written off from 'Australia's' foreign debt. Hence, the current account 'constraint' was itself largely a product of the way in which balance-of-payments accounting recorded how capital from Australia had internationalized in the 1980s.

References

ABS (Australian Bureau of Statistics) (1999) *Labour Force, Australia*, ABS Cat. no. 6203.0, July.

ABS (2001a) *International Investment Position, Australia. Supplementary Country Statistics, 2000–01*, ABS Cat. no. 5352.0.

ABS (2001b) *International Merchandise Trade, Australia, Feature Article – Export and Import Currencies*, ABS Cat. no. 5422.0, March.

ABS (2001c) *Labour Force, Australia Special Article – Unemployment and Supplementary Measures of Underutilized Labour*, ABS Cat. no. 6203.0, February.

ABS (2002a) *Australia Now: Persons Unemployed*, www.abs.gov.au/Ausstats/abs%40. nsf/94713ad445ff1425ca25682000192af2/164b9a9eda3f619aca256cbf00172a15! OpenDocument.

ABS (2002b) *International Merchandise Trade, Australia*, ABS Cat. no. 5244.0, June.

Australian Treasury (2001) *Unit Labour Costs*, Australian Treasury.

Bell S. (1997) *Ungoverning the Economy: The Political Economy of Australian Economic Policy*, Melbourne: Oxford University Press.

Blainey, G. (1966) *The Tyranny of Distance: How Distance Shaped Australia's History*, Macmillan: South Melbourne.

Bryan, D. (2001a) 'Accounting for National Economic Identity', *Review of Radical Political Economics* 33: 57–71.

Bryan, D. (2001b) 'The Rush to Regulate: The Shift in Australia from the Rule of Markets to the Rule of Capital', *Australian Journal of Social Issues*, vol. 35, no. 4: 333–49.

Bryan, D. and M. Rafferty (1997) 'Still Calling Australia Home: International Integration and the Framing of National Economic Problems in Recent Official Reports', *Australian Journal of International Affairs*, vol. 51, no. 1.

Bryan, D. and M. Rafferty (1999) *The Global Economy in Australia*, Sydney: Allen & Unwin.

Buchanan, J. and I. Watson, (2001) 'The Failure of the Third Way in Australia: Implications for Policy about Work', *Competition & Change* 5: 1–37.

Burgess, J. and I. Campbell (1998) 'Casual Employment in Australia: Growth, Characteristics, a Bridge or a Trap?' *The Economic and Labour Relations Review*, vol. 9, no. 1: 31–54.

Campbell, I. (2001) 'Cross-National Comparisons – Work Time around the World', commissioned paper for Australian Council of Trade Unions' Reasonable Hours Test Case.

Capling, A., M. Considine and M. Crozier (1998) *Australian Politics in the Global Era*, Melbourne: Addison Wesley Longman.

Cawthorne, P. (2000) 'Fiji's Garment Export Industry: An Economic and Political Analysis of Its Long-Term Viability?', School of Economics and Political Science, University of Sydney Working Paper ECOP 2000–03.

Gust, C. and J. Marquez (2000) 'Productivity Developments Abroad', *Federal Reserve Bulletin*, October: 655–81.

HSBC (1998) *The Fifth Global Currency*, Australia: HSBC.

Journal of Australian Political Economy (2000) 'Round Table on the Falling Australian Dollar', no. 46.

Kelly, P. (1994) *The End Of Certainty: Power, Politics and Business in Australia*, Sydney: Allen & Unwin.

Kitching, G. (2002) *Seeking Justice through Globalization*, University Park, PA: Penn State Press.

OECD (Organization for Economic Cooperation and Development) (1992) *International Direct Investment: Policies and Trends in the 1980s*, Paris: OECD.

Productivity Commission, Australia (2001) *Trade and Assistance Review 2000–01*, Canberra: AusInfo, December.

Reserve Bank of Australia (RBA) (2002) 'Australian Financial Markets', *Reserve Bank of Australia Bulletin*, June: 6–21.

Scarpetta, S., A. Bassanini, D. Pilat and P. Schreyer (2000) 'Economic Growth in the OECD Area: Recent Trends at the Aggregate and Sectoral Level', OECD Economics Department Working Paper no. 248, June.

Shawcross, W. (1993) *Rupert Murdoch – Ringmaster of the Information Circus*, London: Pan.

Sheil, C. (ed.) (2001) *Globalisation: Australian Impacts*, Sydney: UNSW Press.

Thomas, T. (1997) 'Top Exporters Go North', *Business Review Weekly*, 28 January: 48–50.

Watson, I. and J. Buchanan (2001) 'Beyond Impoverished Visions of the Labour Market', in R. Fincher and P. Saunders (eds), *Rethinking Poverty, Inequality and Disadvantage in Australia*, Sydney: Allen & Unwin.

Wiseman, J. (1998) *Global Nation? Australia and the Politics of Globalisation*, Cambridge and Melbourne: Cambridge University Press.

8

Australia:
Neo-liberal Globalism
and the Local State

Ray Broomhill

World-wide, a powerful coalition of global corporations, right-wing think-tanks, and international political institutions promote neo-liberalism as the only viable framework within which national economies will be able to make a successful transition into the new global economy. While these proponents of neo-liberal globalism focus attention on restructuring the nation-state, many of them also regard it as important to restructure the policies of the state at the local level as well. This chapter examines the impact of 'neo-liberal localism' with a particular focus on the Australian example. It specifically explores the differential impacts of neo-liberal restructuring on states such as South Australia which occupy peripheral positions within an Australian economy, which itself, of course, occupies a semi-peripheral position in international capitalism.

Australia has three levels of government: national, state, and 'local'. However, 'local' (i.e. municipal) governments in Australia have very limited resources and policy responsibilities. 'State' (i.e. provincial) governments, on the other hand, influence some of the nation's key regulatory arrangements affecting both capital accumulation and social reproduction. Consequently, political economy debates about the nature and role of the 'local state' apply most aptly to the 'state' level in the Australian context. Over the past decade or more, Australian state governments have, to different degrees, adopted neo-liberal policies. As in other countries, these policies have quite dramatically increased social and economic inequalities and frequently produced 'fractured local economies, disempowered regions and fragmented local cultures' (Amin 1994: 27). However, state political leaders have argued that the emergence of a very different global economic environment in the wake of global restructuring leaves no alternative to such a shift.

The message of neo-liberalism has been that the rapid globalization of the world economy has made it imperative that local economies must become internationally competitive and the role of government must be totally reshaped in order to survive. In this process, every corner of society and the economy must be brought into the market sphere. Its promoters have successfully created a discourse around economic policy-making that has effectively 're-imagined' the local region itself and its place in the world. In the discourse of neo-liberal localism, the local region is 'imagined' no longer as a political, economic, and cultural community, but rather narrowly as an 'economic' entity. The primary goal of policy-makers then becomes to facilitate entrepreneurial activities within the private sector to achieve increased global economic competitiveness. Proponents of neo-liberalism portray this shift as due to the inevitable failure of Keynesianism and the subsequent restoration of the proper (that is, far more limited) role of government.

Many on the political left also seem to have adopted the view that global changes have left local states with little or no real alterative to neo-liberalism – leading in some instances to predictions about the emergence of an enduring neo-liberal local state form (Patterson and Pinch 1995). The idea that local states and communities are firmly locked into a neo-liberal policy framework as a result of globalization is superficially plausible. However, it is based upon questionable assumptions that warrant critical examination, because there are far-reaching implications for political practice. Acceptance of this discourse of inevitability is politically disempowering and detrimental to the generation of any form of progressive alternative policy. This is undoubtedly at least part of the reason why social-democratic parties, in Australia and elsewhere, have recently displayed a 'disarming enthusiasm' for economic orthodoxy and little or no interest in progressive alternatives (Howell 2001: 33). The aim of this chapter is to question the inevitability of this apparent nexus between global economic restructuring and neo-liberal policies at the local level. It does so by using a 'regulation approach' to question the extent to which neo-liberal policy regimes at the state level are likely to prove sustainable over time.

A regulation framework

The 'regulation approach' to understanding capitalist development originated among left-leaning French social science academics in the late 1970s (Aglietta 1979; Leborgne and Lipietz 1988).[1] As this approach emerged near the end of the long post-war boom, a key research question for early regulation theorists was the need to explain how capitalism, a system with a strong tendency towards recurring instability, crisis, and change, nevertheless regularly manages to experience extended periods of sustained growth and relative stability. Regulationists focused particularly on two features that were central to understanding and explaining the 'systematic coherence' of individual phases of growth within the longer-term unevenness of capitalist development and crisis (Amin 1994: 8). First, each expansionary phase of capitalist development was seen to be characterized by a specific 'mode of accumulation' at the level of the whole economy, representing a more or less coherent process of capital accumulation. Regulationists, and others, have often utilized the Gramscian term 'Fordism' to characterize the accumulation regime that reached its zenith in the post-war period of the long boom with the shift to mass production techniques and mass consumer markets.

Second, regulation theory emphasizes the dialectical nature of the relationship between capital accumulation and capitalism's social, political, and cultural context. The concept 'mode of regulation' is used to characterize the political, economic, and social institutional arrangements within a particular society at a particular time that provide the 'regulatory framework' needed to support and sustain economic growth. At a general level the mode of regulation that accompanied post-war Western capitalism has been characterized as the 'Keynesian welfare state' – a term which is often used as a short-hand summary for the particular framework of political and economic institutions that emerged in conjunction with the mass production and mass consumption phase of capitalism in the post-war decades. The institutional forms that emerged within the Fordist era included nationally specific, but usually Keynesian-inspired, state regulation of labour and wage relations, of competition, and of the national economy's insertion in the international economic regime. Importantly, more informal forms of regulation, including cultural and social processes, have also been critical in creating patterns of mass integration and social coherence – serving to secure capitalist reproduction and to stabilize 'inherent crisis tendencies' during the Fordist era (Peck and Tickell 1992: 349).

Regulation theory emphasizes that the form of any regulatory regime is not predetermined or predictable but is arrived at through political struggles, negotiations, and compromises. The particular form of economic, political, and social regulation is therefore never static but continually evolving through ongoing political interactions and conflicts. Periods of relative stability only arise from political and economic compromises that have been struck between conflicting interests within the society. These temporary 'institutional fixes' (Peck and Tickell 1994a), while playing a crucial role in facilitating capital accumulation during a period of sustained growth, invariably prove to be unstable in the longer term and certainly do not eliminate crisis tendencies and contradictions within the system. Ultimately, as capital accumulation falters and signs of economic crisis re-emerge, the regulatory institutional framework also begins to fracture and come unstuck. In fact, crises in the existing institutional arrange- ments may themselves contribute to, and accelerate, the next crisis of capital accumulation and period of restructuring. Therefore it is not inevitable that there will be a stable and sustainable economic, political, and social framework at any particular stage in the cycles of capitalist accumulation.

While the 'regulation approach' is usually focused primarily upon the nation-state, it is important to develop a more subtle awareness of regional variations within countries since there are significant dif- ferences in the impact of economic, political, and social restructuring at the local level. Such a perspective goes a long way to help explain patterns of uneven development within a nation-state as well as globally. While processes of capital accumulation are increasingly global, the patterns of accumulation, regulation, and social reproduc- tion that emerge in each region are formed within a local context and therefore are different and distinctive. Hence it is pertinent to consider the possibility of distinctive local or regional modes of regulation as well as of accumulation. One significant implication of this analysis is that some regions with particular existing structures of accumulation and regulation may be favoured by global changes and by national accumulation strategies while others may be equally disadvantaged.

The importance of examining regional modes of regulation is particularly significant in countries with federal structures such as

Australia, Canada, the USA, West Germany, and Switzerland. In Australia, in particular, state governments are responsible for a substantial share of total public expenditures, and while the powers of the states vis-à-vis the national government are circumscribed in many ways, these regional governments are responsible for the policy development and delivery of many important economic, social, and administrative services. Australian state governments effectively determine some of the country's key regulatory arrangements affecting both capital accumulation and social reproduction. In the post-war period, state governments have been crucial to the accumulation process, accounting for up to 60 per cent of public investment activity through provision of basic economic infrastructure such as road and rail, and essential utilities such as electricity, gas, and water provision. State governments are heavily involved in social regulation since state public services have been responsible for the majority of government expenditures on education, law and order, some welfare services, some industrial relations, and for most business, workplace, environmental, and social regulations. Through these means, state governments in the post-war Fordist era played a significant role in creating and mediating the series of 'temporary institutional fixes' that constituted the regulatory arrangements underpinning Australian capitalism. Similarly, in the post-Keynesian period, Australian state governments have been at the forefront of the process by which both the accumulation regime and regulatory arrangements have been dramatically restructured.

The rise of local neo-liberalism

The breakdown of the Fordist mode of regulation has been a key factor in the rise of neo-liberalism over the last few decades. During the long boom of the post-war period, successful capital accumulation was supported by Keynesian macroeconomic policies; the development of a welfare state; corporatist class arrangements between capital, labour, and the state; and government intervention to promote investment, stability, and consumption. It was also based upon a set of social relations and gender arrangements which were underpinned by the state and which provided the social and economic stability required to sustain economic accumulation. In Australia these policies involved a relatively high level of local state intervention in the economy primarily by promoting successful capital accumulation and in facilitating political stability and social reproduction. Local states pursued economic strategies that sought to gain maximum benefit from federal industry protection policies, combined with the extensive provision of public economic and social infrastructure and services to attract private investment from foreign investors and away from the other states.

There were clear differences in the processes of regulation and the role of the local state from region to region. The South Australian state government policy approach during this period has been categorized as a 'high revenue–high expenditure type' (Gerritsen 1988: 154). It not only stimulated economic development but also actively promoted increased social development, coherence, and equity, especially in the 1970s, when an actively reformist Labour government was in office under the charismatic leadership of premier Don Dunstan. At the same time, governments in New South Wales, Western Australia, and Victoria maintained fundamentally Keynesian policies to facilitate accumulation but were 'median revenue–median expenditure types' and less interventionist in areas of social reproduction. The ultra-conservative state of Queensland, by contrast, was seen as a 'low revenue–low expenditure type' with a very different, more conservative, pattern of social regulatory arrangements.

By the late 1960s the strain was beginning to show in the post-war Fordist model. A period of restructuring ensued from the 1970s onwards, causing traumatic change at the expense of large sections of the community and, indeed, of sections of capital itself. Capital increasingly perceived the liberal Keynesian political framework and policies of the post-war era as impediments to its desire, and need, to have unrestricted free movement in and out of national economies. This phase of capitalist restructuring is 'global' in scope but is also 'local' in effect. The restructuring of transnational capital and the global marketplace has, in turn, resulted in enormously increased pressure on state governments to adopt 'free market' public policy approaches.

Neo-liberalism has gained widespread support from capital since the collapse of the Fordist regime of accumulation because it seeks to facilitate and reinforce the processes of restructuring, emphasizing their therapeutic role following the 'bust' period of the cycle of capitalist development. By reducing government regulation of business, by reducing government ownership of industry, and by lifting geographical restraints on the free flow of capital and commodities, neo-liberal policies seek to maximize the ability of capital to restructure. In particular, deregulation and privatization permit key sections of capital to shift investment out of areas of declining profitability while creating new areas for potentially profitable investment. At the same time, labour market deregulation, the abandonment of corporatist compromise arrangements between capital, labour, and the state, and the reduction of state welfare expenditures all reinforce the disciplining of the workforce that is occurring anyway as a result of increased unemployment and labour market competition. In regulationist terms, neo-liberalism has been the vehicle for the rationalization and restructuring of the outmoded components of the Fordist mode of social regulation that are no longer perceived by capital as desirable, or necessary, for capital accumulation.

The impact of these pressures on state governments in Australia has been profound. The increased flexibility and mobility of restructured global capital has created a bidding competition between sub-national governments and between local workforces. This phenomenon has been approvingly described within the discourse of mainstream economics in Australia as 'competitive federalism' (Groenewold et al. 2001). In practice, the states have adopted beggar-thy-neighbour policies as they compete ferociously for available sources of investment funds. For example, immediately upon its election to office in 1996 the conservative Queensland state government announced that it intended to engage in 'open warfare' to poach business from the other states (Broomhill and Spoehr 1996). State government policy statements have frequently stressed the need for the local economy to develop 'global competitiveness' (Bryan 1995). It typically means a strong shift towards what might be termed a more entrepreneurial state role. Alain Lipietz identifies its ideological underpinnings as the adoption of a culture of 'liberal productivism', whereby all decisions are determined on the basis of their contribution to growth and productivity (Lipietz 1994: 343–5). The demands of social reproduction have, temporarily at least, been demoted to a second-order priority. The adoption of such a 'liberal-productivist' approach has occurred at the expense of a severe loss of social coherence and political democracy.

This entrepreneurial approach has been endorsed by both major political parties and to varying degrees has been accepted by both local business and the trade-union movement. It has been partly

driven by the pressures on state governments arising from the re-
strictionist fiscal policies of successive federal governments, which
have themselves been dramatically affected by the impact of global
restructuring on their own financial capacity. Because the Australian
states have had financial responsibility for many of the welfare and
social aspects of government activity, the fiscal crisis passed on to
them from the federal government has placed them under further
strain and greatly contributed to their shift to a narrower, and more
economistic, approach to governance.

The limits of local neo-liberalism

Neo-liberalism has played an important role in providing a 'conditioning framework' that has facilitated many of capital's short-term
goals in the restructuring process (Grinspun and Kreklewich 1994).
While advocates of neo-liberal globalism habitually overstate the
achievements and inevitability of local neo-liberalism, the discussion above also suggests that critics of neo-liberalism may have
underestimated the logic and benefits for capital, at least in the short
term, arising from the neo-liberal restructuring of the local state.
However, this does not necessarily mean that neo-liberalism provides
a regulatory framework that can sustain the successful transition to a
new accumulation regime. In fact, there are several indications that
neo-liberalism has so far provided a very unstable framework for any
new post-Fordist regime – particularly at the local level.

A sustainable regime of capital accumulation?

While the shift to a neo-liberal policy approach may have been
successful in facilitating global capital restructuring and in restoring
profitability to some sectors of local capital following the collapse
of post-war Fordism, it is not evident that it has succeeded in
creating new modes of productive accumulation within the majority of regions. A considerable body of international research has
demonstrated the negative effects of the globalization process on
local regional economies and the failures of neo-liberalism to deliver
either economic or employment growth in response to the challenges posed by global restructuring. For example, British geographer
Mike Geddes has argued that, in 'the context of overall levels of

unemployment, neo-liberal industrial policy has ... been associated with the collapse of many local economies' (Geddes 1994: 157). In a study of the impact of restructuring strategies in Europe, Ash Amin and Anders Malmberg conclude that policies of the entrepreneurial model of local economic development have exposed 'local communities to the horrifying prospect of becoming the playing field for a thousand-and-one different entrepreneurial ventures, bound together by nothing more than the profit-seeking adventurism of the private sector' (Amin and Malmberg 1994: 244). The capacity of neo-liberalism to solve the problems of local economies is also questioned by Jamie Peck and Adam Tickell, who argue that evidence of its failure to produce recovery can be found even in the 'showcase' regions of neo-liberalism such as Britain's M4 motorway corridor and the Californian technopoles (Peck and Tickell 1994b: 295).

In contrast to the exaggerated claims of the advocates of neo-liberal localism, it appears that the processes of neo-liberal restructuring are more commonly resulting in ongoing systemic instability for local economies. Of course, not all regions and localities are in decline – even in semi-peripheral countries outside the dominant core economies. Cities and regions are actually being structurally transformed in a very uneven process. A small number of large cities in the core economies have clearly become central nodes in international administrative, financial, commercial, and informational networks. Simultaneously, though, many former industrial centres are unable to make a transition to the informational economy. Only some cities and regions are able to flourish under neo-liberal globalism. Consequently, what we are witnessing is a growing polarization between different economic regions and the exacerbation of spatial inequalities as shifting global markets produce winners and losers in the international competitive arena.

Within Australia, there is clear evidence of the unequal impact of global restructuring and the application of neo-liberal state strategies. The key 'global' cities, Sydney in particular and Melbourne to a lesser extent, are able to use their existing resources to extend and deepen their global reach. Simultaneously, the more peripheral regional centres, such as Adelaide (capital of South Australia) and Hobart (capital of Tasmania), are facing severe obstacles in their attempts to make the transition to the informational economy. To a large extent these different outcomes of the restructuring process are the result of differences in the patterns of accumulation and the regulatory arrangements that emerged during the Fordist era in different states. However, this emerging economic and social polarization has been compounded by federal and state policies following the collapse of the Fordist accumulation regime and the subsequent process of restructuring. Federal government cuts in funding to state governments have impacted more harshly on the smaller states. The shift to a beggar-thy-neighbour approach to attracting international and national investment has greatly disadvantaged the weaker states, which have little hope of winning in such an unequal competition.

For example, the state of South Australia is a particularly vulnerable local economy in the current restructuring scenario. Historically it has occupied a somewhat marginalized position within the overall Australian economy. For over a hundred years after its foundation as a state in 1836 the South Australian economy was dominated by agricultural production. The quarter-century following World War II saw the rapid development of manufacturing, supported by state assistance, to the point where the economy became heavily reliant upon it for employment and economic growth. However, the manufacturing sector provided a brittle and limited base for the local economy. Investment came primarily from outside the state, the sector increasingly comprising branch offices of interstate and transnational firms. When the impact of global economic restructuring hit South Australia during the mid-1970s, the effect was to cause many of these firms to restructure, rationalize, or relocate their production. Furthermore, because of the small size of its economy, manufacturing investment was focused on the production of a rather narrow range of goods, especially in electrical appliances and motor vehicles. With the downturn in these industries in the 1970s, the local economy was left without a broad range of manufacturing activity that could act as the base for diversification. Thus the breakdown of post-war Fordist accumulation and the impact of global restructuring affected South Australia particularly severely.

Importantly, however, the problems faced by South Australia have been compounded by the failures of an economic policy approach heavily influenced by neo-liberal principles over the past two decades. Successive state governments have focused on neo-liberal policy goals of debt reduction, privatization, and labour market deregulation, while cutting public sector infrastructure and employment. The result has been that the South Australian economy has stagnated over the past twenty years. Its unemployment levels have typically been the highest in the country (with the exception of the yet more peripheral state of Tasmania), there has been population loss through labour migration, and extensive capital flight has occurred. The credibility of the neo-liberal policy framework has been severely eroded in all Australian states by its demonstrated failure to achieve the economic benefits that it initially promised.

From the perspective of a regulation approach, the failure of neo-liberalism to restore growth and employment and to provide a new neo-liberal post-Fordist 'mode of accumulation' is unsurprising given that neo-liberalism has actually inhibited the emergence of any potentially new phase of productive investment. The widespread adoption of neo-liberalism by governments, while facilitating restructuring by some sectors of capital and benefiting certain regions, has created a situation which has encouraged capital to withhold new productive investment and to seek short-term profit-making in unproductive areas of speculative investment. This is a scenario that is ultimately unsustainable (Dierckxsens 2000). While capital has enthusiastically embraced a more market-oriented role for government to meet its short-term needs, in the long term it requires the state to actively regulate and facilitate social and economic processes. This point was profoundly made by Karl Polanyi and has been reiterated more recently by neo-Marxist scholars (Polanyi 1957; Bryan 2000: 333). The free-market approach promoted by neo-liberalism is fundamentally incompatible with capital's longer-term need to generate a new post-Fordist 'mode of accumulation' – at both national and local levels.

A sustainable regulatory framework?

The capacity of neo-liberalism to initiate and sustain a new phase of capitalist growth is further called into question by the limited extent to which it has succeeded in actually developing a coherent and sustainable regulatory framework. Of course, a number of analysts have argued that, although neo-liberalism has been destructive to many local economies, it has been successful in entrenching a regulatory framework that is now extensive and effectively comprises a new neo-liberal local state form. However, there is reason to question the validity of this perceived hegemonic spread of local neo-liberalism. While there has been a strong shift to neo-liberal policies at the local as well as the national level, there has also emerged, albeit in a fragmented way, a range of interventionist local economic policies and approaches that are neo-Keynesian in nature. Increasing competition between urban regions since the 1970s has pushed many local governments towards the adoption of a more entrepreneurial neo-liberal approach, but has led others to adopt more interventionist strategies. British geographers Aram Eisenschitz and Jamie Gough argue that, despite the dominance of neo-liberalism at the national level, most of the quite rapid growth of local economic initiatives in developed capitalist countries is neo-Keynesian (Eisenschitz and Gough 1996: 434).

Even in cases where sub-national governments have adopted a fundamentally neo-liberal approach to policy-making in general, their 'basket' of policies sometimes includes elements which are essentially neo-Keynesian in the sense of seeking to use non-market coordination to address particular market inadequacies and failures. These seemingly contradictory policy trends not only represent different responses to restructuring by different local states but often are manifested side by side within the same strategy. Sub-national governments in most industrialized countries have come under pressure from many conflicting sources and have, therefore, faced increasing difficulties in formulating coherent policy responses to the challenges raised by globalization. In Australia, the policy approaches of state Labour governments over the past decade, while increasingly influenced by neo-liberalism, have continued to manifest a number of elements of a more interventionist economic strategy towards promoting growth. In South Australia, for example, maintaining support for tariff protection for local car manufacturing industries is a pragmatic concern taking precedence over neo-liberal policy commitments. In general, state governments have faced considerable pressures to reconcile neo-liberal policies with other, more politically reformist and socially egalitarian, goals – including the ongoing provision of essential social infrastructure.

How, then, are we to explain the continuation of forms of state intervention at the local level even within the context of an increasingly neo-liberal global world? A number of reasons can be identified. Of key importance has been the failure of national governments to resolve the economic problems arising from the end of the post-war boom, leading to greater emphasis on state-led economic growth strategies at the local level in many countries. Moreover, the increasingly uneven impact of global restructuring on sub-national regions has forced many regions, especially those most severely disadvantaged by it, to adopt a more active state economic strategy rather than rely solely on aggregate national growth and the 'invisible hand' of the market.

In addition, it is very important to note that some scope remains for political choice in economic strategy. While neo-liberal policies have been adopted by social-democratic governments, it is nevertheless true that their most consistent, and rigorous, application has occurred only under conservative regimes. In Australia, the initial adoption of neo-liberal policies occurred in New South Wales (NSW) with the election in March 1988 of the Liberal government led by Nick Greiner. This marked the beginning of a decade of domination by conservative governments in all states after the previous decade of domination by Labour. The NSW government was quickly outpaced by the radical free-market policy approach taken by Victorian Liberal premier Jeff Kennett. Kennett's government applied extreme cuts to public services and adopted radical policies of privatization and labour market deregulation. The neo-liberal agenda was then extended by a Western Australian Liberal government headed by Premier Richard Court, who initiated three 'waves' of anti-union industrial relations legislation. Finally, in South Australia the moderate faction of the Liberal government that had been elected in 1993 was replaced in 1996 by a faction that took the neo-liberal agenda to further extremes by privatizing or contracting out not only transport and government services but also the supply of water and power. Significantly, however, the political pendulum swung quite dramatically in the Australian states in the middle and late 1990s. While a federal conservative government replaced Labour in 1996 and toughened up the implementation of the previous government's 'soft' neo-liberal agenda, the conservative state governments began to fall one by one until, by early 2002, all the Australian states and territories were governed by Labour. While state Labour governments are certainly continuing to be influenced by neo-liberalism, they have not applied it with the full enthusiasm of the conservative parties.

Problems of social reproduction

To be sustainable in the longer term, capitalism requires far more than a coherent mode of accumulation. As Polanyi observed, 'the human economy … is embedded and enmeshed in institutions, economic and non-economic. The inclusion of the non-economic is vital. For religion and government may be as important for the structure and functioning of the economy as monetary institutions' (quoted in Jessop 2001: 214). During the post-war Fordist period, growth and stability were underpinned not only by a specific set of economic and political regulatory institutions but also by a more informal set of social and cultural arrangements essential to the reproduction of the post-war capitalist model. A critical question concerning the future sustainability of the neo-liberal model of governance is whether it can provide a stable and sustainable social regulatory framework capable of ensuring secure reproduction in a 'post-Keynesian' era.

A range of nationally and locally specific Keynesian political and economic institutions provided the 'temporary institutional fixes' which were critical to supporting accumulation in the post-war era, but these were integrally related to an emerging set of cultural norms and values that played an important role in securing social reproduction. These included the increasing adoption of the values of mass consumerism, of modernism, of state welfarism, and of the 'male breadwinner model' of the nuclear family. Of course, such values were far from hegemonic and were contested and contradicted by competing values in a dynamic process of evolution. They were also variable and place-specific, reflecting the existing culture of different countries and regions together with the dynamics of the social processes at work in each locality. Also important in influencing the different Fordist patterns of social reproduction were the patterns of class, gender, and race relations within each country and region. For example, gender relations under the Fordist regime of capital accumulation supported the use of women's unpaid labour for the undertaking of a range of productive and reproductive activities within households and communities. Men's paid labour, in turn, was remunerated at levels that could support the household/family system. Together these more informal processes of social regulation were crucial in defining and securing a stable pattern of social reproduction, at least for a lengthy period of time during the post-war decades.

With the collapse of post-war Keynesianism, many of these dominant norms and values, as well as patterns of class, gender, and race relations, have experienced dramatic changes. Of course, these had been undergoing change prior to the onset of global restructuring. Indeed, the changes that were occurring (increasingly rapidly by the 1960s) in these social and cultural phenomena were actually significant contributors to the breakdown of Fordism itself. For example, the male breadwinner model in gender relations was being rapidly transformed by several dramatic changes that were occurring, including the increasing participation of women in the paid labour market, the increasing financial independence of women (from men at least if not from the state) through the introduction of the welfare system, and the transforming influence of the women's movement.

At first glance, over the past couple of decades the discourse of neo-liberalism appears to have been remarkably successful, not only in influencing the thinking of policy-makers, but also in bringing about a significant change in popular culture and values. Many commentators have observed the increasing adoption of the neo-liberal values of competitiveness and individualism – the manifestation of the culture of 'liberal productivism' identified by Lipietz (1994: 343–5). For example, the norms and values of neo-liberal capitalism appear to be increasingly embraced by a new generation of shareholders and small investors. The percentage of shareholders in the population has risen sharply in many countries. Welfare recipients and even prisoners are now conceptualized as 'clients'. Fewer and fewer workers belong to collective trade unions. More and more citizens proudly display the logos of global corporations on their clothing. These all appear to be signs of a widespread adoption of neo-liberal values, auguring well for the success of a new 'mode of social regulation' capable of supporting a more competitive, flexible, and individualized form of capital accumulation.

However, there are reasons to be sceptical of the sustainability of a new neo-liberal cultural hegemony. The adoption by governments of market-oriented policies has resulted in a quite dramatic decline in support provided for essential welfare and social reproduction. In effect, there has been a marked shift away from social welfare to social authoritarianism as the primary strategy for maintaining social control. In Australia, this tendency is most directly reflected in static or even reduced state government expenditures on public health, education, housing, transport, and community services at a time when demands on these services have substantially increased as a result of the social impact of economic restructuring. At the same time, state governments have significantly increased expenditures on 'law and order' areas while strengthening regulatory arrangements governing social welfare recipients.

These policies have further increased the extent of social fragmentation and exacerbated the negative effects of global restructuring itself. They have resulted in the emergence of severe social problems, increasing inequalities and the breakdown of the processes of social cohesion and reproduction in many local areas. In Australia, many households and families have come under greatly increased stress – evidenced by rising poverty levels, crime, violence, and gambling. Cutbacks to social services and infrastructure provision have affected disadvantaged communities disproportionately. Throughout Australia, outer suburban working-class communities have had to bear the real burdens of high unemployment and locational disadvantage resulting from poor access to jobs, services, and infrastructure. Cuts in funding for public housing have further exacerbated the problems of these areas. Homelessness grew steadily during the 1990s and large numbers of people are also now living in marginal accommodation forms such as caravans and other relocatable dwellings. On the other hand, advantaged areas within the major cities have increasingly become the preserve of high-income households. The gap between rich and poor suburbs is dramatically widening, with incomes in Australia's richest suburbs growing at three times the rate of those in low-income areas. Real incomes rose by 7 per cent between 1996 and 2000 in the poorer areas compared to 22 per cent in the richest areas (Harding et al. 2001). Nationally the percentage of the population living below the poverty line increased from 12.5 per cent in 1975 to 16.7 per cent in 1996 (Fincher and Nieuwenhuysen 1998: 4).

Even in those regions and cities that appear to be flourishing, social polarization has been exacerbated as the benefits of restructuring are distributed with growing unevenness through increasing market-oriented policies. For example, although Sydney has been experiencing a building and finance boom that has provided benefits to a core group of workers and property owners, an increasing percentage of the population, especially those located in the peripheral western suburbs, are being left out. A national report on poverty in 2001 found that the state of New South Wales, of which Sydney is the capital, had the highest rate of poverty in the country in spite of also being the wealthiest state (Harding et al. 2001).

However, although the social impact of neo-liberalism has been widespread, it has been especially severe in those states that have already been in the most vulnerable economic position. In South Australia there is particular evidence of widespread social disintegration and household stress resulting from the impact of neo-liberal policies. The number of South Australian households whose incomes were below 60 per cent of average weekly earnings, for example, rose from 25.8 per cent to 41.7 per cent between the 1986 census and the 1996 census. South Australia has experienced one of the biggest rises in bankruptcies of any Australian state. Most of these were not business people but workers affected by excessive use of credit cards, unemployment, domestic break-ups, and the lack of adequate health insurance (*Advertiser*, 11 March 1996). One of the impacts of declining economic security has been a dramatic rise in gambling activity among working-class households. State governments, under pressure from neo-liberal pressure groups to achieve balanced budgets while at the same time reducing taxes, have increasingly turned to income from the rapidly expanding gambling industry to maintain revenues: gambling turnover in South Australia increased by 50 per cent between 1993 and 1998 (*Advertiser*, 30 October 1998). The state also experienced the highest rate of robberies in the country, with these crimes almost trebling over a decade from the mid-1980s to the mid-1990s (*Advertiser*, 3 June 1996).

Economic restructuring and neo-liberalism are also reshaping the responsibilities and the organization of the household/family system, having a profound impact on everyday life and gender relations within many households. The changes by capital and the state to the support of the family/household system have undermined the 'Fordist' arrangements whereby women provided their unpaid socially reproductive labour within the context of a family wage. Many working-class households now depend on two income earners. The number of single-parent households is also rising, requiring other women to seek paid employment to support their dependent children. The rapid rise in single-parent families is one of the biggest causes of impoverishment in the restructuring process as an increasing number of nuclear families disintegrate. As publicly provided welfare services are downsized, the state is facing a 'welfare crisis' as rising numbers of needy people turn to private community agencies which are already stretched to capacity and increasingly unable to cope. A major private welfare agency in Adelaide reported an 80

per cent increase in the demand for emergency assistance over the
five years to 1996 (*Advertiser*, 19 May 1998). A nationwide survey
found that in 1997, 11,800 South Australians experienced at least
one bout of homelessness. These statistics included 3,600 children
and 3,700 women. The most common reasons included violence in
the home, family breakdown, financial crisis, unemployment, and
mental illness (*Advertiser*, 2 March 1998). Meanwhile, at the same
time as the government announced a further 'crackdown' on access
to public housing, the numbers on the Housing Trust waiting list
expanded to 30,000 (*Advertiser*, 2 March 1998). In this context it
is unsurprising to find that there is evidence of increasing levels
of domestic violence within families. For example, the numbers of
confirmed cases of child abuse in South Australia increased by 58
per cent in a twelve-month period in the mid-1990s (*Advertiser*, 25
August 1995). A conference held in Adelaide on the 'overwhelming social problems' facing social workers heard 'stories of poverty,
domestic violence and desperation' being poured out by their rapidly
increasing clientele. One social worker in a women's shelter described
the situation in Adelaide's poor suburbs as like 'living in a war zone'
(*Advertiser*, 2 November 1996).

Ironically, these changes are occurring simultaneously with a
resurgence of rhetoric from governments about the importance
of restoring the nuclear family and family values. In so doing, the
state is effectively attempting to shift the burden of welfare and
social reproduction back onto the 'private' realm of the household
and the individual. Thus the rhetoric of family and individualism
is being used to facilitate a quite deliberate attempt significantly to
restructure social reproduction. This has important consequences
both for individual and family welfare and for the broader process of
social reproduction within the economy and society. The destructive
and fragmenting impact of neo-liberal policies on communities and
households creates severe doubts about the long-term potential to
maintain a structure that effectively secures social reproduction.

Conclusion

In spite of the undoubted influence that neo-liberalism has exerted
over state governments, a regulation analysis suggests scepticism
about its ability to underpin a new post-Fordist era of capital
accumulation. While neo-liberalism has been effectively used as a

vehicle for restoring short-term profitability for certain sections of capital, it has not provided the basis for the emergence of a new localized and flexible post-Fordist regime of accumulation within the majority of regions in core and semi-peripheral countries. In fact neo-liberalism only prolongs this crisis by maintaining unproductive investment and systemic instability. As such, it is the return to the 'jungle' of unfettered national and global markets, creating havoc for local communities (Peck and Tickell 1994b). Nevertheless, because neo-liberalism does serve the short-term class interests of extremely powerful global and local forces, it will require staunch political resistance to overcome its influence.

The breakdown of Fordism has precipitated a crisis of capitalist regulation as well as a crisis of capital accumulation. Despite the hopes of some analysts, and fears of others, there is little evidence that a new stable and coherent neo-liberal regulatory arrangement has emerged to replace the local Keynesian welfare state. Neo-liberal localism is neither universal nor monolithic and a coherent post-Fordist local state structure has yet to emerge or stabilize. On the contrary, governments at the local level have faced extreme difficulties in formulating coherent policy responses to the challenges raised by globalization and economic restructuring. As elsewhere, in Australia this confusion has produced a hotch-potch of policy responses from state governments. Looking from a regulation perspective, it seems that we are now experiencing a period of 'institutional searching'. The partial adoption by state governments of neo-liberal policies can be seen as a temporary and unstable 'institutional fix' – indicative of the regulatory crisis facing local states rather than its solution. Furthermore, the ability of neo-liberalism to provide a stable framework for social reproduction is even more problematic. The destructive and fragmenting impacts of neo-liberal policies on communities and households create severe doubts about its long-term potential to provide a new mode of social regulation, capable of sustaining both capital accumulation and social reproduction for local communities. But as Alain Lipietz reminds us: 'the history of capitalism is full of experiments which led nowhere ... abandoned prototypes and all sorts of monstrosities' (Lipietz 1987: 15).

The embrace of neo-liberal policies by Australian state governments is partly a result of the powerful global economic and political forces that have exerted strong pressures on them. It is also partly because state governments have been squeezed by the effects of the application of neo-liberal policies at the national level. These global and national changes result in the fragmentation and fracturing of local economies and political institutions in a way that has reduced the 'manoeuvring space' available to local states. However, state governments clearly have far more room for manoeuvre than is acknowledged in the discourse of neo-liberalism or, indeed, in some political economic analysis. Contrary to the arguments of proponents and critics of neo-liberalism alike, the extent to which neo-liberalism has become the only viable policy approach for local states has been much more circumscribed than appears to be the case at first glance. Many of the problems faced by state governments in Australia are the result not of the overwhelming impact of globalization at all, but rather of policies that, for a variety of expedient reasons, they have themselves chosen over the past decade or more. Globalization presents a challenge for local regions but it should not be an excuse for governments' failure to seek policy alternatives which support social reproduction and equity together with capital accumulation, thus providing better outcomes for the whole of society.

Notes

An earlier version of this chapter was published in 2001 in the *Journal of Australian Political Economy* 48, December.

1. The term 'regulation' is derived from the French word, which has quite a different and broader meaning than the common English one. Essentially *régulation* refers to all those formal institutions and informal processes by which a particular social, political, and economic order is constituted.

References

Aglietta, Michel (1979) *Theory of Capitalist Regulation*, London: Verso.

Amin, Ash (1994) 'Post-Fordism: Models, Fantasies and Phantoms of Transition', in Ash Amin (ed.), *Post-Fordism: A Reader*, Oxford: Blackwell: 1–40.

Amin, Ash and Anders Malmberg (1994) 'Competing Structural and Institutional Influences on the Geography of Production in Europe', in Ash Amin (ed.), *Post-Fordism: A Reader*, Oxford: Blackwell: 227–48.

Broomhill, Ray and John Spoehr (1996) 'Altered State Governments and Vampire Economics', in J. Spoehr and R. Broomhill (eds), *Altered States: The Regional Impact of Free Market Policies in the Australian States*, Adelaide: Centre for Labour Studies and the Social Justice Research Foundation: 13–25.

Bryan, Dick (1995) 'International Competitiveness: National and Class Agendas', *Journal of Australian Political Economy* 35: 1–23.

Bryan, Dick (2000) 'The Rush to Regulate: The Shift in Australia from the

Rule of Markets to the Rule of Capital', *Australian Journal of Social Issues*, vol. 35, no. 4: 333–48.

Dierckxsens, Wim (2000) *The Limits of Capitalism: Globalization Without Neoliberalism*, London: Zed Books.

Eisenschitz, Aram and Jamie Gough (1996) 'The Contradictions of Neo-Keynesian Local Economic Strategy', *Review of International Political Economy*, vol. 3, no. 3: 434–58.

Fincher, R. and J. Nieuwenhuysen (eds) (1998) *Australian Poverty: Then and Now*, Melbourne: Melbourne University Press.

Geddes, Mike (1994) 'Public Services and Local Economic Regeneration in a Post-Fordist Economy', in Roger Burrows and Brian Loader (eds), *Towards a Post-Fordist Welfare State?*, London: Routledge: 154–76.

Gerritsen, Rolf (1988) 'State Budgetary Outcomes and Typologies of the Australian States', in B. Galligan (ed.), *Comparative State Politics*, Melbourne: Longman Cheshire: 146–63.

Grinspun, Ricardo and Robert Kreklewich (1994) 'Consolidating Neo-liberal Reforms: "Free Trade" as a Conditioning Framework', *Studies in Political Economy* 43: 33–61.

Groenewold, Nicolaas, Alfred J. Haggar and John R. Madden (2001) 'Competitive Federalism: A Political-Economy General Equilibrium Approach', discussion paper, Department of Economics, University of Western Australia, October.

Harding, A., R. Lloyd and H. Greenwell (2001) 'Financial Disadvantage in Australia 1990 to 2000: The Persistence of Poverty in a Decade of Growth', Canberra: National Centre for Social and Economic Modelling (NATSEM).

Howell, Chris (2001) 'Social Democratic Parties and Trade Unions', *Studies in Political Economy* 65: 7–37.

Jessop, Bob (2001) 'Regulationist and Autopoieticist Reflections on Polanyi's Account of Market Economies and the Market Society', *New Political Economy*, vol. 6, no. 2: 213–32.

Leborgne, D. and A. Lipietz (1988) 'New Technologies, New Modes of Regulation: Some Spatial Implications', *Environment and Planning D: Society and Space* 6: 263–80.

Lipietz, Alain (1987) *Mirages and Miracles: The Crisis of Global Fordism*, London: Verso.

Lipietz, Alain (1994) 'Post-Fordism and Democracy', in Ash Amin (ed.), *Post-Fordism: A Reader*, Oxford: Blackwell: 338–58.

Patterson, A. and P.L. Pinch (1995) '"Hollowing Out" the Local State: Compulsory Competitive Tendering and the Restructuring of British Public Sector Services', *Environment and Planning A* 27: 1437–61.

Peck, Jamie and Alan Tickell (1992) 'Local Modes of Social Regulation? Regulation Theory, Thatcherism and Uneven Development', *Geoforum* 23: 347–63.

Peck, Jamie and Adam Tickell (1994a) 'Searching for a New Institutional Fix: The After-Fordist Crisis and the Global-Local Disorder', in Ash Amin (ed.), *Post-Fordism: A Reader*, Oxford: Blackwell: 280–315.

Peck, Jamie and Alan Tickell (1994b) 'Jungle Law Breaks Out: Neo-liberalism and Global–Local Disorder', *Area* 26: 317–26.

Polanyi, Karl (1957) *The Great Transformation: The Political and Economic Origins of Our Time*, Boston: Beacon Press.

9

Global Governance and the Semi-peripheral State: The WTO and NAFTA as Canada's External Constitution

Stephen Clarkson

A particular conundrum for political economists trying to understand the meaning for semi-peripheral countries of continental and global economic governance's recent emergence is its impact on these formerly sovereign states' capacity to manage their own affairs. Global governance is a less urgent question for the understanding of dominant states, which, having historically imposed their own norms on the rest of the world, have shaped the new multilateral institutions to serve their needs. It does not even present much of a problem for analysing peripheral states, for which the current global order is just another iteration of the old story of imperial control. But for those many states in the middle of the globe's hierarchy of power – except for the *sui generis* European Union, which has transformed stateness for the smaller of its fifteen members – the new multilateral economic institutionalization presents a radical challenge to the *modus operandi* they had worked out in the period after World War II, when Keynesian policy activism premissed on national autonomy drove the elite consensus throughout the capitalist world.

This chapter develops the argument that the North American Free Trade Agreement (NAFTA) and the World Trade Organization (WTO), of which Canada became a founding member in 1994 and 1995, respectively, are such intrusive manifestations of global governance that they constitute the country's *supraconstitution*. The recognition that an external constitution has become a standard feature of the territorial state's structure under conditions of advanced globalization then enables strategies for correcting its deficiencies.

Constitutions

Generally understood, an organization's constitution lays down principles that prescribe how it is to function and assign rights plus obligations to its members. In the case of a liberal-democratic state, a constitution generally demonstrates eight principal attributes:

• It expresses the *will* of a would-be community to establish some kind of order for its constituents.

• It may entrench certain *norms* that are inviolate – that is, above the reach of any politician to alter.

• It sets up the rules of the political game by establishing decision-making executive and law-making legislative *institutions* that will have authority over the territory and establishes the administrative structure needed to apply the laws and regulations they create.

• Having empowered institutions, it also constrains them by setting *limits* to what they can do.

• It establishes specific *rights* for its citizens, whether individual or collective.

• It establishes a *judicial function* to interpret the constitution's texts in the light of conflicts over their meaning.

• It provides mechanisms for the *enforcement* of courts' judgments to ensure the observance of all laws and regulations.

• It provides procedures for *amending* or abrogating the constitution in response to systemic changes.

My objective is not to analyse the constitutions of NAFTA and the WTO as organizations in their own right. It is to consider to what extent membership in NAFTA and the WTO adds to Canada's already existing domestic constitution a supraconstitutional matrix understood in terms of these eight categories.

Norms

The WTO and NAFTA entrench norms such as 'national treatment' that are not necessarily incorporated into domestic legislation. There is no Canadian law saying that the federal government must treat foreign-owned furniture companies at least as well as it treats Canadian-owned furniture firms. But since the trade agreements extended the 'national treatment' principle from goods to investments and even to services, if any federal or provincial or municipal government favours a nationally or provincially owned firm, the government of Canada is liable to legal attack by another government belonging to NAFTA or the WTO that deems one of its companies in Canada to have suffered discrimination.

National treatment for investment brought to an end a whole generation of industrial development policies centred on supporting domestic corporations to improve their competitive performance and boost their exports (Sinclair 2000: 44). It also called into question Canadian governments' capacity to bolster their cultural industries through encouraging domestic entities in the private sector. In this way supraconstitutional norms have direct impacts on the domestic legislative and administrative order.

Another type of limit whose enforcement is contingent on foreign complaints is the prohibition of governments from imposing obligations on foreign corporations as a condition for granting them permission to invest. 'Performance requirements', for instance, can include export commitments, undertakings to find local sources for their manufacturing needs, to transfer technology to domestic partners, or to guarantee set levels of employment (Chang 1998: 232–7). Strictly speaking, these norms do not actually *prevent* governments from extracting undertakings from foreign investors or subsidizing domestic firms. But federal or provincial or municipal governments that violate a NAFTA or WTO norm are vulnerable to a partner state initiating a legal action that could result in economic sanctions to restore the damage from which its corporation claims to have suffered.

NAFTA and the WTO's trade principles are thus supraconstitutional because they give legal grounds to foreign corporations to press their home government to launch a suit against Canada through NAFTA's dispute settlement panels or the WTO's dispute settlement board. When Canada persisted in showering public largesse on its champion aircraft builder, Bombardier, to boost its exports, and when Brazil lodged a complaint at the WTO on behalf of its own regional aeroplane builder, Embraer, the dispute panel in Geneva found Canada to have broken the global rules. Ottawa was obliged to mend its ways.

Limits on government

By the very act of signing the earlier bilateral Canada–United States Free Trade Agreement (CUFTA) in 1989, and then NAFTA and the WTO, Canada undertook to make specific changes in a wide range of legislation and regulations. For instance, CUFTA's investment chapter raised the exemption from review of a foreign takeover of a Canadian firm from $5 million to $150 million. Canadian implementation legislation accordingly made the appropriate amendment to the Investment Canada Act. In the WTO's agreement on agriculture, member states committed themselves to transform such quantitative restrictions as import quotas into tariffs, which were then to be reduced. Canada duly proceeded to 'tariffy' its protective regulations for farmers in central Canada. The WTO's and NAFTA's rules are so comprehensive that, in their implementation legislation, Canada had to change hundreds of existing laws.

These changes to laws and regulations mandated by the WTO and NAFTA were supraconstitutional not just because they had to be made automatically but also because they were irreversible. When legislatures enact statutes, they can subsequently amend or revoke these acts in response to changing conditions. But statutory amendments incorporating international trade norms can only be amended if the external regime changes its rules by international agreement. In this respect, accepting changes over which Parliament no longer exercises sovereignty has fundamentally altered the legal order. This is the constitutional significance of free-trade discourse about NAFTA 'locking in' neo-conservative values, making them immune from partisan politics. In practical terms this means that, even if more activist politicians were to win power, they would find their hands tied by these internationally negotiated but domestically implemented political limits to which their predecessors had committed them (Schneiderman 1996). In this light, NAFTA and the WTO enabled their proponents to disempower not just their present adversaries but also future generations who have been disenfranchised pre-emptively from pursuing different legislative goals through the democratic process.

Rights for corporations

The classic corollary of limits on government is rights for the citizenry. Although the European Union (EU) does create direct rights for citizens in member states – for instance to sue their own governments before the European Court of Justice – the only 'citizens' whose rights in Canada were expanded under NAFTA were corporations based in the United States or Mexico. Similarly, under the WTO, rights were created for foreign corporations, not for citizens. National treatment, the right of establishment, and intellectual property rights gave firms owned in other countries greater entitlements when doing business outside their home economy.

NAFTA

Article 1110 of NAFTA provides that no government may 'directly or indirectly expropriate or nationalize', or take 'a measure tantamount to expropriation or nationalization' except for a 'public purpose', on a 'non-discriminatory basis', in accordance with 'due process of law and minimum standards of treatment' and on 'payment of compensation'. In the face of Canada's constitution, which had been amended in 1982 to incorporate a Charter of Rights and Freedoms that deliberately excluded property rights (on the grounds that this would excessively enhance corporate power), this provision created a property right for foreign corporations that neither the government nor the public had at first understood.

Unlike rights in Canada's internal constitutions, this right was not available for Canadian corporations in Canada, where it could only be exploited by American and Mexican companies. Also contrasting with national constitutions, the rights accorded by trade agreements to transnational corporations subject them to no balancing obligations by continental-level institutions with the clout to regulate, tax, or monitor the newly created continental market that has proceeded to emerge (Blank and Krajewski 1995). NAFTA's Chapter 11 expanded the scope of investment rights without requiring transnational corporations to promote the public interest by protecting the environment[1] or public health. In other words, NAFTA supported a regime of continental accumulation less by creating a new institutional structure for it than by reducing member states' capacities to control corporations, which were given a means to discipline governments that stood in their way.

The WTO

Many of the WTO's agreements also contained rights for international corporations but none for citizens. TRIPs, the agreement on Trade Related Aspects of Intellectual Property Rights, required that all member states amend their intellectual property legislation and change their judicial procedures in conformity with the stipulated norms (Kent 1994). The external and constitutional quality of these rights can be seen in their giving European pharmaceuticals firms the legal justification to have the EU successfully take a case to the WTO against Ottawa because its drug legislation did not give European firms the full patent benefits that they claimed were now their due (WTO 2000).

Adjudication

For a foreign government to 'take a case to the WTO' against Ottawa presumes that global governance includes judicial capacity. However, this ability of one state to litigate against another for violating some supraconstitutional norm varies widely depending on each international organization's own constitution. Despite the many international agreements concerning the ecology, global *environmental* governance is notably bereft of adjudicatory muscle. Similarly, many of the conventions negotiated by the International Labour Organization have had little effect on their signatory states, for lack of adjudicatory muscle. The strength of the new breed of intergovernmental *economic* agreements that establish limits on national states and create rights for transnational corporations is due to their strong dispute-settlement mechanisms.

NAFTA

Whereas the WTO, as we shall shortly see, was endowed with an impressive apparatus for adjudicating intergovernmental disputes, NAFTA was created without a supranational judiciary. Instead North American governance is distinguished by some precarious dispute-settlement processes whose supraconstitutional impacts vary from minor (for general disputes between member states) to negligible (for trade disputes between exporting and importing states) to substantial (for disputes between transnational corporations and host states).

General disputes

Continental dispute settlement was meant to depoliticize conflicts between Canada, Mexico, and the United States by having their differences resolved through neutral arbitrators applying common rules. In this spirit, NAFTA's Chapter 20 provides for binational panels to be struck when the member states have been unable to resolve their differences over issues generated by the agreement. Although

'Chapter 20' dispute settlement was considered expeditious at first (Davey 1996: 65), later decisions have proven unable to settle conflicts without resort to power politics (Loungnarath and Stehly 2000: 43). For example, when it lost a panel decision to Canada in a wheat case (CDA-92-1807-01), Washington responded by threatening to launch an investigation into Canadian wheat exports. Closure was only achieved when US pressure caused the Canadian government to give way by agreeing to limit wheat exports during 1994/5 to 1.5 million tonnes (Davey 1996: 56). If such Chapter 20 rulings are unable to constrain the continental hegemon so that it becomes futile to submit general issues to NAFTA arbitration, continental governance appears judicially unable to deliver for its weaker members the rights for which they 'paid' when negotiating the original compact. In this respect the judicial function of NAFTA is faulty as a constitution for North America by failing to have supraconstitutional effect in the American legal order.

Trade disputes

Had NAFTA created a true free-trade area, its members would have abandoned their right to impose anti-dumping (AD) or countervailing duties (CVD) on imports coming from their partners' economies. The United States refused such a real levelling of national trade barriers to create a single continental market. It simply agreed to cede appeals of its protectionist rulings to binational panels which were restricted to investigating whether the administration's AD or CVD determinations properly applied *American* trade law (Trakman 1997: 277).

Generalized to its two peripheral partners in NAFTA's Chapter 19, this putatively binding judicial expedient turned out to be as disappointing as its critics had predicted. When the United States' CVD against Canadian softwood lumber exports was remanded for incorrectly applying the notion of subsidy as defined in US law, Congress changed its definition of subsidy to suit the Canadian situation. Beyond softwood lumber's long-lasting evidence (Howse 1998: 15), Canada has not had a satisfactory experience in using Chapter 19 to appeal other American trade determinations. In 1993, for instance, there were multiple remands in five cases, which led the panels to surpass their deadlines significantly.

Although AD and CVD jurisprudence may have been ineffective supraconstitutionally in helping the peripheral states constrain their hegemon, the opposite is not necessarily true. Canadian trade agencies have had to become more attentive to American interpretations of the standards they apply in AD or CVD determinations out of a concern for what the binational panels, which necessarily include American jurists, may later decide on appeal. Thus Chapter 19 confirms the experience of Chapter 20 that NAFTA's judicial function is asymmetrical in its impact. On the one hand, it does not have supraconstitutional clout over the hegemon's behaviour. On the other, it is used to enforce NAFTA rules in the periphery, with some effects on Canadian administrative justice.

Investor-state disputes

Although barely noticed when NAFTA was debated before its ratification, an obscure dispute mechanism buried deep in Chapter 11 has established a powerful new adjudication procedure to enforce Article 1110's corporate rights. Under these investor-state tribunals, an American or Mexican corporation with interests in Canada can initiate arbitration proceedings arguing expropriation against a municipal, provincial, or federal policy that harms its interests. These 'investor-state' disputes are taken for arbitration before an international panel operating by rules established under the aegis of the World Bank's or the United Nations' procedures for settling international disputes between corporations (Horlick and DeBusk 1993: 52). Since these panels operate according to the norms of international commercial law, Chapter 11 disputes actually transfer judicial authority over government policies from the realm of public national law to private international commercial law.[2]

Beyond shrinking the scope of the Canadian judicial system, 'Chapter 11' arbitrations overlay it with a supraconstitutional process that conflicts with many of its historic values. *Transparency* is the first victim in this secretive world of commercial arbitration: even the existence of a case may be kept secret and the public may never learn what has happened or why. *Neutrality* is the second legal value that falls by the wayside. Since the plaintiff investor has the right to appoint one of the three arbitrators, the defending government already faces a bench that is substantially weighted in favour of corporate rather than public values. *Judicial sovereignty* is a third victim of this extraordinary addition to the Canadian legal order. As the corporate plaintiff and the defendant state choose the panel's chair by consensus, it is likely that there will be just one Canadian in tribunals adjudicating suits launched against Canadian governments. This suggests that when a norm of international corporate law comes into conflict with a Canadian legal standard, the latter is likely to be overridden.

The WTO

In contrast with NAFTA's judicial processes, which are weak at the governmental level and strong at the corporate level, the WTO's dispute settlement excludes corporations from directly using its services and gives governments a powerful tool with which to enforce the global regime's economic rules even against the most powerful non-compliant state. Indeed, the key to the WTO's unprecedented importance lies in the power and neutrality of its dispute-settlement mechanisms. Unlike NAFTA's Chapter 19 and 20 panels, WTO panellists are chosen from countries other than those involved in a particular dispute. Their rulings are based not on the contenders' own laws, as they are in NAFTA's AD and CVD cases, but on the WTO's international rules. They make their judgments quickly on the basis of the WTO's norms, which they interpret in the light of the international public law developed by the prior General Agreement on Tariffs and Trade (GATT) jurisprudence.

The sociology of the WTO's dispute panels fosters a rigid legalism in its jurisprudence (Weiler 2001: 194). Panellists adjudicating WTO disputes are either trade lawyers or professors of international law who tend to stick very close to the black letter of the WTO's texts that they are interpreting, or they are middle-level diplomats who take their cues from the Secretariat's legal staff. In either case, they know full well that their judgment will be appealed by the losing side and that the judges on the Appellate Body will be responding to highly refined legal reasoning.[3] Under these conditions, 'soft' arguments defending cultural autonomy or environmental sustainability hold little weight against the 'hard' logic of applying the WTO's rules.

While the WTO's rules create new supraconstitutional norms for member states to accept, their meaning cannot be anticipated with any certainty. In referring to one contentious concept in trade law, the WTO's Appellate Body memorably compared the notion of 'likeness' to 'an accordion, which may be stretched wide or squeezed tight as the case requires'. This conceptual flexibility did not guarantee cultural sensitivity, as Canadians discovered when the WTO ruled that *Sports Illustrated Canada* – the proposed split-run

Canadian edition of *Sports Illustrated*, produced with the American editorial content but local advertising – was 'like' *Maclean's Magazine* (WTO 1997). This finding meant that several key policy instruments, which had successfully promoted a Canadian magazine industry for several decades, were declared illegal (Magder 1998). Such an expansive approach to the interpretation of the new global rules means that national policy-makers can only be sure that they will never know what Geneva's supreme court of commercial law will decide until a trade dispute concerning this policy is heard (Howse and Regan 2000: 268).

Whether the WTO rulings' supraconstitutional superiority over domestic constitutional norms will be accepted by Canadian courts remains to be seen. As any student of federalism knows, a system containing more than one order of jurisdiction creates conflicts between the cohabiting authorities. A case has yet to be brought to Canada's Supreme Court to test whether a ruling by a global or continental dispute panel necessarily has precedence over a Canadian norm.[4] The introduction of a supraconstitution with judicial muscle suggests that continuing clashes between the external and internal constitutional orders must be expected.

Interconstitutional conflict has already broken out between the global and continental orders, as when the United States challenged in a NAFTA panel Canada's tariffication of its agricultural quotas. The panel ruled that the WTO's tariffication imperative prevailed over Canada's NAFTA obligation not to raise its tariffs (CDA-95-2008-01). Other conflicts between the two regimes' norms are bound to occur, complicating their constitutionalizing impact on their members.

The WTO's dispute system may be procedurally superior to NAFTA's, but multilateralism does not necessarily present Canada with an escape from a Washington-dominated continentalism. Indeed a significant part of the constraint that the WTO has imposed on the Canadian state in the first few years of its existence has been an application of US-driven demands that Canada comply with US-inspired WTO rules (Moon 2000: 346–7) on behalf of US-based entertainment oligopolies. Nor does multilateralism necessarily offer allies to help Canada resist the relentless liberalizing pressure of transnational capital. Another part of the WTO's supraconstitutional pressure on Canadian legislation has come from European pharmaceutical giants exploiting TRIPS to support their American counterparts in their demands that Canada abandon the terrain it reserved for generic drug producers and strengthen the monopoly prerogatives of branded drugs.

Enforcement

NAFTA

As with other trade treaties, NAFTA has no enforcement capacity other than the parties' sense of their long-term self-interest. If one member state does not comply with the judgments of disputes that it loses, it cannot expect its partners to do the same. Under the great asymmetry prevailing in North America, the hegemon is less constrained by such prudential considerations. The US remains able to flout NAFTA's rules even when interpreted by its judicial processes, as was seen when it refused to honour its NAFTA commitment – confirmed by a clear Chapter 20 dispute panel ruling – to open its highways to Mexican truckers.

The WTO

Like NAFTA, the WTO has no police service capable of implementing its judicial decisions. But unlike NAFTA, the enforcement provisions supporting its dispute settlement rulings are significantly stronger.[5] When a final decision on a trade dispute deems a signatory state's laws or regulations in violation of a WTO norm, the offending provisions are supposed to be changed or compensation paid. A non-compliant state is much more likely to be brought to 'justice' by a litigant state because failure to abide by a WTO dispute ruling gives the winning plaintiff the right to impose retaliatory trade sanctions against the disobedient defendant. This retaliation can block any exports of the guilty state. The amount of damage inflicted by the retaliation can equal the harm caused to the complainant by the violation. This self-enforcement system works in the WTO, where there is greater symmetry among the major powers, although Washington still remains leery about obeying the rulings of the global organization to which it gave life (Howse 2000).

In principle, participating in a rules-based system should have given the semi-peripheral state the capacity to have the hegemon play by the same book. In practice it is the hegemon that has used the new rules to cause Canada to yield while thumbing its nose at the international community when it felt vital political issues were at stake. When Canada, along with the EU, prepared to invoke WTO rules to discipline through the Dispute Settlement Body the extra-territorial application of the US Helms–Burton law to Canadian and European assets in Cuba, Washington threatened to boycott the proceedings by invoking the higher norm of national security. When the game was going to go against it, the USA refused to play.

Institutions

With the major exception of the European Union, whose various institutions' decisions can directly affect the behaviour of individuals and corporations in its member states, global governance acts indirectly by affecting the behaviour of the nation-states that have constructed its various organizations by treaty. It would be surprising if, in Canada's case, the WTO and NAFTA would not have some indirect effects on its political institutions as well as their relationship with civil society.

Beyond inhibiting federal and provincial governments in their policy actions, NAFTA and the WTO may also have altered Canadian federalism's distribution of powers between the two levels of government. By making Ottawa responsible for ensuring provincial conformity to its provisions, NAFTA may have restored to the Canadian Constitution a federal power of disallowance that had fallen into disuse. The fact that only the federal government may launch a trade dispute under NAFTA or the WTO and appear in its hearings, even when a provincial grievance or measure is the issue, shifts further power towards Ottawa from the provincial capitals. NAFTA norms also create abnormalities in interprovincial relations. The application of national treatment and investor-state conflict resolution to sub-central governments creates the anomaly that provinces, territories, and municipalities have to give NAFTA investors non-discriminatory treatment, whereas they may still discriminate in favour of their own, locally based firms against Canadian investors from other provinces. In these ways global governance may alter – to a potentially dramatic degree – the country's delicate constitutional balance (Gold and Leyton-Brown 1988).

In offering to have public education and health care brought under the General Agreement on Trade in Services' (GATS) liberalizing rules on services in the Doha Round of WTO negotiations, the federal government made a step that will affect provincial jurisdiction more than its own. This action is also of dubious constitutional validity since it would change the norms governing the provinces without the appropriate amendment having been made in the Canadian Constitution.

Will

Legitimacy among the citizenry is the binding agent sustaining such societal contracts as constitutions. Civil society organizations (CSOs) were not much interested in economic liberalization when free-trade agreements were first being negotiated. Their memberships had little interest in or knowledge of NAFTA or the WTO's contents. As time revealed their implications, activists have discovered that there was nothing neutral about rules which reflected the demands of the continental hegemon and transnational capital but protected neither labour nor the environment.

That popular support for global governance can no longer be taken for granted was suggested by the spectacular and continuing demonstrations that have been mounted since 1999 to protest not just the global WTO and the IMF, but the hemispheric Organization of American States and the Free Trade Area of the Americas as well. Canadian CSOs like the Council of Canadians, have been among the most active within the semi-periphery in mounting vocal opposition to manifestations of global or continental governance.

Canadian participation in polarizing world opinion about globaliz-ation also impinges on the domestic constitutional order. When protesting at the 'wall of shame' – the link-fence barrier erected in Quebec City in April 2001 to keep opposition groups away from delegates to the Summit of the Americas – Canadian citizens were not just making the point that global governance was unfairly privileging the interests of business. They were also contributing to strengthening attitudes that are delegitimizing the Canadian constitutional order. If Canadian leaders are seen to be complicit in the imposition of reviled supraconstitutional norms that negate environmental regula-tion, the amount of deference accorded them by the public diminishes further. In short, the constitutional fallout from global governance's democratic deficit may worsen the democratic deficit from which the domestic legal order already suffers.

Declining deference for politicians may be linked to a growing concern for the deterioration of public services. An efficient,
publicly funded health system has become a defining characteristic
of Canadians' sense of national identity. If the commercialization of
publicly provided health care is the product of the services provisions
in NAFTA and the WTO's GATS, Canadian society will lose a prime
social institution that has played a major role in defining its identity
and so sustaining its cohesion.[6] Should continental and global free-
trade norms accelerate privatization of health care with consequent
increases in inequality of treatment between the rich and the poor,
Canadian political culture would become more fractured.

Instead of developing its social and community cohesion, Canada
appears to be bifurcating into a society of those who can succeed
in the globalized system and a society of those left behind. If this
perception is linked to the norms and practices of the global economic governance regimes, serious repercussions may be felt in the
legitimacy of the country's own representative system (McBride and
Shields 1997). If global institutions have 'hollowed out' the Canadian
state to the point that it risks being seen as incapable of defending
its citizens' interests (Jessop 1997: 561–81), the Canadian political
system will lose credibility at the same time as neo-conservative
globalization loses legitimacy. If the public's commitment to the
institutions of global governance is fragile, we need to consider the
prospects for changing the external constitution.

Amending the supraconstitution

Although the concept of constitution connotes stability, if not per-
manence, constitutions that fail to adjust to changing conditions will
ultimately lose their legitimacy. Typically, constitutional change takes
place through formal amendments, through the evolving concepts
generated by judicial interpretation, and through the way that prin-
cipals comply with judicial rulings.

Formal amendment

Changes to the WTO's or NAFTA's own set of rules can only be
affected through these regimes' members reaching a consensus.[7]
While this gives Canada a veto to block changes to which it
objects, it also means in principle that the government of Canada's

role in making new rules would be proportional to its diminishing effectiveness in representing its interests in these regimes, which each have extremely weak legislative capacities.

The WTO's principal decision-making institution is its biennial ministerial council meeting, which can emit new rules and alter the organization's institutions (Kajewski 2001). It can also mandate negotiating rounds, which have so far been designed to produce new bodies of rules that set limits on governments and define rights for corporations. The Uruguay Round was dominated by the triad of the US, the EU, and Japan, with Canada playing a supportive but not decisive role in the wings. Anger at the WTO in the third world and continuing protests from civil society have given peripheral states and CSOs more weight in its Doha Round of negotiations.

NAFTA's decision-making capacity is limited to the minor annual or emergency meetings of the North American Free Trade Commission, which has no bureaucratic base and is simply made up of the three countries' trade ministers. These trade minister summits are empowered to make whatever changes they deem appropriate (NAFTA Chapter 20). This authority includes the power to make 'interpretations' which Chapter 11 investor-state tribunals are bound to accept. This means that NAFTA's own constitution − that is, Canada's external supraconstitution − can evolve, though without any direct accountability to the Canadian public.

Because of the uproar among Canadian environmentalists over several ecologically adverse Chapter 11 rulings (described by David Schneiderman in Chapter 12), the Canadian government has lobbied its NAFTA counterparts since 1998 to amend the investor-state dispute process. Mexico opposed the change on the grounds that its attractiveness to foreign capital lay in offering iron-clad guarantees of investor rights. The clarification agreed to on 31 July 2001 by the three trade ministers concerning the meaning of 'international law' in article 1105 for use by Chapter 11 arbitrators is deemed unlikely to have much effect.

No more promising are the North American Commissions for Environmental (CEC) and Labour (CLC) Cooperation established under NAFTA's aegis. The CLC has been notably ineffectual in affecting labour standards and cannot be expected to develop a capacity to achieve change. While the CEC has more autonomy, a more substantial institutional structure, and a larger budget, it has failed to moderate the pro-business bias of NAFTA dispute settlement.

Informal amendment

Change in constitutional systems can be brought about through a number of channels, chief of which is the adjudication process. Decisions by judges 'make' law and on occasion amend constitutional meanings. In NAFTA, it is Chapter 11 tribunals which have shown the greatest supraconstitutional capacity for making law in Canada. More accurately, the cases launched by the Ethyl and S.D. Myers Corporations, discussed at greater length in Chapter 12, resulted in *un*making legislation that had been passed. In the first instance Ottawa settled privately by withdrawing the law forbidding the trade of the alleged neurotoxin MMT when Ethyl initiated an investor-state dispute process. In the second Chapter 11 affair the tribunal ruled that a federal law banning the export of PCBs (industrial compounds regarded as environmental pollutants) expropriated the waste disposal company's property, even though its processing plant was in the United States. In affirming the notion that S.D. Myers had suffered action tantamount to expropriation, the tribunal was both invalidating a federal law and amending the notion of expropriation previously employed in the Canadian legal order. If the general trend of legal interpretation of NAFTA and the WTO rules has been towards strengthening corporate rights and weakening governmental powers, amendment through the judicial process offers only a faint hope for a state-friendly rebalancing of global governance. That faint hope lies in the very protests triggered by the trade regime's bias towards neo-conservative values. These denunciations of judicial actions may already have had some effect on judicial decision-making.

As legal theorists advise us, judges working within national legal systems have two audiences in mind when they deliver their judgments. On the one hand, they make determinations in terms of the black letter of the law since they know their peers will scrutinize their reasoning. On the other hand, their rulings are also addressed to the general public, which is sensitive to the respect for basic societal standards. And if citizens find a judgment has overstepped the bounds of the value system to which they are presently attached, the ruling and the judge who made it can be repudiated. While easily observable within domestic courts, this process of informal dialogue between judging and civil society is less prone to observation internationally.

The WTO's asbestos judgment, which allowed the French public's fear of a carcinogenic product to be taken into consideration, may herald an incorporation of civil society's values into the trade adjudication process. Moreover, in revising the famous Shrimp/Turtles decision in order to legitimate regulations that discriminate against harvesting shrimp with nets that killed sea turtles, the Appellate Body adopted what Barfield calls a 'dynamic interpretation' of article XX, arguing that it must look at the text in light of 'contemporary concerns of the community of nations about the protection and conservation of the environment' (Barfield 2001: 92; WTO 1998: para. 128). The point for our analysis is that neither constitutional nor supraconstitutional elements are fixed in stone. They can evolve through the informal alteration of the trade arbitrators' normative framework.

Compliance

The way the rules are interpreted by economic tribunals is no more critical than the behaviour of states in complying with or resisting the international judgments. As we have seen, the hegemon's behaviour can be decisive, but the system's functioning can also be influenced by the behaviour of mid-sized powers like Canada. Were Ottawa to have declared that considerations of national security – in the face of American dominance of the nation's magazine industry – prevented it from accepting the WTO's ruling on the question of the split-run edition of *Sports Illustrated Canada*, it could have set limits to the trade regime's capacity to undermine not only its own carefully constructed cultural policy but other countries' domestic priorities.

Exercising supraconstitutional rights abroad

Transnational global governance limits on government and its rights for corporations have external as well as internal effects. When Sweden joined the EU, it accepted an array of limitations on what its government could do. By the same token, it joined fourteen other member states whose governments were limited by identical constraints and in whose economies the EU gave Swedish corporations and citizens new rights. These limits on other members can be seen as external rights belonging to the citizens of the trade regimes' member states.

Similarly for Canada, the relation between domestic and external constitutional orders is not a one-way street in which autonomy is only lost to transnational institutions or markets. A balancing of political power can be seen when its loss of *internal* autonomy is offset by the capacity to exercise power beyond the national boundaries. This trade-off was visible when Ottawa participated in the deliberative process at the global level that established the norms, regulations, and disciplines it subsequently imposed on itself.[8]

Global governance has given Canada a vehicle for accentuating its own unequal relations of dominance vis-à-vis states in the periphery. However much it has complained about the unfairness of Chapter 11's investor-state dispute settlement, Ottawa has imposed the same provisions on third-world countries. Canada's investment treaty with South Africa requires that Canadian transnationals be granted property rights denied South Africans by their state's newly crafted constitution. However unsuccessfully Ottawa tried to keep the power to impose performance requirements on foreign investors in Canada, Canadian mining companies are nevertheless profiting in several African countries from just such bans on domestic performance requirements. With other semi-peripheral countries of its own size, Canada's experience under the global constitution has produced more balanced results. Although Brazil was able to use the WTO to discipline Ottawa's export subsidies for Bombardier, Canada was also able to use the same supraconstitutional framework to discipline Brasilia's subsidies for Embraer.

Moreover, Canada has been quite energetic in proactively using NAFTA's and the WTO's supraconstitutional status in other countries to defend its corporate interests there. For example, it joined the United States in using the WTO's sanitary and phytosanitary measures to prevent the European Union from banning the import of beef raised with the growth hormone commonly used by North American ranchers.

Conclusion

Historians remind us that a constitution expresses a system's power structure at the moment of its writing. This typically happens at independence, when the ex-colonial elite writes new rules for itself, or occurs in the trauma of military defeat, when the victors try to mould the defeated in their own image – as the Americans did to Japan and Germany after World War II. The WTO expressed the balance of forces in which the US, the EU, and Japan could write rules for the world's economy that favoured their transnational corporations and protected their less competitive interests. On a smaller scale NAFTA represented the continental corporate interests in the three states of North America.

Historians can also tell us that the challenge for any constitution is to respond to emerging forces ineffectively represented in the original power relationship – such as the blacks in the US legal order. Unfortunately for the world, the global economic constitution has actually increased the power of its founding fathers, so that those who are disadvantaged – the third world in general, and the disempowered within the industrial economies – are losing bargaining power. But the fact that global institutions such as the International Monetary Fund and global corporations, as voiced at Davos, are acknowledging the failures of neo-liberal formulas shows that constitutional change is on the global agenda.

In this situation, Canada remains a classic semi-peripheral power-in-the-middle looking up to the powerful centre and down at the weak periphery. Rather than putting its limited diplomatic resources into clinging to its unjustifiable participation in the central powers' G7/G8 summits, the world's interests would be better served by Canada allying itself with other semi-peripheral states in order to remake the rules of the international system.

The precondition of progressive change is reaching a consensus on a viable new globalist paradigm. It then requires mobilizing to implement the new vision. As social-democratic values regain global currency, action must be directed to rebalancing the disequilibrium created by the excessively market-liberating rules of the WTO and its related regional blocs. Environmental, labour, human-rights, and cultural-governance regimes must gain equal weight to that of economic governance so that the supraconstitution for Canada and other states becomes an instrument not for denying but for achieving human welfare and social justice.

Notes

1. Steven Shrybman notes that 'the powerful private enforcement machinery of international investment treaties has now been invoked by several transnational corporations to assail water protection laws, water export controls, and decisions to re-establish public sector water services when privatization deals have gone sour' (Shrybman 2002: 7).

2. For example, in the Metalclad case (see Gutiérrez-Haces, Chapter 5; Schneiderman, Chapter 12), the tribunal ruled that the local municipality had exceeded its constitutional authority – a judgment that hitherto only the judges of the Supreme Court of Mexico had the power to make (Dunberry 2001: 1).

3. Robert Howse, personal communication. While, strictly speaking, Appellate Body (AB) rulings are not precedent setting, it is generally recognized that the logic of one panel's decision can be carried over from case to case as the situation dictates (Bhala 1999: 847). David Palmeter and Petros C. Mavroidis also note that the AB 'operates on a collegial' basis. While only three of the seven members sit on any one 'division' to hear a particular appeal, and the division retains full authority to decide the case, views on the issues are shared with the other AB members before a decision is reached. Consequently, in considering prior decisions, members of the AB are likely to be confronting their own decisions, or those of their close colleagues. This relationship seems likely to lead to a stronger attachment to the reasoning and results of those decisions (Palmeter and Mavroidis 1998: 398, 405).

4. 'WTO decisions generate international governmental rights/obligations but not necessarily for judicial arms of government at the national level' (communication from Howard Mann, trade lawyer, to the author, January 2001).

5. Indeed, Sylvia Ostry has called the Dispute Settlement Body 'the strongest dispute settlement mechanism in the history of international law' (Ostry 2001: 6).

6. Christopher Arup writes that 'the main thrust of the GATS is deregulatory: it attacks non-conforming national government measures'(Arup 2000: 96).

7. Claude E. Barfield has recognized this principle as a serious deficiency of the WTO. He argues that it encumbers the legislative function of the organization to the extent that most of its rule-making is done through litigation rather than legislation, compromising the regime's democratic nature (Barfield 2001: ch. 2).

8. Wolfgang Streeck (1996) has suggested a similar hypothesis for the member states of the European Union.

References

Arup, Christopher (2000) *The New World Trade Organization Agreements: Globalizing Law through Services and Intellectual Property*, Cambridge: Cambridge University Press.

Barfield, Claude E. (2001) *Free Trade, Sovereignty, and Democracy: The Future of the World Trade Organization*, Washington, DC: AEI Press.

Bhala, Raj (1999) 'The Myth about State Decisions and International Trade Law', *American University International Law Review* 14: 845–956.

Blank, Stephen and Stephen Krajewski (1995) 'US Firms in North America: Redefining Structure and Strategy', *North American Outlook*, vol. 5, no. 2.

Chang, Ha-Joon (1998) 'Transnational Corporations and Strategic Industrial Policy', in Richard Kozul-Wright and Robert Rowthorn (eds) *Transnational Corporations and the Global Economy*, Tokyo: The United Nations University: 225–43.

Davey, William J. (1996) *Pine and Swine: Canada–United States Trade Dispute Settlement; The FTA Experience and NAFTA Prospects*, Ottawa: The Centre for Trade Policy and Law.

Dunberry, Patrick (2001) 'The NAFTA Investment Dispute Settlement Mechanism: A Review of the Latest Case Law', *Journal of World Investment* 2: 151–99.

Gold, Marc and David Leyton-Brown (eds) (1988) *Trade-offs on Free Trade: The Canada–US Free Trade Agreement*, Toronto: Carswell: 131–67.

Horlick, Gary and Amanda F. De Busk (1993) 'Dispute Resolution Under NAFTA: Building on the U.S.–Canada FTA, GATT and ICSID', *Journal of World Trade*, vol. 27, no. 1: 51–71.

Howse, Robert (1998) 'Settling Trade Remedy Disputes: When the WTO Forum is Better than the NAFTA', *C.D. Howe Commentary*, no. 111: 1–24.

Howse, Robert (2000) 'The Canadian Generic Medicines Panel: A Dangerous Precedent in Dangerous Times', *Journal of World Intellectual Property*, vol. 3, no. 4: 493–508.

Howse, Robert and Donald Regan (2000) 'The Product/Process Distinction: An Illusory Basis for Disciplining Unilateralism in Trade Policy', *European Journal International Law*, vol. 11, no. 2: 249–91.

Jessop, Bob (1997) 'Capitalism and Its Future: Remarks on Regulation, Government, and Governance', *Review of International Political Economy*, vol. 4, no. 3: 561–81.

Kajewski, Markus (2001) 'Democratic Legitimacy and Constitutional Perspectives', *Journal of World Trade*, vol. 35, no. 1: 167–86.

Kent, Christopher (1994) 'The Uruguay Round GATT, TRIPS Agreement and Chapter 17 of the NAFTA: A New Era in International Patent Protection', *Canadian Intellectual Property Review*, vol. 10, no. 3: 711–33.

Loungnarath, Vilaysoun and Céline Stehly (2000) 'The General Dispute Settlement Mechanism in the North American Free Trade Agreement and the World Trade Organization System: Is North American Regionalism Really Preferable to Multilateralism?' *Journal of World Trade Law*, vol. 34, no. 1: 39–72.

McBride, Stephen and John Shields (1997) *Dismantling a Nation: The Transition to Corporate Rule in Canada* (2nd edn), Halifax: Fernwood.

Magder, Ted (1998) 'Franchising the Candy Store: Split-Run Magazines and a New International Regime for Trade in Culture,' *Canadian–American Public Policy* 34 (April).

Moon, Bruce E. (2000) 'The United States and Globalization', in Richard Stubbs and Geoffrey R.D. Underhill (eds) *Political Economy and the Changing Global Order*, Don Mills: Oxford University Press: 342–52.

Ostry, Sylvia (2001) 'Global Integration: Currents and Counter-Currents', Walter Gordon Lecture, University of Toronto, 23 May.

Palmeter, David and Petros C. Mavroidis (1998) 'The WTO Legal System: Sources of Law', *American Journal of International Law* 92: 398–413.

Schneiderman, David (1996) 'NAFTA's Takings Rule: American Constitutionalism Comes to Canada', *University of Toronto Law Journal* 46: 499–537.

Shrybman, Steven (2002) 'The Impact of International Services and Investment Agreements on Public Policy and Law Concerning Water', paper presented to conference 'From Doha to Kananaskis: The Future of the World Trading System and the Crisis of Governance', Robarts Centre for Canadian Studies,

York University and Munk Centre for International Studies, University of Toronto, 1–3 March.

Sinclair, Scott (2000) *GATS: How the World Trade Organization's New Services Negotiations Threaten Democracy*, Ottawa: Canadian Centre for Policy Alternatives.

Streeck, Wolfgang (1996) 'Public Power beyond the Nation-State: The Case of the European Community', in Robert Boyer and Daniel Drache (eds) *States Against Markets: The Limits of Globalization*, London: Routledge: 299–315.

Trakman, Leon (1997) *Dispute Settlement under the NAFTA*, New York: Transnational Publishers.

Weiler, J.H.H. (2001) 'The Rule of Lawyers and the Ethos of Diplomats' Reflections on the Internal and External Legitimacy of WTO Dispute Settlement', *Journal of World Trade*, vol. 35, no. 2: 191–207.

WTO (World Trade Organization) (1997) *Canada – Certain Measures Concerning Periodicals: Ruling by the Appellate Body*, Geneva: World Trade Organization.

WTO (1998) *United States – Import Prohibition of Certain Shrimp and Shrimp Products*, Report of the Appellate Body, Geneva: World Trade Organization.

WTO (2000) *Canada – Term of Patent Protection*, Report of the Panel, Geneva: World Trade Organization, 5 May.

10

International Forces Driving Electricity Deregulation in the Semi-periphery: The Case of Canada

Marjorie Griffin Cohen

Question: How many economists does it take to change a lightbulb?
Answer. None. The invisible hand will do it.

Two main and related policy decisions in the United States are behind major changes in the electricity sector in Canada. One was the regulation that allowed US electricity companies to invest in other electrical utilities throughout the world. The other was the deregulation of the US market that shifted production and distribution from a system of regulated regional monopolies to a price-driven system controlled by market mechanisms. Both of these events (which themselves had significant political antecedents) increased the power of large new private players in the US energy sector and gave them strong incentives to pressure Washington to pursue international trade agreements on electricity to meet their investment needs. From the beginning of the deregulation exercise the interests of private power producers have had a decisive impact on the regulatory changes that have occurred – not only in the US but also in international regulatory bodies that condition the way electricity markets will work throughout the world.

As a result, Canada, a country that had no compelling economic reasons to deregulate its electricity sector, has been profoundly affected by both the regulatory changes within the US and those that are cemented through international trade agreements like the North American Free Trade Agreement (NAFTA) and the World Trade Organization (WTO). As a 'semi-peripheral' country, it recently played a complex role in shaping international economic regulations, a role that has undermined its historical effort to maintain some measure of economic policy autonomy. Other authors in this book have stressed the leading role the government of Canada plays internationally, on behalf of large-scale business, in aggressively pursuing increased trade liberalization. But it is a particularly critical role primarily because, while negotiating on 'trade', it has consciously and deliberately included for negotiation areas of national and subnational jurisdictions that go far beyond issues of trade and deal with areas currently in the public sector. Canada's geography, history, and objectives differ substantially from the US, and, as a result, it has placed much more emphasis on providing services in the public sector. In the case of electricity, this has worked exceedingly well by most measures. But social and economic success in providing this service is proving to be an insufficient insulator against the radical changes that are pushing the sector towards action mimicking the US experience. This shift is happening despite the dismal record of electricity deregulation in the US.

The transformation of the electricity industry in Canada is an important example of how deep and radical regulatory changes in the dominant country (US) can subvert the public provision of an essential utility in a semi-peripheral country (Canada). This chapter will analyse these transformations and show how the underlying principles informing this shift are being codified in international trade agreements like NAFTA and the WTO's General Agreement on Trade in Services (GATS), and so facilitate the march towards further deregulation and privatization. NAFTA is becoming increasingly significant in this sector because moves towards deregulation in Canada create a situation where the NAFTA rules apply, but the most significant international arena for advancing the neo-liberal agenda for utilities is the current round of negotiations on the GATS. These new negotiations coincide with the United States' drive for an integrated continental energy policy and, should it succeed, will considerably enhance the project of a continental electricity market with full-scale continental pricing.

Changes in the electricity industry

Until recently, electricity experienced very little trade in the sense of producing in one country and selling in another. It has been difficult to trade because it is not storable. Certain technical features about its production and distribution meant that it developed as a natural monopoly.[1] Most of the world still does not engage heavily in electricity trade, and that which occurs is regionally based, because of its non-storability and its reliance on limited transmission networks. It exists primarily between Canada and the USA, Paraguay and Brazil; between Russia and other countries in Eastern Europe; and among Western European nations.[2]

In most countries, electricity has been provided either through the public sector or through a highly regulated private monopoly, which is usually confined to serving customers in specifically defined areas (WTO 1998). The American electricity sector developed as a combination of private, public, and cooperative systems that had specific jurisdictions and did not compete with each other. Prices and market areas were highly regulated with prices set in relationship to costs of production.

In Canada the capital costs involved in providing large-scale vertically integrated hydro systems were larger than private corporations wanted to risk, so the establishment of the modern electrical system was accomplished mainly through publicly owned utilities within each province (Froushauer 1999). The primary mandate of these provincial utilities has been to provide electricity to people and industries within a provincial boundary: their operations have been characterized by long-term planning for adequate supply, equitable distribution, and low and stable prices. Exports to the US, while often important for provincial revenues, were usually limited to the sale of surplus electricity through long-term contracts with guaranteed pricing.[3] However, as will be seen later in this chapter, the export market and the desire to increase exports to the US have proven to be the critical factor in accelerating the deregulation and privatization of electricity in Canada.

Market liberalization came more gradually to the electrical industry in the US than to other utilities primarily because of its characteristics as a natural monopoly. The technological advantages of large-scale generation, transmission, and distribution, coupled with a history of public development of the infrastructure, kept this industry firmly under government regulatory control, even when private utilities were significant actors in the sector. The slow, but steady deregulatory process began in 1978 when the Public Utility Regulatory Policy Act required utilities to purchase power from private producers if it could be obtained at costs that were less than those associated with building new facilities (Gilbert and Kahn 1996). This was the initial attempt to introduce competition for electricity supply, a direction that was driven by a US Supreme Court ruling that antitrust laws applied to the electric power industry and that federal regulatory agencies had to take into account the impact of their decisions on competition. At the same time a growing dissatisfaction with nuclear energy heightened the sense that massive public spending on mega-projects to provide energy had not served the public well (Flavin and Lenssen 1994). The monopoly of power utilities, it was argued, had encouraged the huge capital-intensive approaches to supplying electricity, and since costs could be passed on to the consumer, there was little incentive either to seek alternative sources of supply or to develop more efficient facilities. Public policy changes were also influenced by the sharp increases in costs due to the oil crises, the huge cost over-runs from nuclear power generation, and the nuclear disasters associated with Chernobyl and Three Mile Island. The immense cost of maintaining the safety of nuclear facilities made this source of energy particularly unattractive.

Initial regulatory constraints on utilities paved the way for greater private participation in the industry. This 'competition' was greatly accelerated through the Energy Policy Act of 1992, which significantly expanded the number of generating entities that could be exempt from regulatory controls of operations and pricing and created a whole new class of producers called 'exempt wholesale generators' (EWG). These EWGs could be owned by the electric utilities or could be private, independent entities. The 1992 act also accelerated competition by allowing greater access for wholesale transmission (wholesale wheeling) so that any EWG could be assured transmission either to its own utility or to other utilities at distant locations. These changes were further strengthened by regulatory changes in 1996 by the Federal Energy Regulatory Commission (FERCs) under orders 888 and 889, which removed monopoly power from utilities and mandated the separation of transmission from generating and other functions of the utility. These regulatory changes increased competition between utilities and generated a significant supply outside traditional utilities. Utilities have historically not competed with each other, but with the rise in wholesale wheeling, they were encouraged to attempt to increase their market shares at the expense of other utilities. As a result, the relative cost structure of other utilities became more significant to the security of markets that previously had been protected from competition.

Eliminating the natural monopoly aspects of electricity relied heavily on 'unbundling', a concept that emerged when deregulation of telecommunications successfully introduced competition in that industry. Unbundling the formerly integrated aspects of the electricity system requires that the advantages (and efficiencies) of vertical integration be dismantled so that new private suppliers can have access to transmission and distribution networks. The argument used to justify unbundling the three major components of electricity entities (generation, transmission, and distribution) is that existing vertical integration leads to natural monopolies unfairly capturing the electricity market. This train of thought is reinforced by the promise (at least when the concept was initially discussed) that a competitive, deregulated market would elicit more supply, be more efficient, and produce lower prices. However, the attractiveness of the market for private companies relies heavily on the availability of a well-developed and highly regulated infrastructure for transmission and distribution, because new technologies have not changed the natural monopoly of these components of delivering electricity to where it is needed.

The other major factor usually identified as accelerating changes in the industry relates to the technological changes that have occurred in the generation of electricity and that have made investor-owned, relatively small-scale electrical generation more viable (Jess 1997). It is true that the economies of scale that have historically characterized the industry have been undercut by new technologies such as combined cycle gas turbines that make smaller-scale production cheaper and environmentally cleaner (Linden 1995). However, the significance of new technologies as the driving force behind deregulation is grossly overstated since it really applies only to those jurisdictions that have turned away from coal and nuclear energy to gas, such as Great Britain and California. The main significance of technological change lies in providing an important lever for independent power producers to promote a competitive environment.

Once the ability to penetrate the regulated system occurred, the significant factor in accelerating the changing shape of the industry was the spectacular rise in the role of power traders like Enron and Duke Energy and the regulatory change that allowed US owners of electrical utilities to invest in utilities in other countries. The

Table 10.1   Fuel sources for electricity generation (% of total electricity production)

Fuel source	USA	Canada
Coal	52	19
Nuclear	20	13
Natural gas	16	3
Hydropower	7	61
Oil	3	2
Renewables	2	2

Sources: Cheney et al. 2001; OECD/IEA 2001.

increased trading and investment possibilities that arose from the deregulated system greatly expanded the size of electricity markets within regions and made the interconnectedness of regions more prominent.

The US experience demonstrates that relatively minor initial regulatory changes can have far-reaching repercussions throughout the entire system. The initial changes that only applied to wholesale wheeling did not appear as threatening as would total competition and complete deregulation of the market. But the small initial steps constituted an important first stage towards introducing competition at both the wholesale and retail levels. Competition at the retail level was mandated through the Comprehensive Electricity Competition Act (2001), which allows all customers in the US to choose their electricity supplier.[4]

The movement towards competition in the industry in Canada was even slower than in the US and was driven in most jurisdictions primarily by the perceived need to conform to US regulations in order to export into that market.[5] Most provincial utilities in Canada did not experience the same problems of inadequate supply and high prices as had their US counterparts. This was mainly because Canadian utilities are considerably more water-based than are those in the US, and hydro-based systems are much more cost-effective than are thermal-based and nuclear systems (Kwoka 1995). Most of the electricity in the US comes from nuclear fission or steam from burning fossil fuels, while in Canada it is primarily hydro-generated

Table 10.2 Comparative electricity prices in North America
(Canadian cents/kWh)

Cities	Residential	Medium power	Large power
Canada			
Winnipeg	5.89	4.44	2.96
Montreal	6.03	6.10	3.83
Vancouver	6.12	4.56	3.36
Ottawa	7.36	6.88	5.78
Edmonton	7.51	5.81	5.30
Toronto	8.32	7.31	6.24
St John's	8.37	6.22	3.49
USA			
Seattle	6.75	5.28	4.92
Miami	10.22	7.79	5.77
Chicago	12.26	10.98	7.09
Detroit	14.63	10.53	7.39
Boston	16.82	14.76	11.96
New York	21.24	17.52	12.63
San Francisco	17.18	12.76	7.33
Average	10.62	8.64	6.29
Power (kW)		1,000	50,000
Consumption (kWh)	1,000	400,000	30,600,000

Note: Average prices on 1 May 2000. This was before deregulation in Ontario and Alberta. Since then prices have increased considerably in these provinces.

Sources: Hydro Québec 2001; National Energy Board 2001; Toronto Hydro Electric System 2001.

(see Table 10.1). Once a hydroelectric system is in place, it is much cheaper and cleaner than other sources of large-scale electricity production.[6] Three of the four main electricity-exporting provinces in Canada – BC Hydro, Hydro Québec, and Manitoba Hydro – all rely primarily on waterpower.[7]

As a result of the abundance of low-cost electricity (see Table 10.2), Canadian utilities were not experiencing the serious problems encountered by many US utilities. Internal pressure for deregulation has come from the private sector's desire to gain entry to a market from which it has been excluded. The American deregulatory model, and the increased pressure from US regulators on Canada's exporting provinces to conform to US regulations, have reinforced this trend. This has meant shifting a closed, vertically integrated system to an open system where private access to transmission lines, if not actual generation itself, is permitted. All exporting provinces in Canada have opened their transmission systems for wholesale access, although only Ontario had planned for a fully deregulated market. Most provinces (with the exception of Alberta) have pursued a cautious route, and even Ontario, an exporting province that had planned to deregulate fully, is proceeding slowly.

US drive for energy

The drive for secure sources of supply is a critical feature of US energy policy. The major report prepared by Vice President Dick Cheney, Secretary of State Colin Powell, and others of the National Energy Policy Development Group (NEPD) in May 2001 documented not only the dire shortages the US faces – 'a fundamental imbalance between supply and demand defines our nation's energy crisis' – but also the relationship with foreign energy suppliers required to meet future needs (Cheney et al. 2001). The document describes, in dramatic words, how 'millions of Americans find themselves dealing with rolling blackouts or brownouts', employers who 'must lay off workers or curtail production to absorb the rising cost of energy', and of the families who 'face energy bills two to three times higher than they were a year ago' (Cheney et al. 2001: viii).

The critical situation is accentuated by the estimate that US electricity demand will increase by about 45 per cent within the next twenty years. This will require between 1,300 and 1,900 new electricity generation plants, which would mean bringing into production about one new plant a week over the next two decades (Cheney et al. 2001: 5–6). This ratcheting up of supply is something that even the most optimistic supporters of a deregulated market think unlikely. Despite its perceived failure, deregulation remains the cornerstone of US electricity policy. On the belief that in a completely deregulated market private companies will assume the requisite financial burden of increasing electricity supplies, there is no deliberate public planning for expanding future electricity supply.

In the face of recent market responses to deregulated markets, this assumption seems curiously optimistic. Although twenty-five states have opened their retail electricity markets to competition, very little new generating capacity has come on-line. The NEPD says new capacity is expected to come into production before 2005, but the clear message of the US policy report is that there will be a mismatch between generation of electricity and demand where it is needed. At present, the major problem areas for electricity are California, New York, and New England, all areas that could dramatically increase their supply from Canada.

As was amply demonstrated in California, the major problem with the electricity shortages in the US is that prices can fairly easily be manipulated through the deregulation process. While new domestic sources of electricity could come on-line if prices escalate very rapidly, this is a politically unsettling solution to what is clearly a serious problem. As the Chair of the Western Governors' Energy Committee noted at a 2001 conference in Whistler, BC, 'the best way to drive prices down is to increase supply'. As he observed, the heavy reliance on Canada by the US can create conflicts, particularly if Canadian companies gouge US customers. (This was a clear reference to the allegation that BC Hydro gouged California during the disastrous deregulation exercise.) But, as this official noted, these kinds of problems with price spikes can be averted if Canada assures adequate supply through an 'energy policy for the Americas' (Skelton 2001).

Developing a continental market for electricity to make sure resources are available from Canada and Mexico is clearly the goal of the National Energy Policy. The Cheney document stresses that 'energy security must be a priority of US trade and foreign policy', and makes clear that this security will be achieved by supporting a 'North American Energy Framework to expand and accelerate cross-border energy investment, oil and gas pipelines, and electricity grid connections' (Cheney et al. 2001: xv).

Canadian and Mexican resources are to be the US energy storehouses, and policies that increase these storehouse supplies are seen as crucial to US domestic security. Promoting the liberalization of the global energy sector means not only securing access to supply but also promoting US energy investments in other countries. To this end the NEPD recommends that the US focus on meeting energy objectives through international trade agreements. This can be done, the document argues, by supporting 'American energy firms competing in markets abroad and us[ing] our membership in multilateral organizations ... and our bilateral relationships to implement a system of clear, open, and transparent rules and procedures governing foreign investment; to level the playing field for US companies overseas; and to reduce barriers to trade and investment' (Cheney et al. 2001: 8/6).

The outlines of US energy policy are eminently clear – the objective is not simply to secure adequate trade in energy resources, but also to secure the right of US energy investors' capacity to exploit the resources of other countries. It is particularly important that the NEPD has targeted the opportunities to ensure this through the trade agreements: it specifically refers to the opportunities at the WTO to open markets 'for private participation in the entire range of energy services, from exploration to the final customer' (Cheney et al. 2001: 8/7).[8]

Electricity trade

Canada exports between 5 per cent and 10 per cent of its electrical generation, levels that are highly dependent on weather conditions and water levels in dams. Between 1988 and 1996 only 6 per cent of total production was exported to the US on average. Export sales are primarily to the New England states, New York state, the upper Midwest, the Pacific Northwest, and California. But despite the small share of total production that is sold across the border, export markets are a significant factor in the future because of the revenues these sales have generated for provincial governments in recent years. For example, in British Columbia revenues of the crown corporation BC Hydro changed considerably in a very short period: in the 1990s, revenues from exports were normally between 6 and 8 per cent of total revenues; however, by 2000, exports represented 32 per cent of total revenues and rose to 69 per cent of total revenues the following year. While the huge revenues in 2001, which were generated by the California deregulation debacle, are unlikely to be repeated, the anticipation that export revenues will continue to be substantial raises the incentive to meeting US demands for regulatory changes.

For all exporting provinces, US trade is more important than interprovincial trade (see Table 10.3). The Canadian electricity system is oddly structured, reflecting the historical peculiarities of federal/

Table 10.3 North American world electricity trade (billion kWh, 1999)

Country	Exports	Imports
Canada	42.91	12.95
Mexico	0.01	1.00
United States	14.00	42.92
North America total	56.92	56.87

Source: USEIA 2001.

provincial jurisdictions and competition between the provinces. Rather than developing a national grid system, or even substantial regional grids, to take advantage of efficiencies and low-cost production capacity of some provinces, the bickering between provinces at crucial times prevented the development of a mechanism that could have encouraged and regulated the transmission of electricity across provincial boundaries. Instead, each province developed electricity for distribution within its borders and, when the opportunity arose, preferred exporting electricity to the US rather than to other provinces. The result is that north/south inter-ties are considerably more developed than those between the provinces (Frouschauer 1999).[9] This has produced unfortunate results, such as Ontario developing nuclear power rather than importing significant amounts of hydroelectric power from Québec, and Alberta relying on coal rather than importing much hydroelectric power from British Columbia or Manitoba. Most exports of British Columbia, Manitoba, New Brunswick and Québec, all very low-cost producers, go to the USA.

Since the electricity industry developed primarily within provincial boundaries, most of its regulation is under provincial control. Until recently all provincial governments either directly owned the major electrical utilities or, in a few minor cases, asserted strong regulatory control over private monopolies. This meant that the security of supply and prices was firmly in the public sphere. The federal government regulated the export of electricity to the US and regulatory approval was needed from the National Energy

Board (NEB) for any export agreement. Export agreements were subject to public scrutiny through hearings to determine the effect on various groups and the environment. This federal control and public scrutiny began to change, however, with the gradual opening of the market to comply with Federal Energy Regulatory Commission (FERC) demands and the signing of the Free Trade Agreement and NAFTA.

The oversight of the NEB diminished considerably with changes to the NEB Act that removed the necessity to consult the public about the economic and social significance of proposed exports. Now export permits are allowed to proceed in a more routine way without public hearings and in most cases without any federal scrutiny. In response to changes in the market, and in particular with the rise of power trading and the increase of Canadian utilities' actions on spot markets, blanket export permits are issued to exporting companies. As a result, virtually no control or oversight exists over Canadian exports of electricity. This is especially important because changes in the entire industry are being made as a result of US policy directives, rather than from an assessment of the best interests of Canadians. When relatively small amounts of electricity are exported, the lack of federal review did not appear to place the security of electricity supply in jeopardy. However, the relative size of the export market is much less significant than the fact that the export market is the stimulus for an 'open access' policy that itself triggered increasing demands from US electricity companies and power traders to have access to the Canadian market. Since Canada is blessed with such a huge supply of the basic materials for generating electricity, few could imagine a decade ago that international trade would threaten domestic consumption. The difference now is that the powerful trade agreements that support an export-centred energy strategy can compel markets to open in ways that will jeopardize the stability of both supply and pricing that Canadians take for granted.

The major risk for Canadians in a deregulated market is that the new private producers, who will have access to the transmission grid, will focus on exporting to the more lucrative market in the US. Since public utilities would no longer plan for future supply, but rely on the private sector's investments, and since prices would no longer be regulated to reflect the cost of production, Canadians would be forced to compete with customers in the US for access to their own domestically generated electricity.

NAFTA and the GATS

While trade liberalization is not itself the primary cause of changes under way in the industry, the existence of NAFTA has contributed to the restructuring and ensures that any changes towards deregulation are permanent. This section will examine how NAFTA rules affect the electricity sector, but will also show how, despite the strength of these rules, NAFTA has limited power. The fact that NAFTA powers are limited is extremely important because it means Canadian provinces could maintain public monopolies in electricity, should they choose to defy US pressure to deregulate and privatize markets. It also means that because the deregulation of electricity is in a rather precarious situation and NAFTA rules are unable fully to achieve US objectives, Washington has had to pursue much more dramatic rule changes through the WTO. This is occurring in the negotiations on the General Agreement on Trade in Services (GATS). If the US proposal for energy in GATS succeeds, it would support complete electricity deregulation, privatization of electrical generation, and full-scale continental pricing.

NAFTA and electricity

According to the NAFTA Commission for Environmental Co-operation (CEC), NAFTA rules will be increasingly significant for the electricity sector, even though the trade agreement itself includes only a few provisions directly referring to trade in electricity. This is because NAFTA reinforces the market pressures for a competitive market in North America and because it continues to 'expand on the institutional frameworks within which the economic integration of the Canadian, US and Mexican electricity markets may take place' (CEC 1999: 288).

Several sections of NAFTA contain provisions that can affect the electricity market. The most important of these include the chapter specifically on energy (Chapter 6), all provisions dealing with investment (Chapter 11), and the sections dealing with monopolies and competition policy (Chapter 15). As the CEC notes, the rules on energy specifically aim to reduce the capacity of government regulators to involve themselves in cross-border energy sales by removing restrictions on exports and preventing the creation of new restrictions (CEC 1999: 289). In addition, regulatory measures of all governments are subject to 'national treatment' (see below).

While the federal government had few regulatory powers over electricity production in Canada, when NAFTA was signed it was heavily involved in controls over exports. As was noted earlier, all exports from utilities required permits from the National Energy Board, which had the authority to make decisions to grant or deny permits based upon several legal criteria. These criteria included consideration of the effects of the proposed exports on the environment and whether Canadian customers had equal access to the purchase of electricity under the same terms (Howse and Heckman 1996: 127). Since the signing of NAFTA, the federal government's oversight over exports has become much more flexible and much less rigorous. Blanket long-term export permits are routinely granted both to public utilities and to private corporations which have not yet entered the international market. For example, when Duke Energy purchased the Canadian gas company West Coast Energy, it applied for and received a long-term electricity-exporting permit, even though it is not yet in the electricity-producing business.

While it is clear that Canada could retain the right to monitor and regulate electricity exports under the NAFTA regime, it would need to make a case that this control was necessary in order, for example, to protect the reliability of the system or to prevent a critical shortage of electrical power (Howse and Heckman 1996: 127). But it is equally clear that Canada has not chosen to exercise its power under NAFTA and has voluntarily relinquished, at least in practice, a good deal of its regulatory control over electricity trade.

A similar self-censoring type of action seems to be occurring with regard to the interpretations of 'national treatment'. National treatment means that granting market access to domestic producers requires the same kind of access be given to foreign corporations as well.[10] But the situation is less satisfactory for the US in a deregulating climate where US deregulation is proceeding at a much more rapid rate than it is for most of Canada. The Canadian electricity-exporting provinces that have not fully deregulated (which is most of them) have greater access to US markets than American firms have to Canadian markets, creating what the US perceives to be highly asymmetrical circumstances. Canadian producers (including public utilities) are able to sell into the deregulated US market, but national treatment only allows US producers access to the Canadian market to the extent that Canadian private producers are allowed to participate. This means that as long as the Canadian market remains primarily in the public sphere, the level of private participation is limited. Consequently, US producers are demanding 'reciprocity' for both trade and investment rights. That is, they demand the same kind of access to produce, distribute, and trade in Canada that they (and Canadian utilities) have in the US.

Under NAFTA no country is required to provide reciprocity: the standard to be upheld is 'national treatment', and as long as a province treats domestic and foreign firms in the same way – that is, as long as they are both denied access to the market of a public monopoly – they are not contravening NAFTA (CEC 1999: 290). However, some utilities, such as BC Hydro, have voluntarily agreed to reciprocity, and all exporting provinces, even those who do not intend ever to deregulate fully (like Quebec), have opened their markets to wholesale wheeling. This means that when the public utilities buy power from independent power producers, they will have to give equal consideration to US producers.[11]

Once Canadian provinces begin the process of deregulation, very powerful NAFTA requirements come into play that considerably enhance the ability of private power producers to curtail the power of public utilities. So, for example, when some measure of competition begins in the generation of electricity, the public utility will be forced to abide by the rules laid out under NAFTA Chapter 15 dealing with competition policy, monopolies, and state enterprises. This requires that state enterprises must act 'solely in accordance with commercial considerations in its purchase or sale of the monopoly good or service in the relevant market, including with regard to price, quality, availability, marketability, transportation and other terms and conditions of purchase or sale' (NAFTA: 1501, 3, b). For a public utility, this could fundamentally undermine the very basis for its existence – that is, to meet needs that are defined more widely than those pertaining to commercial considerations.

While NAFTA has powerful tools to accelerate the deregulation of electricity in Canada, it cannot demand that either deregulation or privatization occurs. The main force compelling Canadian electricity utilities to deregulate is their desire to have access to the US export market and their reluctance to demand this right through NAFTA. Instead, Canadian utilities have entered into the regional transmission grids governed by FERC in the US and understand their interests to lie in conforming to FERC requirements. The Canadian federal government has been inactive in pursuing the interests of public utilities by creating specific rules to protect the Canadian system. According to some analysts, this 'combination of American regulatory activism, Canadian regulatory inertia, international trade law rules, and Canadian interest in continued access to American markets may bring about an integrated Canada/US market' (Howse and Heckman 1996: 134).

The GATS: current negotiating issues

Under the existing GATS agreement, Canada has relatively few commitments to liberalized markets in electricity. Those that exist pertain to construction work on power facilities.[12] However, this is changing through the current negotiations on GATS, particularly considering both the US government's negotiating issues, and the way that very large electricity traders are aggressively pursuing comprehensive coverage for energy in the GATS (Irwin 2000).

According to a leaked document from the US government, 'the United States requests full access to markets for energy services, including those provided to a public entity and used by the public entity to provide a service for commercial sale but not for use for governmental purposes.'[13] Considering that virtually all activities relating to electricity production and distribution can be considered a service, this is an extremely sweeping objective. It is also one that would require the dismantling of public utilities were it to be met.

As can be seen from Appendix I (the list of US market reform objectives and the types of GATS instruments that are useful in achieving these aims), those specific areas that the US wants covered are extremely inclusive.[14] These objectives correspond to the official negotiating objectives of the US, as defined in a WTO document submitted to the Council for Trade in Services which specifically calls for a comprehensive energy section to make it easier to open energy markets for both trade and investment (WTO 2000). The most important objectives relate to the classification of energy services, very broad market access, national treatment, and commitments that address national regulations.

The official statement of the US objective, which is to 'negotiate the broadest possible market access and national treatment commitments' for energy services, expressed the desire to eliminate the 'barriers' US firms face, such as the lack of a 'right of establishment' and an 'inability to provide cross-border services' (WTO 2000). Since in Canada these 'barriers' are constituted by the public sector's existence, it is clearly the public sector that is the target. The US document also discusses the elimination of discriminatory treatment between foreign and domestic service providers, but, significantly, it signals that merely achieving the lack of discrimination between the two is not sufficient to give access to markets. It specifically wants to see regulatory reform because without it 'market access and national treatment commitments, while necessary, may not be sufficient to assure liberalization for energy services'. This would address the US aim to achieve 'reciprocity', in contrast to the existing requirement in all international trade agreements that equal treatment ('national treatment') is the test of appropriate domestic regulation.

All of these objectives of the US, should they eventually become part of GATS, would substantially change the regulation and operations of most electricity utilities in Canada – even those that have already begun to open markets to private providers of electricity. Most certainly these changes would threaten the security of domestic consumption at differential prices – that is, at prices that currently relate to the cost of production of electricity, rather than the price established on the market. Also, at a time when power traders are increasingly active in electricity markets, open and non-discriminatory access to transmission systems would have to be accorded not only to those who want to sell to domestic customers but also to foreign traders who may prefer to export electricity. The result would be either less supply for Canadian consumers, or increased prices driven up by export markets.

Conclusions

Electricity market reform in most provinces has proceeded with little consideration for the repercussions of international trade agreements. While many provincial governments have tried to limit their exposure to deregulation and do not intend to submit people to the vagaries of the electricity market, they may have little choice if Canada continues to encourage measures that further liberalize energy markets through international trade agreements. The federal government so far has been silent about its position on how electricity should be treated in the GATS, but, considering its long-standing policy of extending the reach of the trade agreements as quickly as possible, it is likely that it will give in to US pressure on energy issues.

Shifting to a competitive deregulated market for electricity presents considerable dangers to all jurisdictions where the public provision of electricity has provided efficient, low-cost, and highly reliable electricity. While those proposing a competitive market assure the public that it can be achieved while protecting the social objectives of a public system, the experience in the US with competition is not reassuring.[15]

Canadian governments have recklessly let the relatively small export market set the agenda for the future of the country's electricity market. Currently 90 per cent of Canadian electricity production goes to people and industries within the country while only 10 per cent is exported, yet both the security of supply and low prices are at risk through deregulation measures designed, for the most part, to accommodate existing and future exports. When electricity was firmly within government control through integrated monopolies, and when exports proceeded through long-term contracts, international trade agreements could not affect the ways that the public resources were used. Under this type of regime, governments could insist on planning for adequate supply in the future, environmental protection, and ensuring a price to domestic consumers that was based on the cost of production. The process of deregulation has exposed this rational use of resources to the chaotic chance of the market.

Notes

1. A natural monopoly occurs when a single large firm would have the lowest cost of production and could prevent other firms from entering the industry because set-up costs are high and the 'natural monopoly' can sell at relatively low prices.

2. In Europe the major exporter is France (due to its huge nuclear industry), while Germany, Italy, Netherlands, and Spain are net importers (USEIA 2001).

3. This needs to be qualified by the recognition that mega-projects such as Churchill Falls and much of the Quebec and BC Hydro systems had an export objective.

4. This is modified for states that feel a regulated monopoly is more advantageous.

5. The exception to this was deregulation in Alberta, which was driven more by ideological issues than regulatory ones. Since Alberta is not an electricity-exporting province, the regulatory changes in the US had little impact on its decisions to deregulate and privatize the industry.

6. Hydro-based systems are not without problems. The initial creation of large reservoirs and transmissions system results in damage to wildlife, terrain,

local communities, and the socio-economic way of life of many aboriginal people. But once the systems are in place, they provide a secure, reliable supply of inexpensive and clean electricity.

7. New Brunswick is an exporter that relies primarily on thermal sources to generate electricity.

8. That the US is extremely serious in this objective is evident from the section in the National Energy Policy that recommends a comprehensive review of the use of 'economic sanctions' so that energy security can be included in US policy (Cheney et al. 2001: 8/6).

9. Inter-ties are the very large transmission lines between electricity systems.

10. 'Foreign' in this case refers to the national corporations of the signatories of NAFTA.

11. For all intents this is an issue between Canada and the US because Mexico has such a small export market. However, the NAFTA and GATS rules could have very significant implications for the ownership structure and the future development of electricity in Mexico.

12. For a more comprehensive discussion of the GATS and electricity, see Cohen 2001: 1–79.

13. This is a 2002 document that indicated that it was not yet intended for distribution outside the US government and the US Trade Representative.

14. The area identified as 'other' refers to specific language that would need to be written into the agreement in order to meet a specific objective.

15. For an example of this position, see Jaccard 2002.

References

Cheney, Dick, Colin L. Powell, et al. (2001) *National Energy Policy: Report of the National Energy Policy Development Group*, Washington, DC: US Government Printing Office.

Cohen, Marjorie Griffin (2001) 'From Public Good to Private Exploitation: GATS and the Restructuring of Canadian Electrical Utilities', *Canadian–American Public Policy* 48, December: 1–79.

Commission for Environmental Cooperation (CEC) (1999) 'Electricity in North America: Some Environmental Implications of the North American Free Trade Agreement (NAFTA)', Issue Study 3, Montreal: NAFTA/CEC, March.

Flavin, Christopher and Nicholas Lenssen (1994) *Powering the Future: Blueprint for a Sustainable Electricity Industry*, Washington, D.C.: Worldwatch.

Froushauer, Karl (1999) *White Gold: Hydroelectric Power in Canada*, Vancouver: University of British Columbia Press.

Gilbert, Richard J. and Edward P. Kahn (1996) 'Competition and Institutional Change in US Electric Power Regulation', in Richard J. Gilbert and Edward P. Kahn (eds) *International Comparisons of Electricity Regulation*, New York: Cambridge University Press: 179–230.

Howse, Robert and Gerald Heckman (1996) 'The Regulation of Trade in Electricity: A Canadian Perspective', in Ronald J. Daniels (ed.) *Ontario Hydro at the Millennium*, Montreal and Kingston: McGill-Queen's Press: 103–55.

Hydro Québec (2001) *Comparison of Electricity Prices in Major North American Cities*, Montreal: Hydro Québec.

Irwin, John R. (2000) press release, Oil and Gas Drillers Group, 3 May.

Jaccard, Mark (2002) *California Shorts a Circuit*, Toronto: C.D. Howe Institute.

Jess, Margaret (1997) 'Restructuring Energy Industries: Lessons from Natural Gas', *Natural Gas Monthly Special Report*, May.

Kwoka, John E. (1995) 'Public vs. Private Ownership and Economic Performance: Evidence from the US Electric Power Industry', Discussion Paper no. 1712, Cambridge, MA: Harvard Institute of Economic Research, February.

Linden, Harry R. (1995) 'Technology as an Enabling Force in the Global Restructuring of the Electric Power Industry', *The Electricity Journal*, vol. 18, no. 10: 54–64.

OECD/IEA (2001) *Electricity Information 2001*, Paris: OECD.

National Energy Board (2000) *Canadian Electricity: Trends and Issues*, May, Ottawa: National Energy Board.

Skelton, Chad (2001) 'US Delegation in Whistler Clear: BC's Energy Resources in Sights', *Vancouver Sun*, 27 July: D7/13.

Toronto Hydro Electric System (2000) *Important Information about Rates*, Toronto: Toronto Hydro Electric System.

USEIA (US Energy Information Administration) (2001) 'International Energy Database', January.

WTO (World Trade Organization) (1998) *Energy Services: Background Note by the Secretariat*, Council for Trade in Services, 9 September.

WTO (2000) 'Communication from the United States: Energy Services', 18 December, S/CSS/W/24.

PART II

Dealing with the Centre

11

Money on the (Continental) Margins: Dollarization Pressures in Canada and Mexico

Paul Bowles

The rise of regional currencies has been one of the most dramatic changes in monetary governance over the past decade as the historic link between national boundaries and national currencies has been weakened (Cohen 1998; Bowles et al. 2003). This has been most obviously the case in Europe, where the long process of integration now includes the European Central Bank and a new common currency for twelve of the EU member states. Elsewhere, the expansion of the euro to some of Eastern Europe's transitional economies is actively being debated. In Asia, the response to the financial crises of 1997 has included the possibility of developing regional currencies, and Japan has been actively promoting the internationalization of the yen. In West Africa, currency union is also on the agenda. In the Americas, debates about dollarization have been evident throughout the region. Despite the appearance of a common trend, however, the regional dynamics of monetary integration differ significantly.

The regional context for analysing currency developments needs to be taken explicitly into account, and for this reason the focus of this chapter is restricted to the Americas, and to the North American continent in particular. Here, as elsewhere, countries have used a variety of exchange rate regimes over the past half-century; while there has been a general movement towards flexible exchange rates over the past decade, some countries have gone against the trend in this period and others. This reflects the fact that exchange rate choices and monetary regimes depend on both economic and political pressures, and while economic theory may play a role, exchange rate and monetary regimes are not purely technocratic decisions but reflect a variety of pressures in the domestic and international political economies.

In the Americas, dollarization has emerged as a policy choice and has been officially followed recently by a number of small countries, such as El Salvador and Ecuador, following the example of Panama, which dollarized in 1904. A number of microstates and dependencies also use the US dollar as their currency. While these are the only current instances of official dollarization, there has also been widespread unofficial dollarization (or currency substitution),[1] and debates over official dollarization have arisen in three of the largest economies of the region, namely, Argentina, Canada, and Mexico. That is, dollarization, as a policy choice in the Americas has moved out of the periphery and into the semi-periphery. In this chapter, I analyse why dollarization has risen on the policy agenda in Canada and Mexico, what the pressures are for this form of monetary governance, and what are its implications.

Why is dollarization an issue?

Part of the reason that dollarization and/or adoption of a common currency have risen on the policy agenda in the Americas can be attributed to an intellectual fad of the 1990s spurred, in part, by the European experience. However, this is not the only reason that dollarization has arisen as an issue in both Canada and Mexico. Two of the most important reasons in these countries may be called the 'integrationist' and 'stabilizing' causes, although this should not be taken to imply that these causes are exclusive to these two countries. Indeed, as an example of the former, consider Europe, where monetary union has been designed to meet the objectives of political integration as well as of economic integration. That is, monetary union has been part of an integrationist agenda in both the political and economic spheres. With respect to the 'stabilizing' reason, in some peripheral countries, such as Ecuador, dollarization has been used as a means to attempt to stabilize an economy experiencing an economic crisis. Integrationist and stabilizing examples can therefore readily be found in other countries. What differentiates the debates on dollarization in Canada and Mexico is the extent to which *both* of these factors – the integrationist and the stabilizing – can be found. The fact that both factors have been invoked by supporters of dollarization in the two countries reflects the multiple identities of semi-peripheral countries, sharing, as they do, characteristics of both the periphery and the core. In the discussion of the arguments and pressures for dollarization in Canada and Mexico both integrationist and stabilizing factors are therefore analysed.

Canada

Consider, first, the integrationist factors in Canada. Since Canada and the USA signed the Free Trade Agreement in 1989 and NAFTA in 1994, the value of trade between Canada and the USA has increased greatly, as indicated in Table 11.1. Also indicated in the table is that the proportion of Canada's exports destined for the USA has increased over the past decade from an already high level of around three-quarters to almost 85 per cent.

Table 11.1 indicates the growing dependence of Canada on US markets, a dependence further emphasized by the fact that the export sector was Canada's main growth driver during much of the 1990s when domestic demand was relatively restrained and when, as a result, Canada's export/GDP ratio rose dramatically from around 25 per cent in 1990 to close to 45 per cent by 2000.

At the level of theory, this growing integration of trade has inevitably raised the question of whether this might increase the need for, and benefits of, using a single currency. The need to hedge against exchange rate movements and the costs of changing currencies when engaging in cross-border trade impose transaction costs on the business constituency, particularly multinational corporations, which might therefore gain from the adoption of a single currency with the USA.

At the practical level, growing trade and business integration has led to a questioning of whether 'unofficial dollarization' – that is, the use of US dollars by Canadian companies and individuals – is already taking place and creates pressures for considering official dollarization. Certainly, in the business sector, exporters to US markets are typically paid in US dollars and imports are also typically invoiced in US dollars. However, beyond this, and contrary to the frequent assertions in the media, the evidence for unofficial dollarization is weak.

While national newspapers such as the *Globe and Mail* (26 January 2002) may proclaim that 'Canada, by osmosis, has already adopted the US dollar', academic research by Seccareccia, for example, finds

Table 11.1   Canadian Exports, 1985–2000

Year	Total exports ($ million)	Exports to US ($ million)	US share (%)
1985	119,061	93,793	82.25
1986	125,172	97,647	78.01
1987	131,484	99,764	75.88
1988	143,534	105,292	73.36
1989	146,963	108,024	73.50
1990	152,056	111,565	73.37
1991	147,669	108,616	73.55
1992	163,464	123,377	75.48
1993	190,213	149,100	78.39
1994	228,167	181,049	78.35
1995	265,334	205,691	77.52
1996	280,079	222,461	79.48
1997	303,378	242,542	80.95
1998	326,181	269,336	82.57
1999	365,233	309,194	84.66
2000	422,559	359,551	85.09

Source: Canadian Economic Observer 2000/1: 59.

that there has not been 'any dramatic shift in the holding of foreign currency-denominated deposits by Canadians over and above what one would normally expect from the growing share of foreign trade out of GDP' (Seccareccia 2002: 5). Similarly, Murray and Powell argue that 'existing data suggest that informal dollarization is proceeding at a very slow (to non-existent) pace. Indeed, by many measures, Canada is less dollarized now than it was twenty years ago, and bears little resemblance to those economies that are typically regarded as truly dollarized' (Murray and Powell 2002: 1).

In terms of business practices, it is certainly the case that many larger corporations have adopted a dual accounting system in which they report their activities in both Canadian and US dollars.[2] A major reason for this is that Canadian equity markets are argued to be too limited to support the financing needs of large corporations.

Thus, corporations turn to US markets to raise funds, a move which requires meeting US accounting practices and financial reporting standards. This has provoked a lively debate in Canada about the extent to which corporate Canada is 'hollowing out' and heading south of the border. The implications of this for the currency debate are that Canadian firms are argued to be increasingly operating in US dollars and therefore that a dollarized economy might 'naturally' evolve as a result of corporate activities. The head of the Toronto Stock Exchange (TSX), Barbara Stymiest, refutes the 'hollowing out' hypothesis and argues that

> in 1997, for example, 49 Canadian companies were listed solely on a US exchange – the NYSE, Nasdaq or Amex – and the number went up to 53 in the following year. Now [2002], only 35 Canadian companies are solely listed in the USA – down better than a third from the peak. The number of Canadian interlisted companies – that is, companies listed on both the TSX and a US exchange – is down, too, from 213 to 184. There are 11 fewer on the NYSE, 30 fewer on the Nasdaq. (Stymiest 2002: 15)

While these figures cast doubt on alleged trends in Canadian companies listing abroad, it should also be noted that, not surprisingly, it is the largest companies that are listing (solely or cross-listing) on US exchanges. Furthermore, the TSX is seeking to move beyond the borders of Canada for its clients and is open to US investors, and lists some forty foreign companies, including Sony, British Airways, and General Motors (Macklem 2002). Thus, even if there is no trend towards Canadian companies listing in the USA, it is also the case that the TSX is pursuing a continentalist and global strategy itself.

The increasing integration of the two economies through both trade and investment flows over the past decade has therefore led to some business practices and to a part of the business constituency being favourably disposed towards monetary union with the USA. While trade integration, and the benefits of common currencies in reducing transactions costs, have provided one argument for those advocating such arrangements with the USA, this is certainly not a decisive argument for dollarization. For one thing, the data presented above demonstrate that trade integration has increased substantially under a flexible exchange rate regime. Second, around 60 per cent of Canada–US cross-border trade is intra-firm trade. For these firms exchange rate changes lead only to internal transfers, and the extent to which this is seen as a problem depends on whether country subsidiaries are independent profit centres or not. For example, the accounting practices of General Motors (unlike Ford) operate on a continental basis, so exchange rate changes are not important for its country-based subsidiaries. Furthermore, as noted above, the importance of unofficial dollarization is only a moderate factor. That is, while Canada trades to an increasing degree with the USA and this has led to some increase in the US dollar holdings of companies and individuals, it is not the case that the US dollar has been replacing the Canadian dollar in any serious way as a means of undertaking transactions in Canada. The topicality of the dollarization debate requires forces other than an appeal to a general claim that 'it's already happening', despite the frequency with which such appeals may appear in the business press.

Further support for the need for dollarization has been the result of two other factors: the volatility of the exchange rate and the decline of the Canadian dollar relative to the US dollar. Consider, first, the volatility of exchange rates, a volatility which has not only imposed hedging costs on business but has also, according to some academic economists, involved costs for the Canadian economy as a whole. It has been argued that the volatility of Canada–US exchange rates has inhibited cross-border investment and trade, and that further economic integration requires a more stable currency regime (Courchene and Harris 1999). Not only does hedging in volatile currency markets lead to considerable 'currency fatigue' among businesses; it also introduces uncertainty into planning and investment decisions. As an example, companies typically base their investment decisions on a conservative value of the Canadian dollar: for example, while the Canadian dollar has recently been trading around the 63 cent US mark, companies often base their investment calculations on a 75 cent dollar. If a project cannot make money with a 75 cent dollar, it is unlikely to be undertaken. As a result, it is argued, investment levels are lower than they would be with a fixed – and certain – exchange rate. A volatile (and often misaligned) exchange rate, it is argued, results in output and productivity losses to the Canadian economy as a result of lower investment. While a fixed exchange rate might be an obvious choice here, proponents have argued that other options, such as a common currency and adoption of the US dollar, should also be considered. In a world of mobile international capital flows, fixed exchange rates are hard to maintain, and the search for 'hard fixes', such as those provided by

Figure 11.1 US/Canadian dollar exchange rate, 1970–2001

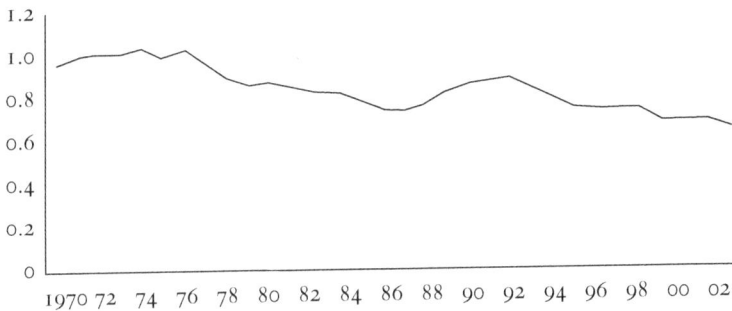

Source: Pacific Policy Analysis Computing and Information Facility in Commerce Exchange Rate Service, University of British Columbia, Canada.

currency boards, or 'superhard fixes', provided by common currencies and dollarization, has also gained a greater prominence in discussion of exchange rate regimes.

How should this volatility argument be interpreted? Certainly, the argument that business investment is lower than it would be in a world of greater certainty has some validity. However, it should be noted that Canada is not unique in experiencing volatility in exchange rates; it has, in fact, been a persistent feature of the international financial (dis)order since the early 1970s and is just as evident in G3 exchange rates. For example, as Frankel and Roubini have noted, 'the short-run volatility of G3 real exchange rates is one of the most robust – and to many observers disturbing – characteristics of the post-Bretton Woods floating exchange rates experience' (Frankel and Roubini 2001: 6). This raises the question of why the dollarization debate has been more prominent in some countries than others, given that all countries seem to be experiencing this phenomenon, and whether global solutions might be more appropriate than countries such as Canada trading one kind of volatility for another by adopting a (volatile) US dollar.

Additional pressures are present from the decline in the value of the Canadian dollar against the US dollar. The Canadian dollar has been falling for the past three decades against the US dollar but, in the wake of the Asian financial crisis, in 1998 it fell to its lowest level in 140 years (although it subsequently fell further still in late 2001 and 2002), as indicated in Figure 11.1.

After decades of the Canada/US exchange rate fluctuating in the 90 cent to $1.05 range, the period since 1970 has seen a discernible decline in the value of the Canadian dollar. The reasons for this decline are subject to debate. It is precisely Canada's position as a staple producer that some have used to explain the depreciating dollar and to justify the continued use of a national currency and a flexible exchange rate. That is, it is because Canada relies, relatively speaking, more heavily on commodity exports that its currency depreciates in times of global economic slowdowns as commodity prices weaken. However, John Murray, chief economist at the Bank of Canada, points out in his analysis that it is this feature of the Canadian economy that distinguishes it from the US economy and why a flexible exchange rate serves as a useful adjustment mechanism in the face of external shocks (Murray 1999). That is, Canada's status as a staple producer is used to justify the need for an independent currency. Adopting a common currency would not remove the need for adjustments to be made; it would merely move them to areas other than the exchange rate, such as nominal wage flexibility, where, at least in the short run until labour is sufficiently weakened, there are likely to be more protracted struggles and higher output costs. It is the case, though, that this argument is more persuasive in Canada's resource-intensive regions than in the manufacturing regions of Ontario and Quebec, provinces which are both the most populous and the most highly integrated with the USA (Beine and Coulumbe 2002). Canada's economic dualism may lead to regional frictions over the desirability of a common currency/dollarization just as such frictions have been evident at various points in Canadian history in the debates over free trade with the USA.[3]

This line of reasoning – that a depreciating currency is a natural market response to a commodity-based economy, a response that is both rational and desirable (since it permits easier adjustment to external shocks) – is not one that is accepted by the pro–dollarization lobby. For them, the fall in the exchange rate relative to the US is a sign of policy failure. For the public, each new low for the Canadian dollar invites criticism of government institutions and policies and invites envious comparison with the strength of the US dollar, with individuals feeling their real wealth reduced if the value of the currency falls.[4] While this is true to the extent that Canadians consume imported goods, there has been a considerable exaggeration of the case for a single currency in response: for example, Mundell argues that 'if Canada and the United States shared a stable common currency or an irrevocably fixed exchange rate, Canada's real income would soar, closing a large part of the gap between the two countries' GDP per capita' (Mundell 2001: 26). One wonders if the Nobel laureate predicts the same outcome for East Timor, Ecuador, and El Salvador, all of which do share a common currency with the United States!

Nevertheless, the depreciating Canadian dollar appears as an immediate sign of failure and resonates with the public, explaining why support for dollarization with the US in Canada has a constituency beyond some business groups and academics. Indeed, CIBC World Markets Chief Economist, Jeff Rubin, argues that the 60 cent Canadian dollar is an important psychological threshold and that if this threshold is broken, then in his view many Canadians would lose confidence in the Canadian dollar (Diekmeyer 2001).

Thus the momentum behind any dollarization initiative depends critically not only on increased integration between the Canadian and US economies but also on the sense of discomfort felt by the public at seeing the value of their currency eroded relative to their neighbour. That is, pressures for dollarization rely in part upon the response to a falling (not simply a volatile) dollar. However, while the public may view the falling dollar with concern, this concern is not unanimously felt by business interests. This points to important differences of interest between business sectors, in respect of which the description provided by Wise in the Latin American context serves as a useful general rule:

> Those producing for export prefer a depreciated but predictable exchange rate policy, while those involved in production for the home market are prone to push for a more flexible monetary policy overall, including an adjustable exchange rate. International investors clearly side with exporting interests in their demands for stable and predictable prices ... workers and middle-class consumers have come to prefer overvalued fixed rates, which they associate with enhanced purchasing power. (Wise 2000: 11)

While this provides a general summary of business and consumer interests, two other sectors should be mentioned in the Canadian context which represent the opposed interests of the old, 'peripheral' resource-based industries and the new, 'core' information technology (IT) industries. Many resource-based industries have benefited from a declining dollar and this has boosted their competitiveness in the US market: Canada's $10 billion exports of softwood lumber to the

US, for example, have been aided by the depreciating dollar in the face of other trade restraints imposed by the US. Thus, while these firms might be willing to support a stabilization of the exchange rate, the *rate* at which any monetary union came about would be of critical concern. Conversely, many high-tech firms, faced with importing IT equipment from the US priced in US dollars and competing for labour in a continental market, have been hurt by the depreciating dollar as it has pushed up their costs and made it difficult to recruit and retain highly skilled, mobile workers. This sector would also support an end to a depreciating dollar through some kind of exchange rate fix or monetary union with as high a rate as possible being the most desirable. This division has added spice to dollarization debates in Canada since pro-single-currency analysts have argued that the current flexible exchange rate regime favours traditional resource exporters and thereby slows Canada's transition to the 'knowledge-based economy', a transition which will see Canada finally escape its semi-peripheral trappings (Courchene and Harris 1999).

Divisions between business interests are evident from surveys conducted by the Canadian Federation of Independent Business. Given concern over the value of the dollar and the prominence of dollarization debates, it asked its members (made up of small and medium-sized firms) for the first time in its 2002 *Business Outlook* whether the low value of the dollar benefited their firm: 23 per cent responded that the lower dollar helped them, whereas 31 per cent saw a higher dollar as being of more benefit (38 per cent reported no effect one way or the other). Similar divisions are also present in larger firms.[5]

The argument so far has been that pressures in Canada for use of a single currency with the USA have come as a result of increasing trade integration, a volatile exchange rate, and a depreciating Canadian dollar. In each case, however, these pressures are not unchallenged: for example, increasing unofficial dollarization is not much in evidence, exchange rate volatility is not unique to Canada, and business interests are split on the response to the depreciating dollar. Does this therefore mean that dollarization pressures in Canada will remain weak? It would be rash to reach this conclusion, because a business coalition in favour of dollarization could still emerge just as it did in favour of free trade a decade ago. Then the organization representing large corporations, the Business

Council on National Issues (BCNI, newly renamed the Canadian
Council of Chief Executive Officers, CCCEO) was instrumental in
forging a business coalition for free trade in the early 1980s despite
close to a century of opposition to free trade from the business
community. The BCNI pushed its agenda with the Conservative
government under Prime Minister Brian Mulroney, which ultimately
opened the way for the Canada–US Free Trade Agreement in 1988.
This represented a large shift in Canadian business orientation, and
the coalition in favour of deeper continental integration, as a way
of ensuring that Canadian companies have access to markets and
technology within a framework of constrained government action,
is still very much in effect. Thomas D'Aquino (1998), President of
the CCCEO, turning his attention to the Free Trade Area of the
Americas, has stated that he has

> never been of the view that globalization was somehow a totally imper-
> sonal force beyond the control of individuals and governments. History
> has taught us that policy choices can be made which could reverse trends
> towards greater global integration.... The Canadian business community
> will do what it can to support the continuing agenda of deeper economic
> and social integration throughout the hemisphere.

This community has not taken a definitive position on dollarization as the next step in the continental integrationist agenda; it is
entirely possible, however, that the longer-term strategic interests of
the business class as a whole may go this route, just as a decade ago
they entered into a neo-liberal trade regime which tied the hands of
future governments in Canada to the neo-liberal agenda. The desire
to keep the border open and to consider all options necessary to
promote a continental perimeter rather than one across the 49th
parallel post-September 11 has pushed the envelope of thinking
and forces for policy harmonization with the USA. Furthermore,
the continuing depreciation of the dollar has been interpreted by
some as indicating that Canada has a 'productivity problem' caused
by excessive regulation and taxation relative to the USA. Adopting
a common currency would force Canadian governments to address
this issue and liberalize the business environment since remaining
competitive through exchange rate depreciation would no longer
be an option.

Certainly some pro-dollarization business commentators have
drawn parallels with the free-trade debate. For example, Sherry
Cooper, Vice-President and Chief Economist with BMO Nesbitt

Burns, remarked that if arguments for monetary integration with the USA and Mexico sound far-fetched, 'so did the idea of a free-trade deal in 1980' (Cooper 2002: D5), a view recently also expressed by Ted Carmichael, Chief Canadian Economist at the US investment bank J.P. Morgan, who argues that 'in the medium term … a common currency has the potential to make the transition from political issue to policy reality in much the same way as Canada–US free trade did in the 1980s' (as quoted in Thorpe 2002). For Cooper, 'the reality of dollarization is difficult. It is a tough-love reality in that it will force us to truly compete through innovation and productivity-enhancing investments' (Cooper 2002: D5). It is precisely this type of masochistic neo-liberalism based on appeals to 'innovation', 'productivity', and 'competitiveness' that has proved dominant in forming business coalitions in favour of neo-liberalism in Canada and elsewhere. For the Canadian business community, integration with the USA is the overriding priority; the possibility that it might throw its weight behind dollarization as the next step in continental integration remains real. Thus, while integrationist pressures narrowly conceived do not point to dollarization, integrationist pressures broadly conceived as a strategic interest of the business class have the potential to be a more potent force.

Mexico

Turning from the Canadian case, these forces for dollarization – drawing on integrationist and stabilizing reasons – bear strong resemblance to the situation in Mexico; trade integration with the US has also increased substantially since the advent of NAFTA, as indicated in Table 11.2.

While oil revenues have decreased from around a quarter of total exports in the early 1990s to half of that level, manufactured exports have taken an increasing share of exports. Manufactured exports are dominated by a few large firms, and it is estimated that fully 40 per cent of non-*maquiladora* manufactured exports are accounted for by just five multinationals.[6] Trade with the US is dominated by large companies operating in the north of the country (especially in the *maquiladoras*). The banking sector, following the banking crisis of 1995, has been largely taken over by foreign banks. Just as in Canada, therefore, there has been an increasing use of US dollars as a result of the integration of trade. In Mexico too, however, unofficial dollarization beyond that has been relatively modest.[7] Even so, for the major

Table 11.2 Mexican exports, 1985–2000

Year	Total exports ($ million)	Exports to US ($ million)	US share (%)
1985	22,105	8,954	40.51
1986	16,120	7,574	46.99
1987	20,526	8,252	40.20
1988	20,765	12,102	58.28
1989	22,975	15,553	67.70
1990	29,982	23,144	77.19
1991	42,688	33,912	79.44
1992	46,196	37,420	81.00
1993	51,886	43,068	83.00
1994	60,882	51,855	85.17
1995	79,542	66,337	83.40
1996	96,000	80,541	83.90
1997	100,267	85,830	85.60
1998	107,747	94,710	87.90
1999	124,247	109,710	88.30
2000	153,247	135,930	88.70

Source: 1985 to 1990: *Mexican Handbook* 1994; 1990 to 2000: IMF 2001.

transnational firms operating in Mexico, using a single currency would reduce transaction costs; as will be shown below, Mexican business associations have taken up the cause of dollarization.

Equally important, the recent debates over dollarization have come after twenty-five years of periodic exchange rate crises. The 1980s were a particularly difficult time – a 'lost decade' – when the 1982 debt crisis and the 1986 oil price collapse sent the Mexican economy into recession. However, by the end of the decade, Mexico was heading in a new direction. The ruling PRI (Institutional Revolutionary Party) government had abandoned its protectionist policies and had turned to neo-liberalism as the solution to the country's economic ills. Adopting the array of policies recommended by the Washington consensus, Mexico introduced a programme of

rapid trade liberalization, privatization, and deregulation. International
investors liked what they saw and capital flowed into the country.
Entry into NAFTA on 1 January 1994 cemented these policy reforms
and Mexican politicians spoke bravely of Mexico's graduation to a
new level of economic and political standing. Quite unexpectedly,
however, by the end of that year Mexico found itself embroiled in
another currency crisis in which the crawling band had ultimately
to be abandoned, the peso devalued by 50 per cent, and GDP fell
by 6 per cent with the financial system left in ruins.

The increase in US interest rates in 1994 did much to stem the
flow of capital to Mexico, as did the increase in political violence.
But while there are country-specific factors, as Kessler notes, 'in
the wake of the devastating devaluations in several of the world's
largest emerging markets, including Russia, South Korea, Indonesia
and Brazil, the Mexican experience is now seen as the harbinger
of a new economic phenomenon: the volatility of global capital
markets' (Kessler 2000: 43).

The collapse of the exchange rate in 1995, shown in Figure 11.2,
came after previous equally large collapses in the mid-1970s and
early 1980s. Following on from this collapse, it is perhaps no surprise
that as the debate over dollarization became increasingly fashionable
throughout Latin America as a form of monetary governance in a
world of volatile international capital flows, it also became a hot
topic in Mexico. In the post-crisis period from 1994 to the end
of the decade, currency reform was on the policy agenda either in
the form of outright dollarization or, following on from the then
successful Argentinian experiment, a currency board. In 1999, the
President of the influential Mexican Businessman's Council, Eugenio
Clariond, called on then President Zedillo to consider dollarization,
a call also supported by the Mexican Bankers Association and the
country's largest industrial chamber. While rejected by Zedillo, the
call for monetary integration into North America was initially supported by the newly elected President Fox in 2000.

The stabilizing pressures for dollarization are stronger in Mexico
than in Canada given the dramatic exchange rate crises which Mexico
has experienced in recent decades. However, in other respects, the
economic case for dollarization in Mexico is weaker than in Canada.
The large differences in the economic structures of the USA and
Mexico and the importance of oil in Mexico's exports make the
asymmetry of shocks to both economies a compelling example of

Figure 11.2   US dollar/Mexican peso exchange rate, 1990–2001

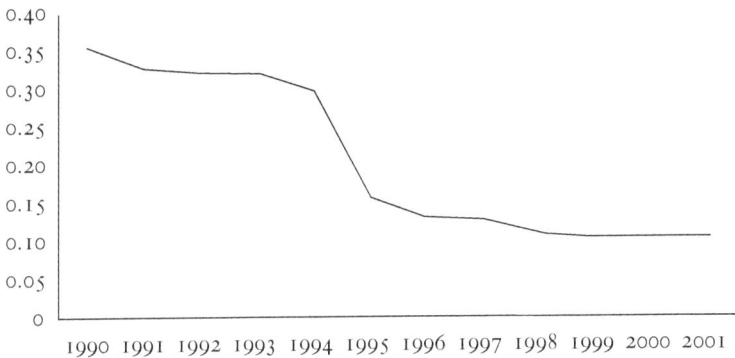

Source: Penn World Tables.

the need to have separate currencies. Without them, adjustments would have to take place entirely through wage and price flexibility in the Mexican economy, with the potential for large output losses and unemployment as a result. In addition, one important function of a national monetary system and of a national central bank is to provide 'lender of last resort' facilities to the domestic banking system: that is, the central bank is charged with providing liquidity to the domestic banking system in order to prevent a generalized banking crisis. Given Mexico's fragile financial system and the fact that it is highly unlikely that the US Federal Reserve would come to its aid if Mexico dollarized, it is a wonder that dollarization is being given such a prominent hearing. However as Ibarra and Moreno-Brid note,

> the unexpectedly wide debate provoked by the proposals in favour of a North American monetary union or the adoption of a currency board reflects, more than the actual soundness of their arguments, ideological dogma or the simple desperation of businessmen, bankers and even workers to find rapid remedies to cure the instability of the financial system and prices in the Mexican economy. (Ibarra and Moreno-Brid 2001: 16–17)

The stabilizing pressures for dollarization as a solution to periodic exchange rate instability and purchasing power reductions are therefore evident both in the business sector and among the public. However, also important, as Ibarra and Moreno-Brid point out, is 'ideological dogma'. In this instance, this refers to the strong anti-government position of the Mexican business community and some academics, a position which regards limitations to state authority and discretionary policies as a key medium-term objective. That is, the continuing neo-liberal agenda in Mexico has placed dollarization on the policy agenda more firmly than might otherwise be expected.

In Mexico too, therefore, the integration of the economy with the US and the presence of currency crises have been important factors in shaping the dollarization debate. The rise in the value of the peso since 2001, combined with the Argentinian collapse, has removed the dollarization issue from the immediate policy agenda. However, it may not remain off the agenda permanently, for a couple of reasons. First, the factors which caused the slight appreciation of the peso in 2001 – investor confidence buoyed by fiscal reform, debt agency upgrading, and Citigroup's takeover of Banamex – may only provide temporary stability to the peso. Second, and more importantly, there remain the longer-term strategic interests of business in policies designed to limit the discretion of governments in their policy dealings. Just as the Free Trade Agreement and NAFTA were seen in Canada as a way of limiting government dirigisme in the economy through adherence to the supranational rules of NAFTA, so they were viewed as preventing a return to past policies of interventionism in Mexico. Taking away the ability of governments to exercise monetary authority would be a further part of this strategic business agenda.

Implications

The pressures for dollarization in both Canada and Mexico come predominantly from the business sector. Admittedly, as noted, especially in the case of Canada, there are significant divisions between various sectors of business on the desirability of such a policy; however, the argument presented above suggests that it would be possible to forge a class alliance between the constituent parts of the business sector if dollarization were seen as a necessary component of economic integration and continentalization of the North American economy. At present, the jury is still out on whether the business community regards this as necessary, but it is clear that, just as the business sector coalesced around pro-free-trade policies in both countries in the debates over the Canada–US Free Trade Agreement and NAFTA, so such a coalition could be put together in favour of monetary union. As the discussions above illustrate, the topic is one which is being keenly followed by the business community. In some respects, monetary sovereignty is one of the few remaining economic levers left to governments; it is not surprising to find therefore that it has become the latest battlefield for those wishing to limit the possibilities of national economic autonomy.

Nevertheless, there remain significant political obstacles to achieving such an outcome given the surrender of sovereignty that would be implied by dollarization. For this reason, many proponents have argued for a common currency along European lines as the way forward. By appealing explicitly to the European case, proponents suggest that the model of pooled sovereignty which characterizes the European Central Bank would be possible in North America. For example, in Mexico, particularly in the past few years when the US dollar–peso exchange rate has stabilized, the view has been expressed that a movement towards North American monetary union could be seen as a longer-term goal. Reflecting this in public pronouncements, President Fox has typically worked in reference to the EU and has suggested that this might be a model for a North American common market. Similarly, he has also been keen to include Canada in any proposals, thereby linking monetary integration to the wider economic integration taking place under NAFTA rather than simply advocating an unconditional acceptance of US monetary governance. Monetary union is now viewed as a long-term possibility emerging from the 'convergence' of the three North American economies. Again taking its cue from the European experience, monetary union is regarded as one of the last elements of continental integration.

In Canada, proponents of monetary integration such as Courchene and Harris (1999) and Grubel (1999) favour the creation of a new common currency, the North American Monetary Unit (NAMU) and the Amero, respectively. In arguing for such a currency, they are clearly suggesting that Canada might be able to enter into a new currency regime with the USA on the basis of some presumed national equality and shared sovereignty. Courchene and Harris have drawn explicit parallels with the European model and argued that 'the easiest way to broach the notion of a NAMU is to view it as the North American equivalent of the European Monetary Union and, by extension, the euro. This would mean a supranational central bank with a board of directors drawn in part from the central banks of the participating nations' (Courchene and Harris 1999: 22). Grubel, in discussing the governance structure for the Amero, has proposed that the three NAFTA signatories adopt a common currency with each member country appointing members to a common central bank's governing body on the basis of population and each country's relative wealth. While this would lead to US domination of the governing body, Grubel nevertheless believes that regional alliances, such as Prairie populations on both sides of the Canada–US border, would temper the influence of national interests.

However, such analogies are implausible as the regional dynamics of Europe are substantially different from those in North America; regional context matters. Assessing the European project and the role of monetary union is a controversial issue, as can be seen by the animated debate among the European left. For some, the European Central Bank (ECB) represents an undemocratic, monetarist-inspired institution which cements neo-liberalism in Europe (Arestis and Sawyer 1999). For others, such as Notermans, for example,

European economic integration is not necessarily a threat to a full employ-ment welfare state. Under a growth-oriented regime in which the ECB pursues a cheap money policy backed by a functioning system of nominal wage moderation, mass unemployment may not be the inevitable phe-nomenon that many have come to believe it is. (Notermans 2000: 42)

Such debates, however, are irrelevant in the North American case. Here it is very clear that the integration of the continental economy is taking place on neo-liberal lines. If Germany was reluctant in accepting an ECB under some kind of pooled sovereignty, such an arrangement is a non-starter in the North American context. As argued by John McCallum, the chief economist at one of Canada's four major chartered banks, in 2000, 'the European Union model, in which independent states share decision-making and sovereignty, is alien to American thinking and American history' (McCallum 2000: 2); and he described the USA as being 'light years' away from allowing any other country a formal role in formulating US monetary policy. The total absence of any discussion in the USA about sharing a new common currency with Canada (or anyone else) is also telling. The relevance of the European experience for the political dimensions of potential North American monetary integration is therefore strictly limited.

The pressures for dollarization in North America come therefore from the same sources as the pressures for other forms of economic continentalism and form part of the same agenda. That neither Canada nor Mexico has dollarized does not mean that this integrationist agenda is not still dominant. Although at this point a broad business coalition has not formed around the need for dollarization, such a coalition is far from impossible; for example, it might emerge in response to further exchange rate collapses or perceptions that governments in either country are losing faith in integration and considering more nationalist economic policies. If that were the fear, then the desire to tie the governments' hands in their use of monetary policy would undoubtedly spur business interests to seek a strategic solution in the form of dollarization. Such an outcome would further entrench neo-liberalism in continental North America and further enhance the power of the US in continental decision-making.

Notes

I am grateful to Karine Peschard and Jackie Lytle for their research assistance with this chapter.

1. For details of unofficial dollarization in Latin America, see Balino et al. 1999.
2. This is likely to remain the case, although Guy Legault, President of the Certified General Accountants Association of Canada, has recently argued that Canada should not harmonize its accounting standards with those of the US as it increases the chances of an Enron-style debacle happening in Canada. See 'Quit Trying to Harmonize Accounting with US', *Financial Post*, 4 May 2002: 7.
3. In fact, the sovereignist government in Quebec is in favour of dollarization and views the use of a single currency in North America as a way of further integrating the Quebec economy into the continental economy and of opening up new political space for the sovereignty movement.
4. As Harris notes, 'most Canadians see a large depreciation of their currency as a policy "mistake" even if, while the currency has been depreciating, the Bank has hit its inflation targets' (Harris 2001: 36).
5. Personal interview with the Canadian Association of Manufacturers and Exporters, 25 April 2002. In fact, I was told that firms belonging to this organization were 'all over the place' in terms of their response to the depreciating dollar.
6. I am grateful to Jorge Basave Kunhardy of the Universidad Nacional Autónoma de México for providing this information.

216   GOVERNING UNDER STRESS

7. In Mexico, the ratio of foreign currency deposits to broad money is estimated to be 7.2 per cent, substantially below the level of other Latin American countries (Balino et al. 1999).

References

Arestis, P. and M. Sawyer (1999) 'The Deflationary Consequences of a Single Currency', in M. Baimbridge, B. Burkitt, and P. Whyman (eds) *A Single Currency for Europe?*, London: Macmillan: 100–12.

Balino, T., A. Bennett and E. Borensztein (1999) 'Monetary Policy in Dollarized Economies', IMF Occasional Paper 171.

Beine, M. and S. Coulumbe (2002) 'Regional Perspectives on Dollarization in Canada', mimeo.

Bowles, P., O. Croci, and B. MacLean (2003) 'Globalization and Currency Convergence: What Do the Regions Tell Us?', in J. Busumtwi-Sam and L. Dobuzinskis (eds) *Turbulence and New Directions in Global Political Economy*, London: Palgrave: 169–85.

Canadian Economic Observer (2000/1) Statistics Canada, Cat. No. 11-210-XPB.

Cohen, B. (1998) *The Geography of Money*, Ithaca, NY: Cornell University Press.

Cooper, S. (2002) 'Common Currency is a Tough Love that Will Force Us to Truly Compete', *Edmonton Journal*, Sunday, 3 February.

Courchene T. and R. Harris (1999) 'From Fixing to Monetary Union: Options for North American Currency Integration', C.D. Howe Institute Commentary, no. 127.

D'Aquino, T. (1998) 'Hemispheric Integration After the Santiago Summit: A Canadian Business Perspective', Canadian Council of Chief Executives, Media Centre Speeches, 2 October.

Diekmeyer, P. (2001), 'Is the Loony Drowning? Hemispheric Integration is Reducing the Advantages of an Independent Currency', *CMA Management*, June: 54–5.

Frankel, J. and N. Roubini (2001) 'The Role of Industrial Country Policies in Emerging Market Crises', NBER Working Paper 8634.

Grubel, H. (1999) 'The Case for the Amero: The Economics and Politics of a North American Monetary Union', *Critical Issues Bulletin*, September, Vancouver: The Fraser Institute.

Harris, R. (2001) 'Mundell and Friedman: Four Key Disagreements', *Policy Options/Options Politiques*, May.

Ibarra, D. and J. Moreno-Brid (2001) 'Currency Boards and Monetary Unions: The Road Ahead or a Cul De Sac for Mexico's Exchange Rate Policy?', in M. Anyul and L. Punzo (eds) *Mexico Beyond NAFTA: Perspectives for the European Debate*, London: Routledge.

IMF (International Monetary Fund) (2001) *Mexico: Selected Issues*, IMF Country Report No. 01/91, October.

Kessler, T. (2000) 'The Mexican Peso Crash: Causes, Consequences and Comeback', in C. Wise and R. Roett (eds) *Exchange Rate Politics in Latin America*, Washington, DC: The Brookings Institution.

McCallum, J. (2000) 'Engaging the Debate: Costs and Benefits of a North American Common Currency', *Current Analysis*, April, Royal Bank of Canada Economics Department.

Macklem, K. (2002) 'Stocks: Had "X" Today?', *Maclean's Magazine*, 6 May.

Mexican Handbook (1994) 'Economic and Demographic Maps and Statistics'.

Mundell, R. (2001) 'One World, One Money? Symposium', *Policy Options/Options Politiques*, May.

Murray, J. (1999) 'Why Canada Needs a Flexible Exchange Rate', Bank of Canada Working Paper no. 99–12.

Murray, J. and J. Powell (2002) 'Dollarization in Canada (The Buck Stops There)', mimeo.

Notermans, T. (2000) 'Europeanization and the Crisis of Scandinavian Social Democracy', in R. Geyer, C. Ingebritsen, and J. Moses (eds) *Globalization, Europeanization and the End of Scandinavian Social Democracy?*, London: Macmillan.

Seccareccia, M. (2002) 'North American Monetary Integration: Should Canada Join the Dollarization Bandwagon', mimeo.

Stymiest, B. (2002) 'Corporate Myths', *Financial Post*, 10 May.

Thorpe, J. (2002) 'New Model for Common Currency', *Financial Post*, 25 May.

Weston, Alan, Robert Summers and Bettina Aten, Penn World Version 6.1, Center for International Comparisons at the University of Pennsylvania, October 2002.

Wise, C. (2000) 'Introduction: Debates, Performance, and the Politics of Policy Choice', in C. Wise and R. Roett (eds) *Exchange Rate Politics in Latin America*, Washington, DC: The Brookings Institution.

12

Taking Investments Too Far: Expropriations in the Semi-periphery

David Schneiderman

The dominant themes that emerge from a reading of the literature on globalization are those of speed, movement, and uncertainty. Zygmunt Bauman, for instance, equates globalization with a 'political economy of uncertainty' that gives rise to political regimes of 'permanent and ubiquitous' insecurity (Bauman 1998: 173–4).[1] For many people in the world, it is true that 'globalization' means economic shocks and destabilization. But there is in much of this literature an indifference towards the structural elements that help generate the phenomenon we associate with economic globalization. Predictability and certitude, for instance, are goals that the emergent transnational regime for the protection and promotion of foreign investment aims to secure. What is often overlooked in current analyses, then, is the rigid legal architecture under construction to protect foreign investment abroad.

The standard-bearer for this regime is the North American Free Trade Agreement (NAFTA). In previous work I have argued that NAFTA and the investment rules regime have constitution-like features.[2] To borrow from Jon Elster (2000), the rules and institutions comprise a strategy of precommitment that binds future generations to certain, predetermined institutional forms that limit the possibilities for political practice. Like constitutions, they are difficult to amend, include binding enforcement mechanisms together with judicial review, and sometimes are even drawn from the language of domestic constitutions. Tantamount to a bill of rights for investors, NAFTA's investment chapter (Chapter 11) entitles investors to sue state parties for damages before international trade tribunals for violations of the agreement's investment protections. NAFTA's 'takings' rule – the prohibition on expropriation and nationalization and measures 'tantamount to' expropriation – more particularly, can limit governmental capacity in constitution-like ways.

The takings rule, as articulated in NAFTA, emerged as an important element in US foreign trade policy strategy. The intention, according to Vandevelde, was to develop a body of state practice in international law establishing high standards in regard to expropriations (Vandevelde 1992a: 25). It should be uncontroversial to suggest that the rule is informed by the US constitutional experience under the fifth and fourteenth amendments. Attempts at this kind of 'transference' of national property rules on to the international plane are not uncommon. Lauterpacht argued many years ago that in international law the 'conduct of its members must to a certain extent occupy the place of a source of law' (Lauterpacht 1929: 89).[3]

With the goal of securing predictability and optimal returns for investors in the realm of foreign investment, the investment rules regime places legal limits on the authority of government, isolates economic from political power, and assigns to investment interests the highest possible protection.[4] Premised on a distrust of political power – an idea familiar to the framers of the US Constitution – the regime institutionalizes a version of constitutionalism that primarily is concerned with freezing the regulatory status quo while inhibiting the possibilities for future political action. Karl Polanyi observed how, though the nineteenth century saw the spread of markets all over the world, there arose a corresponding 'network of measures and policies ... integrated into powerful institutions designed to check the action of the market relative to labour, land and money' (Polanyi 1944: 76). It is this capacity for taking self-protective measures that is threatened by the constitution-like features of the investment rules regime.

The object of this chapter is to examine the preliminary impact of the takings rule on two countries, Canada and Mexico, both of which are partners with the United States in the enterprise that is called NAFTA. The impact of transnational investment rules, admittedly, may be felt differently across the constitutional regimes of the semi-periphery – the Mexican constitutional regime may be more different than the Canadian one is to the United States version reflected in NAFTA, and so the impact may be felt more profoundly in the former than in the latter. Rather than engage in these sorts of comparisons, however, this chapter seeks to measure, more generally, the reach of some of the rules entrenched in the NAFTA text that will significantly hamper state action. This chapter complements, then, Clarkson's larger claim that the continental and transnational manifestations of economic globalization – via agreements like NAFTA and institutions such as the World Trade Organization – cumulatively amount to a 'supraconstitution' that has significantly reconstituted the Canadian state (Chapter 9, this volume).

Others also have observed the potential limiting effects of NAFTA's investment rules on the regulatory ability of state parties. Wagner writes that NAFTA's takings rule likely will have a 'serious chilling effect on the ability and willingness of governments to implement' legitimate environmental regulations. He likens the right to sue for economic impacts of environmental regulation to a 'legally enforced protection racket' (Wagner 1999: 467, 526). The International Institute for Sustainable Development observes that NAFTA's investment disciplines have been 'misappropriated' by foreign business owners seeking to prevent a change in regulatory environments (Mann and Moltke 1999: 15).[5] Similar concerns helped to give rise to vociferous opposition to the Multilateral Agreement on Investment negotiated in Paris, which would have imposed similar disciplines on the twenty-nine state members of the Organization for Economic Cooperation and Development. The same anxieties helped to mobilize opposition to the WTO in the streets of Seattle in December 1999, and later protests in Prague, Washington, Genoa, and Quebec City.

Many of these observations and anxieties were based upon an early assessment of NAFTA's disciplines. They were informed by investor–state disputes. No arbitration panel, however, had issued a ruling on the substantive scope of NAFTA's strictures. In this essay we test the earlier hypothesis about NAFTA's constitution-like effects on the semi-periphery in light of recent arbitral jurisprudence. This is not a comprehensive review of all of the work of NAFTA tribunals constituted under Chapter 11.[6] Rather, the chapter focuses on the work of three NAFTA panels – those established in the *Pope & Talbot*, *Metalclad*, and *S.D. Myers* claims – in cases concerning Canadian or Mexican environmental/regulatory policies. A review of this recent arbitral jurisprudence suggests that the fears about NAFTA's takings rule and associated provisions – looming more important is the rule mandating the 'minimum standard of treatment'

– have not been unfounded. The panels have acknowledged that non-discriminatory regulatory takings fall within the scope of the prohibition, and that those measures that are 'substantial enough', 'significantly deprive', or that 'unreasonably interfere' with investment expectations will give rise to a taking under NAFTA. The scope of compressible takings remains quite broad – the rule can catch all varieties of legitimate regulatory initiatives that do not discriminate against foreign investors – while the categorial distinction between compensable and non-compensable regulatory action remains imprecise. Though only one of the three panels found a compensable taking, the panel decisions confirm that NAFTA generates a legal architecture that institutionalizes a regime of limited government with constitution-like disciplines on state regulatory capacity.

This conclusion is fortified by recent initiatives to reform the treaty language. The Canadian Minister for International Trade, troubled by the breadth of these claims, has been seeking an interpretive note that would provide guidance to future NAFTA tribunals. His objective is to provide 'clearer and more specific understandings of Chapter 11's obligations' reflecting the original intentions of the drafters. Canada initiated this campaign several years ago, but the other state parties remained cool to the initiative (Jack 2000b, 2001a, 2001b; McKinnon 2000; Scoffield 2000). Even Canada's Prime Minister, Jean Chrétien, expressed some doubt about the need for clarification. 'The clause is working well', he is reported to have said (Jack 2001c). Recently, the United States, also troubled by this experience, has signalled a willingness to reform the scope of the takings rule in future investment treaties. Treaties now must mirror US Bill of Rights protections, so that foreign investors receive no greater rights than do American citizens under their constitution (Alden 2002) – a position perhaps in accord with the Canadian one. As a restatement of the objectives of the investment rules regime, it is reasonable to expect NAFTA's constitution-like effects to carry on far into the future.

NAFTA rules

Many of the obligations undertaken in NAFTA are organized around the idea of 'non-discrimination'. States may not distinguish for the purposes of legal regulation between domestic and foreign investors.

According to the national treatment rule, foreign investors are to be treated as if they were economic citizens within the host state. 'Most-favoured nation' status mandates that foreign investors receive the best treatment accorded by the host state to investors from any other state. Also connected to the principle of non-discrimination are prohibitions on performance requirements, such as rules that call for the use of local labour, goods, and services.

Other rules do not just mandate equality of treatment, but also place substantive limits on state control. Among these are the 'minimum standard of treatment' rule and the takings rule. The former is an omnibus standard of 'civilized' justice that includes both procedural and substantive components, including possibly the prohibition on takings (Roth 1949; Borchard 1939: 51–63; Dunn 1928: 166–80; Oppenheim 1949: para. 155d; Friedmann 1956: 500–502; Weiler 2000: 207–11). It was described earlier in the twentieth century as being 'nothing more nor less than the ideas which are conceived to be essential to a continuation of the existing social and economic order of European capitalistic civilization' (Dunn 1928: 175). The latter has been described as the 'single most important goal' of the US bilateral investment treaty programme (Vandevelde 1998: 621–41, 1992b: 534). The takings rule typically prohibits measures that 'directly or indirectly' expropriate or nationalize investment interests or measures that are 'tantamount to' expropriation. The classic candidate caught by this prohibition is outright takings of property by the state – the nationalization of the forces of production under socialism, for instance. Outright expropriations, however, have greatly diminished in number and pose little threat to current investment. One study recorded eighty-three expropriations in 1975 alone and yet only eleven between the years 1981 and 1992 (Wells 1998: 15) and, no doubt, these numbers continue to decline. Rather, what is of concern here is not express takings but what are called 'creeping' expropriations (measures that cumulatively amount to expropriation) and regulatory expropriations (measures that so impact on an investment interest that they are equivalent to a taking). According to Vandevelde, measures that only 'partially' expropriate – 'expropriations of a portion of an investment' – are intended to be prohibited (Vandevelde 1992a: 121). Regulatory changes that (in the words of US Supreme Court Justice Oliver Wendell Holmes) 'go too far'[7] are intended to be caught by this rule. The underlying premiss is that governments can be expected to perform only minimal regulatory functions, all of which are inescapably subordinated to the private market.

One could seek clarity about the rule from the decisions of international tribunals, but, as Dolzer and Stevens note, 'there is no clear definition of the concept of indirect expropriation' – referring to a range of actions that include 'creeping', 'de facto', and 'regulatory' expropriations – but rather, a 'wide variety of measures are susceptible to lead to indirect expropriation' (Dolzer and Stevens 1995: 100).[8] The rulings of the Iran–United States Claims Tribunal might be considered an authoritative source in this area, but no clearer distinction between compensable takings and non-compensable regulations emerges from its jurisprudence. Moreover, caution is necessary as the jurisdiction of the claims tribunal is both wider – it has authority to rule upon 'expropriations and other measures affecting property rights'[9] – and narrower – it does not encompass the minute range of investment interests included in the definition of 'investment' – than that under NAFTA. Nor do the writings of international law scholars 'shed much light' on the distinction between regulations and compensable takings (Sornarajah 1994: 301; Herz 1941: 252 – 'it is very difficult to draw a sharp line'; US Library of Congress 1963: 4–5 – 'extremely difficult to determine when normal regulation ends and expropriation begins'; Wortley 1959: 51 – 'line is not always easy to draw'; Friedman 1981). Burns Weston, for instance, refers to regulations that 'retard global well-being by hindering economic development' as requiring compensation (Weston 1975: 112–13). Rosalyn Higgins argues that the distinction between regulations and takings is not even 'intellectually viable' (Higgins 1982: 331). In each case an owner has suffered a loss and should be compensated.

One also could seek guidance from US constitutional experience under the fifth and fourteenth amendments. In the case of regulatory activity that gives rise to a taking, one finds that a variety of factors are determinative: the character of government action, economic impact, and interference with investment-backed expectations.[10] As Kelman notes, the distinction between regulations that are permitted without compensation – so-called exercises of the 'police power' – and those that require payment 'is hardly an obvious one' (Kelman 1999: 21). The least controversial cases concern the forced taking of title, but even here the scope of what constitutes a taking has been expanding while the category of non-compensable (police power) regulations has been contracting.[11] Though the US takings rule mostly is congruent with the presuppositions of the NAFTA rule, the scope of US law is more narrowly drawn than NAFTA. The fifth and fourteenth amendments are concerned largely with takings of physical property, so it is rarer that a regulation will rise to the level of a compensable taking under US constitutional law[12] (though this remains a possibility, see *Eastern Enterprises* v. *Apfel* 1998).

One can search far and wide in vain for a clear and workable distinction between regulations and expropriations. The failure of the state parties to respond meaningfully to this problem contributes, in my view, to continued questions regarding the legitimacy of NAFTA. The muddled thinking among trade scholars is best evinced by an opinion piece authored by Ostry and Solway (1998; see also Soloway 1999: 89). Writing about the settlement of the Ethyl Corporation claim (discussed below), they bemoan the fact that the Ethyl complaint was settled so early and before an international trade tribunal could rule on whether the ban on the use of the gasoline additive MMT amounted to an expropriation under NAFTA. They wrote:

> It would have clarified a great deal for legal scholars, and for others affected, if this question had been put before an arbitral panel: At what point does legislation enacted under the sovereign right of a government amount to an expropriation? ... Those of us anxious to know what governments will – and won't – be allowed to do in the name of national regulation will have to monitor other cases now pending, involving US companies in Mexico.

Regulatory measures of an uncertain magnitude are prohibited entirely unless they are for a 'public purpose' (as opposed to a 'private interest'), are 'non-discriminatory' (that is, are general laws that do not target foreign investors), and are in accordance with the 'due process of law'. If a taking does not meet these preliminary criteria, the expropriating state must then provide compensation according to the strictest available criteria: compensation equivalent to fair market value, paid without delay, fully realizable and transferable. This is the standard of compensation promoted by US Secretary of State Cordell Hull in 1938 and long touted by the United States as the one required by customary international law.[13] These disciplines are enforceable not just by states party to NAFTA but by foreign investors themselves.

Given the variety of measures caught by this rule, it comes as no surprise that firms have invoked the NAFTA takings rule (or its earlier incarnation in the Canada–US Free Trade Agreement) to challenge market regulations that impair all variety of investment interests. There were reports that Ontario's proposed public auto insurance plan (Campbell 1993: 92–3) and the cancellation of contracts to transfer public property into private hands (Toronto's Pearson Airport, *Globe and Mail*, 20 July 1994) triggered threats of litigation. I have written elsewhere about a challenge to Canadian federal government proposals to mandate the plain packaging of cigarettes by two large US tobacco manufacturers (Schneiderman 1996). The tobacco companies alleged that there would be a compensable taking of their trade dress and trade marks should the Canadian government proceed with its proposal to reduce tobacco consumption by mandating the packaging of all cigarettes sold in Canada in plain, brown paper wrapping. More recently, the US tobacco giant Philip Morris threatened to sue the government of Canada for banning the use of terms such as 'mild' and 'light' on cigarette packages sold in Canada (Chase 2002a). Though each of these cases concerns merely threatened action under NAFTA's investor-to-dispute process, one reasonably can conclude that these threats play a role in circumscribing the range of social policy choices available to these governments.

Of the arbitral proceedings launched under NAFTA, the Ethyl Corporation challenge of a Canadian ban on the import and export of the toxic gasoline additive MMT is perhaps the most notorious. The classification of MMT as a 'dangerous toxin', Ethyl claimed, amounted to an expropriation under NAFTA. The Canadian federal government settled the Ethyl claim for US$13 million subsequent to losing an interprovincial trade dispute under Canada's non-binding Agreement on Internal Trade (Schneiderman 1999a: 12–13).[14] In other disputes, United Parcel Service is claiming $230 million in lost profits as a result of Canada Post cross-subsidizing courier services with profits generated from its publicly funded regular delivery service (Jack 2000a).[15] The Connecticut-based chemical manufacturer Crompton Corporation is seeking $100 million in damages for a Canadian ban on the use of its canola-seed pesticide, lindane, a product banned in the United States by the US Environmental Protection Agency (EPA) (Chase 2001). Not all disputes emanate from US firms, however. In a reverse-Ethyl case, Vancouver-based Methanex is suing for losses suffered by the phasing out of the gasoline additive MTBE in the state of California (Scoffield 1999).

In the balance of the chapter, I focus on three recent arbitral rulings under NAFTA's Chapter 11. Emphasis is placed on interpretations of NAFTA's takings rule, though discussion occasionally extends to other claims made by investors that are the subject of NAFTA panel rulings. I argue that these panel decisions, though somewhat attentive to anxieties expressed over the breadth of investor rights under NAFTA, do not assuage concerns that the investment rules regime imposes constitution-like limits on state regulatory capacity.

Pope & Talbot

The interim award in the *Pope & Talbot* case has helped to fill out significantly the scope of NAFTA's takings rule.[16] The US forestry company, Pope & Talbot Inc. of Portland, Oregon, launched arbitral proceedings under NAFTA's investment chapter seeking compensation for losses suffered in the allocation of logging quotas in the province of British Columbia. These quotas were assigned to logging operators in the province pursuant to the Canada–US Softwood Lumber Agreement. The panel issued a number of rulings, resulting ultimately in a finding that Canada had breached NAFTA's terms by engaging in 'combative' and 'threatening' behaviour after Pope & Talbot filed its NAFTA complaint. By treating the company as an adversary subsequent to the initiation of the NAFTA claim, the panel ruled that Canada's behaviour – disassociated from the company's complaint regarding the allocation of lumber quotas – amounted to a denial of the minimum standard of treatment required under international law.[17]

What is of particular interest is an interim decision issued by the panel concerning the argument that the allocation of logging quotas was a measure 'tantamount to expropriation', a claim the panel ultimately dismissed. While the arbitrators rejected Pope & Talbot's broad interpretation of the takings rule, they accepted a number of its key postulates. First, the panel agreed that the definition of a protected 'investment' under NAFTA included market access to the US. According to the panel, access to the US market 'is a property interest' that is the subject of investment protection under NAFTA. Second, the panel found that the takings rule covers 'non-discriminatory regulation that might be said to fall within an exercise of a state's so-called police powers'. The impugned measures, however, were not 'substantial enough' or 'sufficiently restrictive' to give rise to a claim of expropriation.

It is instructive that the panel found support for its interpretation of NAFTA's takings rule in the American Law Institute's *Third Restatement of the Foreign Relations Law of the United States.* The *Restatement* calls for state responsibility in the event that 'alien property' is subject to 'taxation, regulation, or other action that is confiscatory, or that prevents, unreasonably interferes with, or unduly delays, effective enjoyment' of property (American Law Institute 1987: 201, para. 712, comment (g)). The comment goes on to say that, '[a]s under United States constitutional law, the line between "taking" and regulation is sometimes uncertain' (American Law Institute 1987: para. 99),[18] and the panel also acknowledged this difficulty in a footnote. It is this categorial distinction – between compensable takings and non-compensable exercises of the police power, which is so familiar to US constitutional law – which the *Pope & Talbot* ruling incorporates into the Canadian and Mexican legal orders. Yet the *Pope & Talbot* ruling appears to have gone further: even police powers regulations may command compensation under NAFTA.

Metalclad

Through its US and Mexican subsidiaries, the Metalclad Corporation of Newport Beach, California, purchased in 1993 the Mexican company COTERIN. Metalclad was intent on developing COTERIN's waste management and landfill site at Guadalcazar in the Mexican state of San Luis Potosí. The site previously had been closed by order of the Mexican federal government, as COTERIN had improperly stored industrial waste and failed to contain leakage into local water supplies. Local citizens blockaded the road leading to the plant in September 1991, demanding immediate inspection of the facility, resulting ultimately in the plant's closure (Wheat 1995). When Metalclad announced it was taking over COTERIN's operations, the local populace was mobilized to oppose reopening of the site.

Metalclad rehabilitated the Guadalcazar site, it claimed, with the express authorization and encouragement of the Mexican federal government.[19] The company was assured by federal authorities that all necessary permits were in place and that local permission was not required. It was advised, nevertheless, that it should apply to the municipality for a construction permit so as 'to facilitate an amicable relationship'. As the company had not applied for the requisite permit, the municipality of Guadalcazar ordered a halt to construction in October 1994. Metalclad applied for the permit in November and resumed construction of the landfill site. The hazardous waste site opened ten months later, in March 1995. That same month the municipality denied Metalclad's construction permit, citing denial of a similar permit to COTERIN in 1991 and 1992. Metalclad claimed that this effectively closed the hazardous waste operation. Metalclad abandoned the site when, nine months later and three days before the expiry of his term, the state governor issued an Ecological Decree declaring the site a natural area for the protection of rare cactus. Metalclad sued under NAFTA's Chapter 11, alleging violations of the minimum standard of treatment requirement and the takings rule. The arbitration panel agreed and awarded the investor US$16.6 million in damages.

The panel, headed by Cambridge scholar Eli Lauterpacht, found first that Mexico should be held accountable for the acts of its sub-national governments – here the municipal and state governments. Next, the panel found that there was an absence of a clear rule in regard to the requirement that the municipality issue a construction permit. This lack of transparency, predictability, and procedural fairness (Metalclad was given no notice of the town council meeting where the construction permit was denied) amounted to a denial of 'treatment in accordance with international law, including fair and equitable treatment'. The panel turned then to the expropriations claim. By 'permitting or tolerating' the unfair and inequitable treatment under Article 1005, Mexico was held to have 'participated and acquiesced' in the denial of Metalclad's rights. In this way, Mexico had 'taken a measure tantamount to expropriation'. The panel added that the issuance of the Ecological Decree alone would have amounted to an expropriation requiring compensation.

The panel further filled out the criteria for what constitutes a taking under NAFTA (though there was no reference to the *Pope & Talbot* decision, nor to any other source, in its ruling). NAFTA's takings rule would catch not only the outright seizure of property by the host state – the most obvious case – but also 'covert or incidental interference with the use of property which has the effect of depriving the owner, in whole or in significant part, of the use or reasonably-to be-expected economic benefit of property even if not necessarily to the obvious benefit of the host state'. Non-discriminatory exercises of regulatory power could give rise to compensation under NAFTA where the regulation wholly or significantly deprives reasonable expectations of beneficial use of that investment.

The panel made little mention of the troubles that gave rise to the local populace's opposition to Metalclad's operation. Yet this local opposition was entirely foreseeable given the mobilization against the hazardous waste site under COTERIN's prior management. When a new state governor took office in 1993, before NAFTA even came into force, Metalclad was pressed to move its waste facility to an alternative site. Metalclad resisted, having already invested several millions of dollars acquiring a large percentage of COTERIN's stock, banking on the ratification of NAFTA and Mexico's 'tradition of political centralism' (Tamayo 2000: 7) to overcome local resistance. Despite broad-based opposition to the operation of the facility at the municipal and state government levels, Metalclad 'never agreed even to consider the possibility of locating the industrial waste landfill site elsewhere in San Luis Potosí' (Tamayo 2000: 12). The panel would not admit that local resistance to the operation of the facility on public health grounds and the requirement of a municipal construction permit were, even according to the panel's own standards, a reasonable investment-backed expectation which could not have caught Metalclad by surprise.

More startling is the manner in which the panel dismissed Mexico's reply that there was no denial of the minimum standard of treatment. Mexico maintained that the municipality was acting wholly within its constitutional jurisdiction when it refused to issue a construction permit. This was disputed by Metalclad's expert on Mexican law.[20] The panel mysteriously preferred Metalclad's interpretation. Referring to a federal law that grants power to authorize hazardous waste sites to the federal government, the panel was of the view that federal authority 'was controlling and [that] the authority of the municipality only extended to appropriate construction considerations'. In other words, Guadalcazar had no constitutional authority to refuse a permit other than for reasons having to do with the 'physical construction or defects in that site'. According to the panel, the municipality had no constitutional authority even to take into account environmental concerns in the issuance of a municipal construction permit. This was despite the express language of the Constitution – the municipality had jurisdiction to 'control and supervise' land use – and state law authorizing the municipality to take into account environmental impacts in the issuance of municipal construction permits ('Petitioner's Outline of Argument' 2001: 135–6). Whatever the procedural irregularities that gave rise to Metalclad's claim (and on the face of the record there were some), it is remarkable the confidence with which the panel – sitting as if it were a constitutional court – arrived at definitive conclusions regarding the constitutional authority of Mexican municipal governments. This precisely is where the state party itself offered a very different, and more authoritative, interpretation.

The implications of the panel's ruling are mitigated somewhat by an appeal launched by Mexico and heard by a Canadian court (as the original hearing had taken place in the City of Vancouver). Justice Tyose vacated part of the panel's ruling – that part which imposed transparency obligations under the minimum standard of treatment and expropriations articles (precisely the same point that the state parties tried to make clear in an 'interpretive note' issued two months after the court ruling; see NAFTA Free Trade Commission 2001: 139–40). Justice Tysoe confirmed the ruling, however, in so far as the panel found a taking by reason of the Governor's Ecological Decree, issued several months after Metalclad abandoned the Guadalcazar site. The panel's very broad interpretation of the takings rule was considered beyond the purview of a reviewing court. Justice Tysoe warned, however, that the panel's interpretation 'is sufficiently broad to include legitimate rezoning of property by a municipality or other rezoning authority'.[21]

S.D. Myers

Within days of Canada's settlement with the Ethyl Corporation, S.D. Myers Inc. of Tallmadge, Ohio, initiated a claim under NAFTA for losses following a temporary ban on the export of PCB-contaminated waste from Canada to the United States for the years 1995 to 1997 (Scoffield 1998a, 1998b). Myers was in the business of PCB remediation – the transportation, extraction, and destruction of hazardous PCB and PCB waste material. The company established a subsidiary, Myers Canada, to undertake lobbying and promotion of the US-based enterprise and to arrange transportation of waste to its waste facility site.[22]

At the time that Myers began looking to Canada as a new source of business, the importation of PCB waste into the US was prohibited by the US Environmental Protection Agency (EPA). Myers lobbied the US EPA hard and, in November 1995, and without consulting the government of Canada, Myers was permitted to import waste into the US. The Canadian government responded by closing the border to the export of PCB waste from November 1995 until the reversal of its decision in February 1997. The EPA permit order, which Myers secured ultimately, was overturned by a decision of the US Court of Appeals in July 1997 and the border closed once again.

Myers claimed that the government of Canada's ban on PCB exports to the United States for almost a sixteen-month period offended Chapter 11's minimum standard of treatment, national treatment, performance requirements, and expropriation provisions. The government of Canada defended its temporary ban on the basis that it merely was promoting sound environmental management of hazardous waste by seeking domestic solutions to disposal. Also, as a signatory to the Basel Convention, Canada was required to keep the transboundary movement of hazardous waste to a minimum. Myers claimed that Canada merely was protecting the interests of Myers' Canadian competitor, Chem-Security, the waste management firm with operations in Swan Hills, Alberta. Myers claimed damages for the sixteen-month period in lost profits of about US$10 million.

The panel found that Canada was motivated to impose the ban because of threats to the continuing economic viability of the Canadian Swan Hills facility and those commitments were made to Chem-Security to this effect. Nor was the panel convinced that this policy was motivated by sound environmental risk management. Disposing of hazardous waste at the Myers site in the United States was, as three Canadian Department of Environment officials noted, a 'technically and environmentally sound solution for the destruction of some of Canada's PCBs'.

Maintaining the ability to process PCBs within Canada may have been a 'legitimate goal' and consistent with the Basel Convention, but the means employed had to be consistent with NAFTA's strictures. NAFTA permitted state parties to pursue legitimate policy objectives via alternative exempted measures, like government procurement and subsidies or grants. That these less restrictive measure were available but not adopted by Canada amounted to discriminatory treatment against Myers 'in like circumstances' with Canadian competitors. This denial of national treatment also amounted to a denial of the minimum standard required by international law. The panellists agreed, however, that there was no deprivation of an investment interest giving rise to a claim of expropriation.

The panel, in its award and in a separate opinion by one of the panellists, Bryan Schwartz, attempted to fill out the categorial distinction between a non-compensable regulation and a compensable taking. Schwartz's opinion admitted that the imprecise nature of Article 1110 has precipitated vocal opposition to NAFTA and the associated fears and anxieties about the decline of state sovereignty and democratic accountability. Attempting to assuage these fears, the panel wrote that, though regulatory action can be caught by the takings rule, it was 'unlikely that regulatory conduct by public authorities' would be 'the subject of a legitimate complaint under Article 1110', though the panel could not 'rule out that possibility'. The distinction between expropriations and regulations was an analytically helpful one, the panel explained. The distinction 'screens out most cases of complaints concerning economic intervention by a state and reduces the risk that governments will be subject to claims as they go about their business of managing public affairs'.

In contrast to mere regulations, expropriations amount to a 'lasting deprivation of the ability of an owner to make use of its economic rights', though the deprivation may be 'partial or temporary'. In the case of S.D. Myers, there merely was a temporary denial of business opportunity as a result of Canada's conduct. Nor could the phrase 'tantamount to' expropriation expand coverage 'beyond the customary scope of the term under international law'. Citing the *Pope & Talbot* ruling, the *Myers* panel concluded that the word 'tantamount' was intended to catch 'so-called creeping expropriations' rather than expand upon customary international law.

Schwartz's separate opinion admitted that trade agreements like NAFTA 'have an enormous impact on public affairs in many countries'. He went so far as to liken these agreements to 'a country's constitution': 'They restrict the ways in which governments can act and they are very hard to change.' While governments usually have the right to withdraw with notice, Schwartz allowed that this 'is often practically impossible to do': 'Pulling out of a trade agreement may create too much risk of reverting to trade wars, and may upset the settled expectations of many participants in the economy.' Amendment is made no easier, he writes, 'just as it is usually very hard to change a provision of a domestic constitution'. As if to prove the point that Clarkson and others have made about NAFTA as an 'external constitution', (Clarkson, Chapter 9; Schneiderman 1996, 2000), the separate opinion in *S.D. Myers* underscores the claim that NAFTA succeeds in limiting state capacity in constitution-like ways.

Conclusion

The work of these NAFTA arbitration panels admittedly has been made difficult by the opacity of the NAFTA text. They have attempted to provide clarity in regard to some matters that are not at all clear. It should have been expected that the *Pope & Talbot* panel would seek guidance from the national law of the United States and would embrace the categorial distinction between regulatory non-compensable events and takings requiring compensation. The distinction, as under US law, is not easily discerned and so NAFTA panels have begun to define the outer limits of the takings rule.

These NAFTA panels also have been less cautious in their interpretive approaches. Nowhere is this more evident than in the *Metalclad* case. There the panel issued a ruling seemingly divorced from events on the ground that laid down expansive interpretations of the minimum standard of treatment rule and expropriations provision. The confident ability with which the panel dispensed with questions of Mexican constitutional law is striking. The panels in *S.D. Myers* and *Pope & Talbot* reached for the minimum standard of treatment rule to censure a variety of government conduct. The *S.D. Myers* panel, in particular, adopted an aggressive stance via-à-vis the regulatory initiative: here the government could not pursue a policy, consistent with the Basel Convention, in which Canada would be made responsible for the disposal of the waste that it generates. There always will be less restrictive alternatives, according to the panel, in the form of direct subsidies to business or through government purchasing preferences.

It is not unreasonable to have concluded, then, that NAFTA's regime of investment protection institutionalizes a constitution-like regime of limited government. As many critics feared, this is a regime in which policy alternatives are to be constrained and the imagination of alternative futures, not organized around the logic of the market, are to be discouraged.

Notes

Earlier versions of this chapter were presented to the Fulbright Symposium at Golden Gate University School of Law, the Association of the Bar of the City of New York, and the Globalism Project meetings in Mexico City. I am pleased to acknowledge the support of the Canada–US Fulbright Program and the Social Sciences and Humanities Research Council. Many thanks to Stephen Clarkson and John Erik Fossum for their comments.

1. Bauman's work on the poor in an age of economic globalization, on the other hand, is exemplary (Bauman 1998).

2. See Schneiderman 1996: 499; 1999b: 90–95; 2000: 757.

3. '[T]he concept of the minimum standard [of treatment] historically emerged as a result of the strong influence of these internal legal notions' (Dolzer 1981: 568).

4. I am paraphrasing Polanyi 1944: 225.

5. Also see Samrat 1999: 1113; Banks 1999.

6. A more comprehensive review can be found in Dumberry 2001.

7. I deliberately refer here to the language of Holmes in *Pennsylvania Coal* v. *Mahon* (1922): 'The general rule at least is, that while property may be regulated to a certain extent, if regulation goes too far it will be recognised as a taking.'

8. Also see Sacerdoti 1997: 383.

9. 'Iran–United States: Settlement of Hostage Crisis' (1980) at 231 (Art. II).

10. See *Kaiser Aetna* v. *United States* (1979); *Eastern Enterprises* v. *Apfel* (1998); Chemerinsky 1997: 511–15.

11. See *Lucas* v. *South Carolina Coastal Council* (1992); Michelman 1988: 1621.

12. See *Tahoe–Sierra Preservation Council, Inc.* v. *Tahoe Regional Planning Agency* (2002); and see, generally, McUsic 1996; Dolzer 1981: 568.

13. See the exchange of letters between Secretary of State Cordell Hull and the Mexican Ambassador [reproduced] (1938).

14. An arbitral panel did issue a ruling refusing Canada's challenge to the panel's jurisdiction to hear Ethyl's complaint. See *Ethyl Corporation* v. *Government of Canada* (MMT) (2000); and the discussion in Gaillard 2000: 3; and Wilson 2000.

15. UPS recently secured a ruling from the European Commission along the same lines, that the German postal service illegally used profits from its monopoly over postal delivery to subsidize its courier service in competition with UPS (Andrews 2001).

16. *Pope & Talbot Inc and the Government of Canada* (26 June 2000) (2001a); see McCarthy 2000.

17. See *Pope & Talbot and Government of Canada* (10 April 2001) 2001b. The panel awarded $705,000 (Can) in damages. The company originally sought some $80 million (US) in damages for the allocation of logging quotas (Chase 2002b).

18. For a glimpse at the political nature of the restatement drafting process, particularly in the context of expropriations, see Dezalay and Garth 1996: 175–9.

19. This recitation of facts is drawn from the panel decision *Metalclad Corporation and the United Mexican States* (24 August 2000) (2001); and the 'Petitioners Outline of Argument' (2001).

20. A 1994 law graduate of the University of Arizona who was pursuing a Master of Laws in Monterrey, see 'Petitioner's Outline of Argument' (2001): 138.

21. *The United Mexican States* v. *Metalclad Corporation* (2001).

22. These facts are drawn from the panel decision, *S.D. Myers, Inc.* v. *Government of Canada* (2001).

References

Alden, Edward (2002) 'US Does About-Face on Expropriation', *National Post*, 2 October, FP16.

American Law Institute (1987) *Restatement of the Law Third, The Foreign Relations of the United States*, vol. 2, St Paul, MN: The American Law Institute.

Andrews, Edmund L. (2001) 'Backing UPS Complaint, Europeans Fine German Postal Service', *New York Times*, 21 March: C6.

Banks, Kevin (1999) 'NAFTA's Article 1110: Can Regulation Be Expropriation?' *NAFTA: Law and Business Review of the Americas* 5: 499.

Bauman, Zygmunt (1998) *Work, Consumerism and the New Poor*, Buckingham: Open University Press.

Bauman, Zygmunt (1999) *In Search of Politics*, Stanford: Stanford University Press.

Borchard, Edwin (1939) 'The "Minimum Standard" of the Treatment of Aliens', *Proceedings of the American Society of International Law* 33: 51–63.

Campbell, Bruce (1993) 'Restructuring the Economy: Canada into the Free Trade Era', in Ricardo Grinspun and Maxwell A. Cameron (eds) *The Political Economy of North American Free Trade*, Montreal: McGill-Queen's University Press: 89–104

Chase, Steven (2001) 'Ottawa Faces Suit Over Banned Pesticide', *Globe and Mail*, 10 December: B1.

Chase, Steven (2002a) 'Tobacco Firm Warns "Mild" Cigarette Ban May Violate NAFTA', *Globe and Mail*, 16 March: A6.

Chase, Steven (2002b) 'Ottawa Loses Pope Lumber Spat', *Globe and Mail*, 1 June: E1.

Chemerinsky, Erwin (1997) *Constitutional Law: Principles and Policies*, New York: Aspen.

Dezalay, Yves and Bryant G. Garth (1996) *Dealing in Virtue: International Commercial Arbitration and the Construction of a Transnational Legal Order*, Chicago: University of Chicago Press.

Dolzer, Rudolf (1981) 'New Foundations of the Law of Expropriations of Alien Property', *American Journal of International Law* 75: 553–89.

Dolzer, Rudolf and Margrete Stevens (1995) *Bilateral Investment Treaties*, The Hague: Martinus Nijhoff.

Dumberry, Patrick (2001) 'The NAFTA Investment Dispute Settlement Mechanism: A Review of the Latest Case Law', *Journal of World Investment* 2: 151–95.

Dunn, Frederick Sherwood (1928) 'International Law and Private Property Rights', *Columbia Law Review* 28: 166–80.

Eastern Enterprises v. *Apfel* (1998) 524 US 498 per O'Connor J., US Supreme Court.

Elster, Jon (2000) *Ulysses Unbound*, Cambridge: Cambridge University Press.

Ethyl Corporation v. *Government of Canada* (2000)

Friedman, S. (1981) *Expropriation in International Law* [reprint 1953], Westport, CT: Greenwood Press.

Friedmann, W. (1956) 'Some Aspects of Social Organization in International Law', *American Journal of International Law* 156, no. 50: 475–513.

Gaillard, Emmanuel (2000) 'A Strong Start for NAFTA', *New York Law*, 3 February: 3.

Herz, John (1941) 'Expropriation of Foreign Property', *American Journal of International Law* 35: 243–62.

Higgins, Rosalyn (1982) 'The Taking of Property by the State: Recent Developments in International Law', *Recueil des Cours*, vol. 176, no. 259: 259–351.

Hull, Cordell, US Secretary of State and the Mexican Ambassador (1938) 'Mexico–United States: Expropriation by Mexico of Agrarian Properties Owned by American Citizens', *American Journal of International Law* 32 (Supp.): 181–207.

'Iran-United States: Settlement of Hostage Crisis' (1980) International Legal Materials 20: 230.

Jack, Ian (2000a) 'UPS Suing Ottawa for $230M', *National Post*, 22 April: D1.

Jack, Ian (2000b) 'Ottawa Wants to Trim NAFTA Powers', *National Post*, 30 May: A9.

Jack, Ian (2001a) 'New Debate on Controversial NAFTA Clause', *Financial Post*, 6 March: C4.

Jack, Ian (2001b) 'Canada Loses Bid to Change NAFTA Chapter 11', *Financial Post*, 5 April: C4.

Jack, Ian (2001c) 'Prime Minister Contradicts Trade on Chapter 11', *Financial Post*, 24 April: C8.

Kaiser Aetna v. *United States* (1979) 444 US 164, 175, US Supreme Court.

Kelman, Mark (1999) *Strategy or Principle? The Choice Between Taxation and Regulation*, Ann Arbor: The University of Michigan Press.

Lauterpacht, H. (1929) 'Decisions of Municipal Courts as a Source of International Law', *British Yearbook of International Law*, vol. 10, no. 65: 65–95.

Lucas v. *South Carolina Coastal Council* (1992) 112 S. Ct. 2886, US Supreme Court.

McCarthy, Shawn (2000) 'Ottawa Wins Round in Lumber Suit', *Globe and Mail*, 28 June: B3.

McKinnon, Mark (2000) 'Canada Seeks Review of NAFTA's Chapter 11', *Globe and Mail*, 13 December: B1.

McUsic, Molly S. (1996) 'The Ghost of Lochner: Modern Takings Doctrine and Its Impact on Economic Legislation', *Boston University Law Review* 76: 605–67.

Mann, Howard and Konrad von Moltke (1999) 'NAFTA's Chapter 11 and the Environment: Addressing the Impacts of the Investor–State Process on the Environment', Winnipeg: International Institute for Sustainable Development.

Metalclad Corporation and the United Mexican States (24 August 2000) (2001) *World Trade and Arbitration Materials* 13: 47–80.

Michelman, Frank (1988) 'Takings, 1987', *Columbia Law Review* 88: 1600–29.

NAFTA Free Trade Commission (2001) 'Notes of Interpretation of Certain Chapter 11 Provisions', *World Trade and Arbitration Materials* 13, 31 July.

Oppenheim, L. (1949) *International Law: A Treatise* (8th edn), vol. 1, ed. H. Lauterpacht, London: Longmans Green.

Ostry, Sylvia and Julie Soloway (1998) 'The MMT Case Ended Too Soon', *Globe and Mail*, 24 July: A21.

Pennsylvania Coal v. *Mahon* (1922) 438 US 393: 1569, US Supreme Court.

'Petitioners Outline of Argument', 5 February 2001 (2001) *United Mexican States* v. *Metalclad Corporation*, Supreme Court of British Columbia, no. L002904, Vancouver Registry.

Polanyi, Karl (1944) *The Great Transformation*, Boston: Beacon Press.

Pope & Talbot Inc and the Government of Canada, Interim Award (26 June 2000) (2001a) *World Trade and Arbitration Materials* 13: 19–59.

Pope & Talbot and Government of Canada, Award on Merits Phase 2 (10 April 2001) (2001b) *World Trade and Arbitration Materials* 13: 61–155.

Roth, Andreas H. (1949) *The Minimum Standard of International Law Applied to Aliens*, Leiden: A.W. Sijthoff's Uitgeversmaatschappij.

S.D. Myers, Inc. v. *Government of Canada* (2001) *International Legal Materials* 40: 1408.

Sacerdoti, Giorgio (1997) 'Bilateral Treaties and Multilateral Instruments on Investment Protection', *Recueil des Cours* 269: 251–460.

Samrat, Ganguly (1999) 'The Investor–State Dispute Mechanism (ISDM) and a Sovereign's Power to Protect Public Health', *Columbia Journal of Transnational Law* 38: 113–68.

Schneiderman, David (1996) 'NAFTA's Takings Rule: American Constitutionalism Comes to Canada', *University of Toronto Law Journal* 46: 499–537.

Schneiderman, David (1999a) 'MMT Promises: How the Ethyl Corporation Beat the Federal Ban', *Encompass Magazine*, vol. 3, no. 3: 12–13.

Schneiderman, David (1999b) 'The Constitutional Strictures of the Multilateral Agreement on Investment', *The Good Society*, vol. 9, no. 2: 90–95.

Schneiderman, David (2000) 'Investment Rules and the New Constitutionalism', *Law & Social Inquiry* 25: 757.

Scoffield, Heather (1998a) 'US Firm Hits Ottawa With NAFTA Suit', *Globe and Mail*, 21 August: B1.

Scoffield, Heather (1998b) 'PCB Export Ban Breached NAFTA, Firm Says', *Globe and Mail*, 1 September: B2.

Scoffield, Heather (1999) 'Methanex Set to Sue Uncle Sam under NAFTA over Gas Additive', *Globe and Mail*, 3 November: B7.

Scoffield, Heather (2000) 'Mexico Holds Firm on NAFTA Investment Rules', *Globe and Mail*, 2 September: B3.

Soloway, Julie (1999) 'Environmental Trade Barriers under NAFTA: The MMT Fuel Additives Controversy', *Minnesota Journal of Global Trade* 8: 55–95.

Sornarajah, M. (1994) *The International Law of Foreign Investment*, Cambridge: Cambridge University Press.

Tahoe-Sierra Preservation Council, Inc. v. *Tahoe Regional Planning Agency* (2002) 535, US Supreme Court.

Tamayo, Arturo Boja (2000) 'The New Federalism, Internationalization and Political Change in Mexico: A Theoretical Analysis of the Metalclad Case', *Documento de Trabajo* 59.

The United Mexican States v. *Metalclad Corporation* (2001) *BCSC*, vol. 664: paras 72, 79, 99, and 100.

US Library of Congress (1963) *Expropriation of American-Owned Property by Foreign Governments in the Twentieth Century*, Washington, DC: US Government Printing Office.

Vandevelde, Kenneth J. (1992a) *United States Investment Treaties: Policy and Practice*, Deventer: Kluwer.

Vandevelde, Kenneth J. (1992b) 'The BIT Program: A Fifteen-Year Appraisal', in ASIL Proceedings, Washington, DC, 1–4 April.

Vandevelde, Kenneth J. (1998) 'The Political Economy of a Bilateral Investment Treaty', *American Journal of International Law* 92: 621–41.

Wagner, J. Martin (1999) 'International Investment, Expropriation and Environmental Protection', *Golden Gate University Law Review* 29: 465–527.

Weiler, Todd J. (2000) '"The Minimum Standard of Treatment" in International Law: Some Old Cases, Some New', *Canadian International Lawyer* 3: 207–11.

Wells, Louis T., Jr. (1998) 'God and Fair Competition: Does the Foreign Direct Investor Face Still Other Risks in Emerging Markets?', in Theodore H. Moran (ed.) *Managing International Political Risk*, Oxford: Blackwell: 15–43.

Weston, Burns H. (1975) '"Constructive Takings" under International Law: A Modest Foray into the Problem of "Creeping Expropriation"', *Virginia Journal of International Law* 103: 103–75.

Wheat, Andrew (1995) 'Toxic Shock in a Mexican Village', *Multinational Monitor*, vol. 16, no. 10.

Wilson, Timothy Ross (2000) 'Trade Rules: *Ethyl Corporation* v. *Canada* (NAFTA Chapter 11)', *NAFTA: Law and Business Review of the Americas* 52: 952.

Wortley, B.A. (1959) *Expropriation in Public International Law*, Cambridge: Cambridge University Press.

13

The Rule of Rules:
International Agreements
and the Semi-periphery

Stephen McBride and John Erik Fossum

Nation-states are enmeshed in an interlocking series of international and supranational agreements, organizations, and institutions. As signatories and participants, they are bound by the rules they helped establish.

Nation-states vary in resources and power, ranging from the sole superpower, the United States, through countries that play key roles economically and politically, to important but essentially semi-peripheral countries, to those on the outer fringes of influence – the truly peripheral. The nature of states' interactions with international and supranational organizations will vary with their size, resources, and status. But how much variation is there? Are we witnessing a neo-liberal convergence – through the emergence of a set of neo-liberal international institutions and through the embrace of neo-liberal principles and practices in most states? How uniform and encompassing is such a trend? What generates it?

Here, we address these questions through exploration of the interaction of two semi-peripheral countries, Canada and Norway, with a global organization, the World Trade Organization (WTO), and two regional organizations. These are the North American Free Trade Agreement (NAFTA), of which Canada is a member, and the European Union (EU), with which Norway is associated through the European Economic Agreement (EEA) (Claes and Fossum, Chapter 4). NAFTA and the WTO are market-type organizations that lack independent democratic legitimacy. The EU has established a common market and a monetary union but it is clearly also more than a market. It has emerged into a polity in its own right – with market-moderating components – but whose democratic quality is highly contested. Whilst not a state, it officially subscribes to those democratic standards associated with states (which no state fully complies with). When assessed in relation to the democratic standards applied to states, it suffers from deficiencies in rights, representation, accountability, and transparency (Abromeit 1998; Beetham and Lord 1998; Eriksen and Fossum 2000; Greven 2000; Weale and Nentwich 1998).

One way of thinking of neo-liberal convergence is to see international economic agreements and organizations as systems of power in both the senses advanced by C.B. Macpherson as characteristic of liberal-democratic regimes domestically. For Macpherson, the relationship between liberalism and democracy was more problematic than is often assumed (Macpherson 1965, 1977). He depicted liberal democracy as a *double* system of power. First, most obviously, it is a system by which people are governed. Second, in a liberal democracy, the democratic government 'exists to uphold and enforce a certain kind of society, a certain set of relations between individuals, a certain set of rights and claims that people have on each other both directly, and indirectly through their rights to property' (Macpherson 1965: 4). This second aspect was less widely noticed and, when Macpherson drew attention to it, less accepted. For Macpherson, liberal democracy exists to maintain property-based relations between people; these are power relations that need 'a superior power to keep them in order' (Macpherson 1965: 40) because a transfer of powers from property-less individuals to the propertied occur within a specific type of system, the market economy (Macpherson 1965: 46–75). Liberal democracy and capitalism tend to go together, and, for Macpherson, the primary purpose of the political system of liberal democracy is to uphold the power relations embedded in capitalist society.

International agreements like the WTO and NAFTA are certainly liberal, but these organizations preclude certain types of national (and supranational) political control of the operation of markets, hence also constrain the reach and operation of national democracy. Thus enforcement of market relations is unmoderated by the kind of democratic pressures and procedures that historically, at the nation-state level, grafted democracy onto a pre-existing liberal society. The extent to which the EU has the potential to be a regional-level equivalent of the hyphenated liberal-democratic system, which Macpherson saw operating domestically, with its potential to moderate though not transform market systems, will be explored subsequently.

The international political economy as a system of power

In extending the idea of domestic liberal democracy to the international level, the dominant liberal school of international political economy (IPE) does not and cannot acknowledge the 'systems of power' image of the new international economic regime. It refuses to recognize that the global market society is one of structured inequality where international institutions also can maintain this inequality. Liberal IPE proceeds on positive-sum assumptions. In this view, the motivation behind the new generation of economic agreements is that all parties gain or, at a minimum, are no worse off than they would have been without joining. Thus notions of mutual gain drive international economic agreements, and there are no losers, except particular sectors of national economies, which may require temporary assistance to adjust to new circumstances. States' willingness to participate, given this efficiency rationale, is thus unproblematic.

There are scholars, however, whose work runs contrary to the conventional liberal wisdom and who provide a Macpherson-type analysis of the new international economic regime. These scholars talk of a 'new constitutionalism' and 'disciplinary neo-liberalism' that result from international economic agreements (Clarkson, Chapter 9; Gill 1995; Grinspun and Kreklewich 1994). Within this school, international economic agreements are seen as forces to reverse the market-moderating effects of national-level democracy. These agreements tighten the connection between liberalism and market capitalism, highlight economic over political liberalism, and correspondingly narrow the scope for democratic decision-making domestically.

There are strong grounds for questioning the assumptions that lie behind liberal IPE interpretations of the international economic agreements. First, recent international economic agreements reach far beyond measures that might be sufficient to ensure compliance with generally perceived positive-sum agreements (Goldstein 1998: 134).

The terms of international economic agreements can directly affect the outcomes of the balance of domestic political forces by significantly diminishing the legal potential for states to take (sovereign) decisions on matters of concern to their citizens. The agreements specifically preclude certain outcomes that used to be within the purview of states. Second, the assumption that the new international regime is a positive-sum exercise is itself unjustified. Rather than demonstrating these positive outcomes empirically, the benefits are often assumed by virtue of the fact of increased cooperation. However, the growing inequality between states and classes challenges the assumption that liberalization of trade and capital movements improves economic growth rates (Weisbrot et al. 2001).

Yet, if outcomes are negative, why would the leaders of sovereign states relinquish sovereignty (Gruber 2000: 62)? One answer is that the state actors who initiate and drive today's international economic agreements – that is, the powerful states – are 'free to impose their own institutional choices on other actors in the system. Because the "enacting coalition" can shift the institutional status quo unilaterally, its members do not need to take account of their current partners' institutional preferences. When it comes to matters concerning in-stitutional design, the enacting coalition is in the driver's seat, and everyone else better look out' (Gruber 2000: 81). Essentially, powerful states leave weaker states no palatable option but to get 'on board'. Thus the hegemonic state or coalition possesses 'go it alone' power, which removes the status quo as an option for other states, who must get on board and cut their losses. The international institutions are prone to such influence precisely because they have too weakly developed democratic foundations and are too narrow in scope.

The effect of the rules chosen by the enacting coalition is to erode sovereignty, and thus the scope for democratic decision-making, in countries outside the enacting coalition. To insure against changes in domestic political direction, this applies to some countries inside the enacting coalition. These aspects of institutional design are constitution-altering for most participants. Through these changes, international power relations between states are defined; but more importantly, domestic power relations, both institutional and more broadly political, are redefined. The constraints thus created are not external in origin. They are driven by domestic factors, such as the desire of governing elites to lock policy changes in place (Krasner 1999: 22).

International economic agreements are systems of power whose effect is to enhance liberalism and the liberal market society and to diminish democracy – in so far as that concept includes the potential to go against or even modify significantly the results of market processes. Notwithstanding the key role that the state has played in promoting neo-liberal globalization, limiting certain of its capacities is a central goal of international economic agreements. This is because of the 'tremendous potentialities of the state as a centre for alternative forms of economic organization' (Petras and Veltmeyer 2001: 55).

These restrictions on state actions may be particularly significant on the semi-periphery, where state-centred policies aimed at achieving more autonomy, diversified development, and redistribution of incomes were common as a response to the influences of powerful core countries.

Strong states are catalysts and facilitators of globalization (Weiss 1997). In North America the USA has consolidated a regional bloc in which common trade and investment rules apply. The Canadian state, responding to business preferences, facilitated this process. Canada initiated the original free trade agreement with the United States and remains deeply wedded to market liberalization at home and abroad (McBride 2001: ch. 3).

Public opinion in Canada was divided about the deeper integration with the United States that flowed from market liberalism (Ayres 1998). Ultimately, however, the opponents failed to prevent the enactment of, first, the Canada–US Free Trade Agreement and, subsequently, NAFTA.

In Norway, public opinion, which is also divided about Norwegian membership in the EU, proved on two occasions able to thwart the state's efforts to join. Even so, as Øyvind Østerud (Chapter 3) comments:

> The EEA treaty implies that the parties are obliged to follow EU regulations, laws, and directives in areas that are not explicitly exempted from the treaty, like agriculture and offshore resources.... The crux of the treaty, as far as legislative sovereignty is concerned, is the clause saying that EU regulations have priority above national law in case of conflict. The parties may veto certain decisions that are considered as detrimental to their interests, but the political barriers towards activating the potential veto are high. Legal experts have criticized the EEA treaty for transferring nearly as much sovereignty as would have been the case with full EU membership, but without participation in the legislative institutions.

Towards a post-national constellation?

Are power differentials among states enough to account for the transformations that are taking place, or are we witnessing deeper and more systemic types of changes that will reshape the international system? Power differentials between states have considerable impact on the transformations that are taking place, but this is occurring in the context of deeper and more systemic changes that are reshaping the international system.

Many analysts see international economic agreements as intrinsic parts of a wider pattern of systemic change associated with the decline of the nation-state system. The process of globalization helps undermine the centuries-old dominance of the nation-state as a model for political organization and, instead, a post-national constellation of institutions develops. According to Habermas, this

> means that the globalization of markets and of economic processes gener-
> ally, of modes of communication and commerce, of culture, and of risk,
> all increasingly deprive the classical nation-state of its formerly assured
> bases of sovereign power, which it depended on to fulfil its equally classic
> functions: to secure peace internally and defend its borders abroad, to
> set fair conditions for a domestic market economy and to exert what
> influence it can on domestic markets via macroeconomic policies, to
> raise taxes and allocate budgets to assure the maintenance of a minimum
> social standard and the redress of social inequities, to enforce individual
> rights and take measures to secure conditions for their effective realization.
> (Habermas 2001: xiii)

The implications are systemic, but the process is far from even or structurally determined. The Habermas quotation underlines struc-tures, but these are forged by a wealth of actors – domestic and international – whose conception of the world increasingly favours the instrumental rationality underpinning market-based efficiency.

Clearly, considered at the level of *states*, international economic agreements have increased the external constraint on policy-making. In particular, resort to state activism is far more problematic than formerly. Considered at the level of *class interests* within countries, this situation may be unproblematic and even welcome for some interests (capital), and deeply disempowering for others (labour).

Globalization has obvious implications for power relations, as we see in the role of semi-peripheral and peripheral countries. However, it is not clear that the assessment of changes in power relations will shed sufficient light on the *systemic character* of the transformation.

Habermas argues that this process is better captured using the notion of different steering media – that is, market regulation replacing other types of regulatory mechanisms more directly related to democracy: 'The regulatory power of collectively binding decisions operates according to a different logic than the regulatory mechanisms of the market. Power can be democratized; money cannot. Thus the possibilities for a democratic self-steering of society slip away as the regulation of social spheres is transferred from one medium to another' (Habermas 2001: 78). Two key observations can be derived from this. One is that the transformation takes place in a peaceful international setting, less based on military coercion and power than what usually marks the international scene.

The second is that the nation-state was based on a mix of market-facilitating and market-correcting measures. This entailed a significant element of *closure* to the world around it, a closure that included economic, political, legal, and cultural factors. The present situation, by contrast, is one in which states are *opening themselves up to* a globalizing world along all these dimensions, but where the pattern of opening is deeply shaped and conditioned by the logic of the market. This process – structural in its implications – is also intentional, in that it is driven by a neo-liberal ideology based on faith in the market as a regulatory system. To semi-peripheral and peripheral states it is also a system of power, as they are more often rule-takers than rule-makers (Clarkson, Chapter 9).

The main question is whether the deregulatory opening we are now experiencing will be followed by re-regulatory measures that can re-establish democracy as sovereign popular rule. To address this, more needs to be known about specific patterns of market-based opening: how extensive it is, how it came about, and what the prospects of renewed closure are. How this re-regulation would look and what effects it would have on semi-peripheral countries in North America and in Europe are integrally related to the specific conditions existing in these countries.

International market-making systems: rules for efficiency

The argument that the Canadian and other liberal-democratic polities are being liberalized at the expense of their democratic elements can be illustrated by efforts to bind the state permanently to an

economically liberal conception of the state's role. One way this
is achieved is by entrenching the values of economic liberalism in
international agreements. This results in diminished state capacity and
increased reliance on international rules and norms, liberal in nature,
and difficult to alter, once ratified. Barry Appleton argues that

> The NAFTA represents the supremacy of a classical liberal conception
> of the state with its imposition of significant restraints upon the role
> of government.... NAFTA appears to approach an extreme. It does
> this by the extensiveness of its obligations which attempt to lock-in
> one perspective of governmental role for all successive North American
> governments. (Appleton 1994: 207)

NAFTA may be extreme, but Appleton's claim also seems applicable
to other major trading agreements, such as the WTO.

Core states, in close association with a set of international institutions that they themselves have contributed to foster and sustain,
embrace a limited set of steering media that actively deter or organize
out other concerns. The core concern is with efficiency and the
dominant mode of rationality is instrumental. The problem is that
the whole conception of ends becomes instrumentalized, so that what
remains is concern with and debate over means. The question of ends
is depoliticized, which serves to preserve the underlying neo-liberal
ideology. Some examples will serve to underline this concern with
efficiency and how it has crowded out other ones.

The WTO and NAFTA embed neo-liberal ideology as the key
reference point for state decision-makers. Space prohibits a comprehensive treatment, but some examples can be given. The WTO
Agreement on Technical Barriers to Trade[1] permits government
regulation of matters like national security, and health and safety.
However, it privileges economic efficiency criteria above other
legitimate policy goals by stipulating that regulations should not be
more trade-restrictive than necessary, must be non-discriminatory,
and respect the national treatment principle.

Similarly, the extension of GATT into the WTO transformed
shallow or negative integration, based on reciprocal reduction of
border measures (GATT), into '"deeper", positive or "behind the
border" integration which can permit the challenge of almost any
national policy likely to have spill-over or external effects across
borders' (Wolfe 1996: 692–3). Wolfe notes the familiar line-up of
social forces around this issue. Business groups are supporters of deep
integration, social and environmental groups oppose it.

In signing the WTO agreement, countries committed to further liberalization (Das 1998: 110). Through the General Agreement on Trade in Services (GATS), which is tilted towards progressive 'opting-in'. The WTO Secretariat is very open about the GATS' capacity to intrude into national decision-making:

> The reach of the GATS rules extends to all forms of international trade in services. This means that the GATS agreement represents a major new factor for a large sector of world economic activity. It also means, because such a large share of trade in services takes place *inside* national economies, that its requirements will from the beginning necessarily influence national domestic laws and regulations in a way that has been true of the GATT only in recent years. (WTO 1999b)

The ideological roots of this are explicit: in a related document, the secretariat cited as advantages the ability of bindings, once undertaken, to 'lock in a currently liberal regime or map out a future liberalization path' (WTO 1999c: 1) while overcoming domestic resistance to change.

A form of property rights has been conferred on foreign investors through NAFTA Article 1116, which permits investors to launch a claim directly without 'their' government acting as an intermediary. Such provisions confer rights on multinational corporations, in particular, that strengthen their hand vis-à-vis states and also privilege 'corporate citizens' in relation to 'natural' or human citizens.

Protection of intellectual property rights is strengthened under both NAFTA and WTO. Other provisions, such as Article 2010 of the Canada–US Free Trade Agreement, entitling a company to compensation if government action reduces its financial prospects, and Article 1605, which stipulates 'fair market compensation' be paid, featured in the successful insurance company lobby against proposed public no-fault auto insurance in Ontario in the early 1990s. In essence the provisions guarantee enjoyment of future profits, or compensation for loss thereof, to investors.

Rule enforcement in market–making systems: accountability/monitoring/review

Concomitant with the weakening of democratic systems of accountability, through restricting the scope of democratic governance, new forms of scrutiny and accountability are emerging. Domestic policy is continuously monitored by international organizations. Conducted in the name of 'transparency', this applies 'moral suasion' for compliance with the letter, and also with the neo-liberal spirit, of the agreements. The Uruguay round of GATT established a Trade Policy Review Mechanism (TPRM). The trade policies of member nations are regularly reviewed to improve their adherence to WTO rules and commitments, to achieve greater transparency surrounding trade policy and practices, and to facilitate collective evaluation of the impact of individual trade policies on the multilateral trading system of the WTO (Qureshi 1999: 314). The effect is to condition state behaviour:

> It inculcates at the earliest possible moment a 'WTO' approved pattern of behaviour – both through the impregnation of the national policy framework by substantive WTO trade prescriptions, as well as through the provision of conditions, including institutional, necessary for the evolution of WTO approved trade policies. The 'conditioning' stems particularly from the probing of policy, policy formulation and the objectives of policies. (Qureshi 1999: 320)

The TPRMs have been effective in detecting use of anti-dumping measures, subsidies, state aids, and tax concessions in support of industrial and regional development policies. They have drawn attention to the importance of domestic deregulation to ensure that the effects of trade reforms have not been offset by domestic firms' strategies. Through its monitoring role the trade policy review process has 'not only contributed to the fulfilment of commitments in the multilateral trading system but has also contributed to the development of national policies' (Laird 1999: 760). It could be argued that these extra-territorial monitoring mechanisms are more effective in influencing policy than are elected domestic institutions in some countries. In addition, they serve to identify practices within countries that become the targets for increased areas of 'liberalization' in successive rounds of negotiations.

As a member of the Quad, the inner circle of the WTO, Canada undergoes a Trade Policy Review (TPR) every two years (WTO 1997, 1999d, 2001b). The procedure results in a mixture of praise for Canada's policies, since it is acknowledged to be committed to liberalization, combined with expressions of concerns about remaining deviations from liberal principles. In responding to questions and concerns, Canadian delegates sometimes acknowledge that the TPRM has an impact on the domestic policy process. In 1998, for example, a Canadian representative stated that the TPR contributed to public support for Canada's trade policy, and that initiatives like the tariff simplification exercise were a concrete expression of the influence of the TPR (WTO 1999d: ix).

Norway gets a similarly positive assessment in the TPRM process for its liberal trade regime, though with complaints about agricultural protectionism, and perceived investment barriers to investors who are not from the European Economic Area (WTO 2000: xvii). One delegate noted that Norway had never, to that time, been involved as either plaintiff or defendant in a WTO dispute (WTO 2000: 189).

NAFTA also contains transparency provisions that open up national policy processes to the early intervention of NAFTA partners. Contact points must be established to facilitate communications and provide information. All measures affecting the agreement are to be made public in a timely manner and each party is to provide notification of any measure affecting the agreement that it proposes to adopt, and provide other parties a reasonable opportunity to comment. Little research has been done on how these provisions operate. On paper, at least, they would seem to create structured opportunities for intrusion into the policy process by partner states.

Rule enforcement in market-making systems: adjudication

The weakening of state sovereignty and the state-based system of law is accompanied by the emergence of new rules and their adjudication at the international level. Under NAFTA a bi-national review panel displaced judicial review of most issues concerned with dumping and anti-dumping, at least for disputes between NAFTA members. In the investment chapter, foreign investors are given the option of pursuing disputes through domestic courts or arbitration panels. Under the anti-dumping and countervailing subsidies provisions, the panels apply domestic law; under the investment chapter, they apply international law and are able to award damages and impose other sanctions (Lemieux and Stuhec 1999: 146).

Over these issues Canada has ceded decision-making to international panels. The Canadian courts have been diminished. Moreover, the enforcement of property rights has been partially transferred to investors themselves.[2]

Disputes arising under the WTO are referred to dispute panels once attempts at consultation and mediation have failed. The
Uruguay Round strengthened dispute-resolution mechanisms to
eliminate delays and the right of the 'guilty' party eventually to
veto decisions. Enforcement mechanisms include elimination of
the regulation or legislation found to be in breach of WTO provisions, payment of compensation, or, should the offending party fail
to implement panel findings, sanctioned retaliation by the injured
party. The WTO has already deemed the Auto Pact and Canadian
magazine legislation defending Canadian culture to be contrary to
WTO provisions. These examples alone indicate the scope of the
WTO and its extra-territorial adjudication mechanisms.

Countries that fail to comply with rulings can opt to pay compensation or endure sanctioned retaliatory measures instead. Small
and medium states are less able to bear the costs of retaliation, and
'winning cases' are less enforceable by them if they are unable to
mount effective retaliatory measures. Furthermore, rulings are more
intrusive for states that are less committed to the neo-liberal view
of the proper relationship between states and markets.

In disputes over the scope of the rules, few cases so far have
sustained the ability of nation-states to regulate on health, environmental, labour, or other issues that might stand in the way of
economic liberalization.[3] For example, analysis of WTO cases related
to labour standards and health issues showed that the private interest prevailed over the public interest. That is, free traders generally
prevailed over those who wished to erect social regulations, where
these were judged to have infringed on free trade (Drache et al.
2000: 39–45, 71–2).

Mainly, therefore, though countries may enter disputes about
specific cases according to their perceived interests, and 'win' or 'lose'
their case, the pattern of the outcomes reinforces the liberal rules that
constrain state action. If these are democratic states, the scope for
future exercise of democratic decision-making is also constrained.

The EU: neo-liberal copy-cat or novel polity?

Does the EU exhibit the same traits of global opening as was the
case with the WTO and NAFTA? The EU was initially launched as
an economic-type organization, but without a neo-liberal agenda. In

fact, it was a case of economics in the service of politics – that is, to ensure peace after two devastating world wars. Binding cooperation, it was thought, would tie former enemies closely together and preclude future wars. This process has been successful (European Council 2001). The EU has also moved well beyond that of a market and has become a political system, albeit not a state. The former Commission President, Jacques Delors, referred to it as an *objet politique nonidentifié* (Olsen 2001: 329). Many analysts also claim that it has a constitution (Weiler 1999). Precisely how far it has moved in polity terms is a highly contested point, but it is clear that it has never been motivated by neo-liberal ideology *as such*.

There have been neo-liberal influences at work, however, particularly since the 1980s, with the Single European Act. This recently prompted the German Chancellor, Gerhard Schröder, to accuse the EU Commission of being more neo-liberal than the United States.[4] Similarly, EU proposals on the GATS triggered a storm of NGO denunciation for the 'extraordinarily aggressive' content of the proposals.[5] In the view of the *Guardian*, the EU 'was demanding full-scale privatisation of public monopolies across the world as its price for dismantling the common agricultural policy'.[6] While the EU document is, of course, only a negotiating position, its implications are far-reaching and thoroughly consistent with the neo-liberal ethos prevalent at the WTO. One assessment of the EU's proposals for Canada to open up its services sector concluded that '[a] broad range of Canadian policies at every level of government would have to be eliminated or changed' (Gould 2002: 1). A list of some eighteen areas followed, including water privatization, energy, postal and express delivery services, and cultural products, including books, magazines, newspapers, journals, and periodicals. All these have been contentious issues in past Canadian efforts to retain some sovereignty in the face of globalization. In Gould's view the package adds up to a generalized attack on publicly delivered services. With the exception of continued protectionism in textiles and agriculture, the EU has been praised in a recent WTO trade policy review document for opening its markets and pursuing trade liberalization (WTO 2002).

So whilst the EU was not *intended* as a neo-liberal project,[7] the particular approach to integration that was adopted does now seem to have a strong economic imprint. This is manifest in the pillar structure of the Treaty of the European Union (Maastricht and later treaties), where the first pillar, the Common Market, is the one with the strongest supranational imprint and the one that is most tightly integrated.

Beyond market-making: from Common Market to polity/political system

What then needs to be established with regard to the EU is:

- the nature of the polity – that is, the character of the institutional system and its basis of support and legitimacy;
- the decision-making character and ability of the system – in particular in non-economic fields and in market-correcting areas;
- the nature of the integration process, with emphasis on the regulatory approach – a regulatory race to the bottom or to the top?

In terms of the nature of the polity, there is a general sense of the EU as an entity *sui generis*. It has become quite commonplace to portray it as a system of *multi-level governance* or multi-level polity (Marks et al. 1996). This political system does not fit any fixed mould and there is therefore a major search going on as to how to designate it. It is also a meeting place of polity visions. The December 2001 European Summit Meeting's Laeken Declaration stated that the 'Union stands at a crossroads, a defining moment in its existence' (European Council 2001). Prior to the next reform of the treaties, due in 2004, the EU has committed itself to conduct a major constitutional debate on the essentials of the Union.

The present form of the EU reflects its character as 'entity in motion'. Its political system is a mixture of supranational, transnational, transgovernmental, and intergovernmental structures. Some of the institutions, such as the European Commission, the European Parliament, and the European Court of Justice (ECJ), are 'supranational'. It should also be noted that the European Parliament is the only directly elected supranational parliament in the world. In the last two decades this institution, which started out as a mere advisory body composed of parliamentarians from the member states, has greatly strengthened its decision-making power and its ability to hold the Commission accountable, whilst it is still weak in relation to most national parliaments.[8] The ECJ is also supranational and has devised a set of novel legal principles to mark the special character of EC law. Some of the core principles are 'supremacy' and 'direct effect' of EC law, meaning that they are premissed on the notion of EC law as the 'higher' law of the land. The member states are thus profoundly shaped by EC law. National courts of last instance also have a duty to refer cases to the ECJ. Further, all national courts are bound by the judgments of the ECJ (Weiler 1999). This system leaves small states with considerable influence over the large ones.

The central institutions of the EU do not operate in a vacuum but are linked to interest organizations, lobby groups, and social movements directly and through a range of intermediary bodies. The bulk of these represent functional interests, but as the integration process has proceeded further, a larger number and range of non-economic groups and organizations have related to the EU. The establishment of European citizenship – albeit deficient in relation to the established Marshallian conception of citizenship – has given credence to the idea of a citizens' Europe.

The Charter of Fundamental Rights of the European Union, whilst in formal terms a political declaration, is already an important source of legal interpretation. Its actual role is more than that of a political declaration because it is based on existing law (international law and foremost the European Court of Human Rights (ECHR), EU law, and member-state law) (Eriksen et al. 2001; Lenaerts and De Smijter 2001). It was intended to make the EU's growing commitment to basic individual rights more visible. The political system of the EU also has a set of feedback mechanisms through which groups and individuals respond to outputs and seek to foster new outputs that reflect their values and interests.

The integration process picked up pace from the late 1980s on and has helped to alter the conception of the EU, which up until then had been largely technocratic. It was seen as an elite game in the hands of economic interests and bureaucrats. The key role of the EU was devised as that of handling the problems that were beyond the reach of the individual nation-state. Its legitimacy was related to its outcomes and seen as 'indirect' or 'derivative'; that is, it was ultimately conditioned by the legitimacy of the democratic nation-states of which it was composed.

Developments during the 1980s and early 1990s have clearly rendered inadequate the indirect and derivative mode of legitimation. The EU is now a polity in its own right, and requires *direct legitimation*. To some extent, the very success of this mode of integration has contributed to the present legitimacy deficit. EU citizens can still not see themselves as self-legislating citizens.

In political terms, there is a noticeable shift in the perception of the EU from the early and mid-1980s to today. During the process of launching the Common Market, many analysts thought of the EU in neo-liberal terms, and this was reflected to some extent also on the political arena in that right-wing parties were quite favourable to it. Today, the strongest opposition to the EU comes from the political right, whereas the left is increasingly seeing it as a means of salvaging the welfare state and of devising buffers against global capitalism. This political change emanates from changes in the structure of the EU. It also is based on the fact that the EU has not promoted a 'race to the bottom'. The EU does not propound neo-liberal globalism as ideology. Neither is it an entity bereft of capacity to develop market-correcting or offsetting means and ways. To what extent does it represent a case of opening up to the global market?

The four freedoms (free movement of goods, services, capital, and persons within the EU), the Economic and Monetary Union (EMU) and the convergence criteria, and the provisions against discrimination on national grounds clearly emasculate or constrain the scope for domestic policy-making. But the EU is less directly exposed to international competition because of the close economic ties and strong patterns of trade and investment across regions within Europe.

The EU is also more appropriately thought of as a case of re-regulation than of deregulation. In some policy fields, such as environment and consumer protection and health, standards have been consistently raised. European law provisions were framed so that 'the opening of markets was to be had only at the cost of modernizing the relevant regulatory machinery and enhancing its quality' (Joerges 2002: 27). There are also provisions that enable member states that have high regulatory aspirations to 'go it alone'. The inability of the EU to implement its regulations has compelled it to develop national certification bodies that ensure product safety standards. The 'go it alone' provisions can have positive spiralling effects:

> Article 100a(4) (now 95) allows nations to 'go it alone' nationally, on condition that they regulate in more detail. At the same time, all these reservations for national policy-making are opportunities for action. The restriction of national autonomy compels the taking of 'foreign' interests

into account; and conversely, one's own regulatory concerns may be 'exported' beyond one's own territory. (Joerges 2002: 15)

The EU also does not take away much of the fiscal resources of the member states. Its total budget is at 1.27 per cent of GDP and the states have great control of the amounts and sources of their funds. The flip-side of this is that the EU is highly asymmetrical in that it has a strong monetary union but not a commensurate fiscal union. Thus, market correction through fiscal means is not available at present, although it is being discussed. The EU has a cohesion fund and regional development funds, and these have been important in establishing far more equal living standards in Europe. They are used not for redistribution among individuals but for regional development. Their redistributive effects at the individual level are therefore indirect.

The general impression we get from this is that there is a certain neo-liberal policy thrust in much of what the EU does, through the onus on efficiency and privatization, but this coexists with a system of re-regulation that takes non-market considerations into account.

The EU has *not* challenged the core of the European welfare states (Hagen 2002). There is also great concern in many quarters with establishing a European alternative to the US model, an alternative based on social justice and solidarity.

The strong economic imprint on the EU also reflects political realities, in that full-scale political union was not possible, so the alternative was to carefully stimulate it through economic means, and through a pragmatic and step-by-step integration process.

The interesting point is that *further integration* is very likely increasingly to weaken the neo-liberal aspects of the Common Market. The constellation of political support for the EU testifies to this. The British Tories are eager to roll back integration and obtain assurances that the EU will remain a Common Market. Further integration will take place in market-correcting fields or in fields where the negative effects of the market can be handled through the development of more democratic steering media. The last few years have put greatly increased stress on the European social dimension. This emphasis is also clearly outlined in the Charter provisions. The Charter is evocative of the increased role and importance of human rights and provisions against discrimination of various forms, as the EU is currently facing a convergence of legal systems (EU law and

ECHR law) that will likely further strengthen the focus on individual human rights and not only economic, market-based rights.

In sum, the EU defies a simple dichotomy of openness or closure to the world market. It is highly ambivalent in that it is both a product of and a response to globalization. The most remarkable feature of the EU is the multiplicity of projects it contains, and hence it conveys a wide mixture of signals. Each state also has considerable overall room to develop in the direction it desires, subject to constraints emanating from the Common Market. These constraints, perhaps ironically, may serve as stronger adaptive signals to countries that are, formally speaking, non-members than to members, as appears to be the case with the formally non-member country of Norway (Claes and Fossum, Chapter 4). It is directly included in all aspects of the market, yet less included in those aspects of the EU that can serve as market-correcting or that may help undo some of the negative effects of the market.

Conclusion

International agreements ostensibly dealing with trade have expanded their reach so as to become part of the constitutional system of each state. These agreements function to constrain, limit, direct, and 'condition' decision-making in areas far removed from trade as traditionally understood. Canada's state, for example, is no longer available for as wide a range of purposes as formerly.[9]

The argument has been that in re-balancing the liberal-democratic order by accentuating its market and diminishing its democratic elements, the new generation of international economic agreements contribute to the transformation of the nation-state system. In systemic terms, this development will weaken the democratic regulatory system or perhaps even replace it with that of the efficiency-based market. This change in steering medium will have profound effects on citizens, whose status will alter from that of self-regulator to customer or market actor.

This process of transformation is far from even across the globe. In Western Europe, the cradle of the state system, the process of developing a new type of polity has proceeded the furthest but this system is *less opened up to* the market than are the NAFTA countries. The EU is at a critical juncture in its existence as it has exploited the integrative thrust of economic cooperation, and has developed a range of, and is committed to the further development of, rectifying regulatory and institutional measures.

These international arrangements are clearly also systems of power, which can serve to discipline states, and hence also the citizens of those states, albeit the means are peaceful. Citizens are confined to a limited range of choices and thus bound to existing property and power relations embodied in the agreements.

In the North American region the disempowerment of states has a more severe impact in the semi-periphery, where use of the state for national development and social security purposes was more significant than in the American core. This may be less true, for reasons outlined, in the European region.

Notes

1. Texts of all WTO agreements can be found in WTO 1999a.

2. These provisions have provoked a constitutional challenge (The Council of Canadians and the Canadian Union of Postal Workers 2001).

3. The main exception to date is the failed Canadian action against French regulations prohibiting the use of asbestos (WTO 2001a).

4. *National Post*, 15 July 2002: A11.

5. *Bridges Weekly Trade News Digest* 2002.

6. Ibid.

7. Economic liberalization was one of the ideas promoting European integration, but certainly not the only one (Parsons 2002: 47–84). This contrasts with the single-minded focus on economic liberalization that is characteristic of NAFTA and the WTO.

8. Typically, national parliaments are, of course, themselves weak in relation to their executives.

9. It is important not to exaggerate the purposes for which it has been used in the past. Nevertheless, its constitutional room for action was wider in the past than it has recently become.

References

Abromeit, H. (1998) *Democracy in Europe*, Oxford: Berghahn Books.

Appleton, Barry (1994) *Navigating Nafta: A Concise Users' Guide to the North American Free Trade Agreement*, Scarborough, ON: Carswell.

Ayres, Jeffrey (1998) *Defying Conventional Wisdom: Political Movements and Popular Contention against North American Free Trade*, Toronto: University of Toronto Press.

Beetham, David and C. Lord (1998) *Legitimacy and the EU*, London: Longman.

Bridges Weekly Trade News Digest (2002) 'GATS: Leaked EC Draft Requests Bring Mixed Reactions', vol. 6, no. 15, 23 April.

Council of Canadians and the Canadian Union of Postal Workers (2001) 'The Council of Canadians and the Canadian Union of Postal Workers Launch A Constitutional Challenge to NAFTA Investment Rules', Ottawa: Council of Canadians and the Canadian Union of Postal Workers, 28 March.

Das, B.L. (1998) *An Introduction to the WTO Agreements*, Penang: Third World Network.

Drache, Daniel, Yunxiang Guan, Amy Arnott, and Kyle Grayson (2000) *An Analysis of WTO Rulings with Respect to Labour Standards and Health*, Toronto: Robarts Centre for Canadian Studies, York University.

Eriksen, E.O. and J.E. Fossum (eds) (2000) *Democracy in the European Union: Integration through Deliberation?* London: Routledge.

European Council (2001) 'The Future of the European Union – Laeken Declaration', Laeken, 15 December, SN 273/01.

Gill, S. (1995) 'Globalization, Market Civilization and Disciplinary Neo-liberalism', *Millennium* 24.

Goldstein, J. (1998) 'International Institutions and Domestic Politics: GATT, WTO, and the Liberalization of International Trade', in Anne O. Krueger (ed.) *The WTO as an International Organization*, Chicago: University of Chicago Press.

Gould, Ellen (2002) *The European Commission's GATS Position: A Bad Bargain for Canada*, Ottawa: Council of Canadians.

Greven, Michael T. (ed.) (2000) 'Can the European Union Finally Become a Democracy?', in Michael T. Greven and Louis W. Pauly, *Democracy Beyond the State? The European Dilemma and the Emerging Global Order*, Toronto: University of Toronto Press.

Grinspun, R. and R. Kreklewich (1994) 'Consolidating Neo-liberal Reforms: "Free Trade" as a Conditioning Framework', *Studies in Political Economy* 43.

Gruber, Lloyd (2000) *Ruling the World: Power Politics and the Rise of Supranational Institutions*, Princeton: Princeton University Press.

Habermas, Jürgen (2001) *The Post-national Constellation*, Cambridge, MA: MIT Press.

Hagen, K. (2002) 'Explaining Welfare State Survival: (How) Does Europe Matter?', mimeo, ARENA, University of Oslo.

Joerges, C. (2002) 'The Law in the Process of Constitutionalizing Europe', in E.O. Eriksen, J.E. Fossum, and A.J. Menendez (eds) *Constitution Making and Democratic Legitimacy*, ARENA Report no. 5.

Krasner, Stephen (1999) *Sovereignty: Organized Hypocrisy*, Princeton: Princeton University Press.

Laird, Sam (1999) 'The WTO's Trade Policy Review Mechanism: From Through the Looking Glass', *The World Economy*, vol. 22, no. 6.

Lemieux, Denis and Ana Stuhec (1999) *Review of Administrative Action under NAFTA*, Scarborough, ON: Carswell.

Lenearts, K. and E.E. De Smijter (2001) 'A "Bill of Rights" for the European Union', *Common Market Law Review* 38.

Macpherson, C.B. (1965) *The Real World of Democracy*, Toronto: CBC.

Macpherson, C.B. (1977) *The Life and Times of Liberal Democracy*, Oxford: Oxford University Press.

McBride, Stephen (2001) *Paradigm Shift: Globalization and the Canadian State*, Halifax: Fernwood.

Marks, G., F.W. Scharpf, P. C. Schmitter, and W. Streeck (1996) *Governance in the European Union*, London: Sage.

Olsen, J.P. (2001) 'Organizing European Institutions of Governance... A Prelude to an Institutional Account of Political Integration', in H. Wallace, *Interlocking Dimensions of European Integration*, London: Palgrave.

Parsons, Craig (2002) 'Showing Ideas as Causes: The Origins of the European Union', *International Organization*, vol. 56, no. 1.

Petras, James and Henry Veltmeyer (2001) *Globalization Unmasked: Imperialism in the 21st Century*, London: Zed Books.

Qureshi, Asif H. (1999) *International Economic Law*, London: Sweet & Maxwell.

Weale, A. and M. Nentwich (eds) (1998) *Political Theory and the European Union: Legitimacy, Constitutional Choice and Citizenship*, London and New York: Routledge.

Weiler, J.H.H. (1999) *The Constitution of Europe*, Cambridge: Cambridge University Press.

Weisbrot, M, D. Baker, E. Kraev, and J. Chen (2001) *The Scorecard on Globalization 1980–2000: Twenty Years of Diminished Progress*, Washington, DC: Center for Economic and Policy Research.

Weiss, Linda (1997) 'Globalization and the Myth of the Powerless State', *New Left Review* 225.

Wolfe, R. (1996) 'Global Trade as a Single Undertaking: The Role of Ministers in the WTO', *International Journal*, Autumn.

WTO (World Trade Organization) (1997) *Trade Policy Review: Canada 1996*, Geneva: WTO.

WTO (1999a) *The Legal Texts: The Results of the Uruguay Round of Multilateral Trade Negotiations*, Cambridge: Cambridge University Press.

WTO (1999b) *About the WTO*, Geneva: WTO.

WTO (1999c) *The GATS: Objectives, Coverage and Disciplines*, Geneva: WTO.

WTO (1999d) *Trade Policy Review: Canada 1998*, Geneva: WTO.

WTO (2000) *Trade Policy Review: Norway 2000*, Geneva: WTO.

WTO (2001a) *European Communities: Measures Affecting Asbestos and Asbestos-Containing Products. AB-2000–11 Report of the Appellate Body*, Geneva: WTO, 12 March.

WTO (2001b) *Trade Policy Review: Canada 2000*, Geneva: WTO.

WTO (2002) *Trade Policy Review Body: European Union, Report by the Secretariat Summary Observations*, Geneva: WTO, 26 June.

PART III

Comparing Economic Performance

14

Zonal Structure and the Trajectories of Canada, Mexico, Australia, and Norway under Neo-liberal Globalization

Satoshi Ikeda

In the 1980s Canada changed its economic policy direction from 'national development' to 'free trade with the US'. The resulting Canada–US bilateral free-trade arrangement was later expanded to include Mexico, a country that suffered from recurring financial crises in the 1980s and 1990s. Mexico changed its economic policy direction from oil-leveraged industrialization to export manufacturing. Australia faced stagnant export markets since its major trade partner Japan suffered from stagnation/deflation in the 1990s. The country expanded exports to other emerging markets in East Asia, but its currency devalued significantly against the US dollar. Norway became one of the world's richest countries on a per capita income base thanks to booming oil and natural gas exports. While rejecting membership in the European Union, it nonetheless deepened its dependence on the EU's market. These are snapshots of national trajectories under neo-liberal globalization, a historical process where barriers to the movement of goods, services, money, and information are greatly reduced to allow corporations to expand their networks of activities over the entire world.

How did the economies of Canada, Mexico, Australia, and Norway fare under neo-liberal globalization? Did they accomplish growth, and if so, how did they achieve it? Did they become more dependent on external trade and investment, or did they manage to raise their levels of economic autonomy? Are the paths taken by these four countries sustainable? These are the questions that motivate the investigations of this chapter, which looks specifically at the increasingly integrated and interrelated international framework of which these economies are a part.

In the following section, the overall changes in the world economy are first examined in order to identify the trajectories of 150 countries including the four above.[1] The tool used here is the core–semiperiphery–periphery zonal structure of the world-system (which is explained in the following section). As the world economy went through substantial transformation from the 1970s, some countries went up the zonal hierarchy while others moved down. The examination of the overall changes in the zonal structure is expected to illuminate commonalties and uniqueness of the trajectories of Canada, Mexico, Australia, and Norway. Also, the changes in the zonal structure as a whole have important implications for the sustainability not only of the paths taken by these four countries but also of the overall world economy in coming years.

The examination of the zonal structure will be followed by the detailed examination of the trajectories of the economies of Canada, Mexico, Australia, and Norway. This is done by using macroeconomic statistics such as national income, external trade, and investment flows to and from the countries. Through an examination of these figures, this section highlights income trends and the changes in external dependency and identifies the typology of external dependency of the four countries. The last section examines the vulnerability of the four economies and discusses the sustainability of world economic trends under neo-liberal globalization.

Neo-liberal globalization and zonal structure

World-system researchers challenge the developmentalist idea that national economies are on the same development path despite being at different stages at a given time (Wallerstein 1974a; Hopkins 1982; Hopkins, Wallerstein et al. 1982). Instead, they suggest that national economies are integrated into a global system structured by a single division of labour and multiple political jurisdictions. The poor countries are poor, according to this perspective, because they are subjected to the rich countries' appropriation of their surplus. The zonal structure captures the unequal distribution of the rewards of accumulation within the system (Wallerstein, 1974a, 1974b; Arrighi and Drangel 1986). The core zone includes strong states that promote accumulation to further enhance their position, while the peripheral zone is the domain of weak states. The semi-peripheral zone is an intermediate category.

In this section, per capita national income is used as the indicator of countries' zonal position on the assumption that the strength (economic, military, and political) of a country is strongly correlated with the income that accrues to it. For purposes of comparison, national income in local currency is converted into US dollars, which serves as the currency of transactions, settlement, and speculation in the globalized economy (Gowan 1999). The market exchange rate is used for conversion instead of the purchasing power parity exchange rate[2] so as to show how much can be bought by local income in the global market, where the US dollar is the predominant currency. In this way, the market exchange rate is better than the purchasing power parity exchange rate as a measure of a country's command over the global accumulation process.

For the examination of the impact of neo-liberal globalization, the year 1980 is used as our starting point. The term 'neo-liberal global-ization' implies that national economies are integrated according to the neo-liberal economic principles of free trade and liberalized financial flow. At the same time this process accompanied the adapta-tion of neo-liberal economic policies in domestic economies. The year 1980 is the beginning date because neo-liberal economic policies that included tax cuts for the rich, welfare spending reduction, the privatization of public and quasi-public enterprises, industrial and corporate deregulation, and financial sector liberalization were initiated by Margaret Thatcher in Great Britain in 1979 and Ronald Reagan in the US in 1981 (McBride and Shields 1997). Through changes that implemented the doctrine that the market mechanism achieves the best resource allocation and income distribution, giant corporations came to dominate the lives of people while transform-ing the middle class into consumers and investors and denying the poor and underprivileged the fruits of the market (Korten 1995). Since then, other countries have adopted neo-liberal policies as the consequence either of debt crisis and structural adjustment imposed by the International Monetary Fund (IMF) and the World Bank or of a political power shift favouring the wealthy and business interests.

The process of international trade and financial liberalization had started much earlier. A liberal trade arrangement was pursued from the late 1940s under the framework of the General Agreement on

Tariffs and Trade (GATT). International financial liberalization came later. Controls on capital movements were lifted by the Western European countries and Japan in the 1960s and foreign exchange arrangements shifted from fixed exchange rates to flexible exchange rates in the early 1970s among the industrialized countries. Developing countries often fixed their currencies to major currencies such as the US dollar and maintained control on private capital flows until the 1980s. From the Mexican financial crisis in 1982, the IMF and the World Bank started introducing liberalized capital movement with more flexible foreign exchange arrangements as part of their structural adjustment programmes (SAPs). For this reason, figures from 1980 and 1999 are compared to examine the impact of globalization on economic trajectories of the countries.

In this chapter a country belongs to the core if its relative per capita income is 80 per cent of the per capita US gross national income (GNI) or above.[3] If relative per capita income is between 20 per cent and 80 per cent, the country belongs to the semi-periphery. Below 20 per cent relative per capita income puts a country into the peripheral zone. Each zone is further divided into 'upper', 'middle', and 'lower' categories since the finer categories help us identify movement of countries across the zones.

Table 14.1 shows the zonal position of 150 countries in 1980 and 1999. By reading horizontally, we can identify which countries belonged to each zone in 1980. For example, the countries that belonged to the lower core in 1980 were Austria, Canada, Finland, and Australia. By reading vertically, we can identify the countries in each zone in 1999. For example, the countries that belonged to middle semi-periphery in 1999 were Kuwait, Saudi Arabia, Australia, Italy, New Zealand, and Israel. By cross-referring to vertical and horizontal positions, we can identify how each country changed (or remained unchanged in) its zonal position between 1980 and 1999. For example, the four countries in the top-left corner cell, Luxembourg, Norway, Switzerland, and the USA, maintained upper core status. Australia, Canada, and Finland, in contrast, dropped from lower core in 1980 to upper semi-periphery in 1999. The shaded diagonal cells represent non-movement in zonal position, whilst those cells above and right of the diagonal cells represent downward movement and those below and left of the diagonal cells represent upward movement.

Table 14.1 Changes in zonal membership, 1980–1999

1980＼1999	Upper core	Middle core	Lower core	Upper semi-periphery	Middle semi-periphery	Lower semi-periphery	Upper periphery	Middle periphery	Lower periphery	Very low periphery
Upper core	Luxem., Norway, Switz., USA	Denmark	Iceland	France, Germany, Qatar, Sweden, UAE	Kuwait, Saudi Arabia		Libya			
Middle core			Belgium, Netherlands							
Lower core				Austria, Canada, Finland	Australia					
Upper semi-periphery	Japan		UK		Italy, New Zealand	Bahrain				
Middle semi-periphery				Hong Kong, Ireland						
Lower semi-periphery				Singapore	Israel	Bahamas, Barbados, Cyprus, Greece, Malta, Portugal, Slovenia	Czech R., Slovak R., Estonia, Mexico, Uruguay, Venezuela	Latvia, Lithuania, Macedonia FYR, South Africa, Suriname	Armenia, Belarus, Bosnia-Herzegovina, Bulgaria, Moldova, Russia, Ukraine	Kyrgyz
Upper periphery						Argentina, Spain	Oman, Trinidad & Tobago	Gabon	Algeria, Ghana, Jordan, Paraguay, Romania, Uganda	
Middle periphery						Antigua & Barbuda, Korea, Seychelles, St Kitts & Nevis	Chile, Costa Rica, Hungary, Iran, Poland, St. Lucia, Syria	Belize, Brazil, Colombia, Ecuador, Fiji, Malaysia, Panama, Tunisia, Turkey	Bolivia, Cameroon, R. Congo, Guatemala, Guyana, Honduras, Ivory Coast, Morocco, Nicaragua, Papua New Guinea, Philippines, Swaziland, Zambia, Zimbabwe	
Lower periphery							Grenada, Mauritius	Botswana, Dominica, Dominican R., El Salvador, Jamaica, Peru	Namibia, Thailand	Benin, China, Egypt, Equatorial Guinea, Gambia, Haiti, India, Indonesia, Kenya, Lesotho, Mauritania, Myanmar, Nigeria, Pakistan, Senegal, Sri Lanka, Sudan, Togo, Vanuatu
Very low periphery									Vietnam, R. Yemen	Bangladesh, Burkina Faso, Burundi, Central African R., Chad, D.R. Congo, Madagascar, Malawi, Mali, Mongolia, Mozambique, Nepal, Niger, Rwanda, Sierra Leone, Tanzania, Bhutan, Ethiopia, Laos

Note: The zonal position of a country is determined based on per capita gross national income relative to US per capita GNI using the market exchange rate.

Source: IMF 2001.

At a glance, it is clear that the bottom-right cells dominate the table. A vast majority of countries belong to the periphery. Also, many countries are in the cells above the diagonal cells, indicating that many countries experienced downward movement. Among the countries that experienced movement from the core to the semi-periphery are the industrialized countries of Europe such as France and Germany and the oil-exporting countries such as Kuwait. Canada and Australia also dropped from the core to the semi-periphery. Many countries that fell from the semi-periphery to the periphery were former socialist countries. Latin American countries also moved down, such as Mexico and Venezuela from lower semi-periphery to upper periphery and Brazil from upper periphery to middle periphery. Many countries in Africa, South Asia, and Latin America also experienced downward movement. In contrast, the number of countries that went up the zonal hierarchy was limited. They included East Asian countries such as Japan and Korea, and some island countries that emerged as tax havens for the global bourgeoisie. The author's calculation shows that a total of 123 countries experienced decline in per capita income relative to the US, while 96 countries experienced absolute income decline when the US consumer price index is used to derive constant dollar income. Neo-liberal globalization, therefore, brought a downward movement of zonal positions for many countries, and relative (to the US) and absolute per capita income decline for the majority of countries. For the peripheral countries, neo-liberal globalization meant further peripheralization and subordination to the global financial system as 'debt slaves' who keep paying interest on loans with no hope of ever escaping debt (Jomo 1998; Bullard et al. 1998; Maull 1999).

The world economy went through turbulence in the 1970s, including the end of gold–dollar convertibility, fixed exchange rates among the major currencies, and oil price increases and resulting global stagflation. This crisis situation, however, provided opportunities for upward movement in the zonal hierarchy (Wallerstein 1974a, 1976). The petroleum-exporting countries increased their income as oil prices increased substantially in the 1970s. But subsequent oil price decline due to supply increases brought down their zonal positions in the 1980s and 1990s. Latin American countries such as Brazil and Mexico introduced private loans to expand industrial activities in the 1970s, but they fell to the rank of heavily indebted countries

Figure 14.1 Zonal population share, 1980–1999

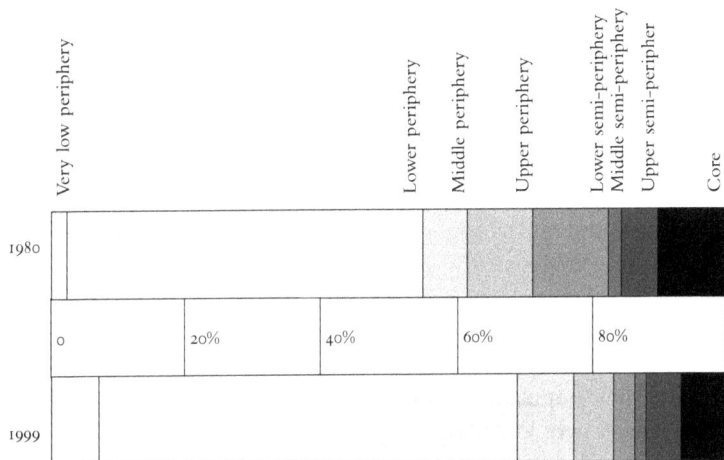

Source: IMF 2001.

in the 1980s. Their aspiration for national economic development was replaced by the cold reality of an indebted periphery. Socialist countries in Eastern Europe in the 1970s appeared to be doing fine, but their economies stagnated in the 1980s until they collapsed towards the end of the decade. These so-called 'transition economies' fell from 'socialist' semi-peripheral status to impoverished peripheral status in the 1990s.

The 1990s was the time when regional economic integration was pursued by many countries as a way of maintaining or raising their economic level. Canada pursued economic integration with the US, but the overall result was a fall from the core to the semi-periphery. The Western European countries continued their effort toward regional economic integration in the 1990s. The formation of the European Union and the introduction of the euro, however, did not help them in terms of keeping up with the US. The major European countries took the downward path from the core to the semi-periphery. Exceptions to these trajectories were observed for the East Asian countries. Upward movement was achieved by Japan, Hong Kong, Singapore, Korea, and so on, although they suffered a setback in the 1990s in the form of stagnation/deflation (Japan) and financial crisis (Korea, Thailand, Indonesia). As predicted by the world-system researchers, upward movement in the hierarchy of zonal structure remained an exception under neo-liberal globalization. To sum up, neo-liberal globalization allowed the establishment of US economic domination in the world economy. At the same time, many other core countries took the path of downward semi-peripheralization, many semi-peripheral countries took the path of peripheralization, and many peripheral countries took the path of further peripheralization.[4]

Just by counting the number of countries in Table 14.1, we can discern the polarizing tendency of the zonal structure. But how do the changes in the zonal structure appear when we count the number of people in each zone? Figure 14.1 was prepared by tabulating the population of the countries in each zone and showing the population share of each zone in 1980 and 1999. The zones that increased their population shares between 1980 and 1999 were lower periphery and very low periphery. Combined, the share of population of countries whose per capita income is less than 5 per cent of US per capita income increased from about 55 per cent to 70 per cent. The size of the periphery (upper + middle + lower + very low) increased from 72 per cent to 83 per cent. As a result of neo-liberal globalization, four in every five people in the world live in the periphery. In contrast, the core and semi-periphery zones shrank in terms of population share. This zonal population shift reflects the 'peripheralization' trajectory of many semi-peripheral countries. Also, the decline in the share of the core population is a reflection of the 'semi-peripheralization' of many core countries.

Within the overall zonal structure changes, Canada and Australia joined the West European countries and some oil-exporting countries that moved downwards from core to semi-periphery, while Norway remained in the core. Mexico fell from lower semi-periphery to upper periphery together with the East European countries and some Latin American countries. From this observation, it appears that Canada, Mexico, and Australia failed and Norway succeeded in the race of moving up or maintaining their zonal position.

Trajectories of Canada, Mexico, Australia, and Norway under globalization

This section examines the macroeconomic trajectories of the four economies by observing income trends and the degree of external dependency in order to identify whether the current path is

Table 14.2 Population and income, 2000

	Population (million)	MER income Total (US$ bn)	Per capita (US$)	Relative per capita	PPP income Total (US$ bn)	Per capita (US$)	Relative per capita
Canada	30.75	679.63	22,102	0.631	849.22	27,617	0.788
Mexico	97.36	549.01	5,639	0.161	852.23	8.754	0.249
Australia	19.16	360.81	18,831	0.537	472.81	24,677	0.704
Norway	4.49	153.77	34,247	0.977	125.13	27,869	0.795

Source: IMF 2001; OECD 2002.

economically sustainable (without considering other limits such as ecological, demographic, social, and politico-military limits). When a country's well-being depends increasingly on external transactions, it becomes vulnerable to changes that are out of its control. Neo-liberal globalization is a process of deepening international interdependence through trade and investment and, as our examination of the zonal structure revealed, it lowered the relative and absolute income of the majority of the countries. Understanding the degree of external dependency and examining what has been achieved in terms of income, therefore, is expected to reveal the forms of vulnerability involved in the trajectories of the four countries.

Table 14.2 shows population size and total income (GNI) in US dollars converted by the market exchange rate (MER) and the purchasing power parity (PPP) exchange rate. To avoid confusion, the difference between MER and PPP needs to be clearly identified. MER income represents how much a country's income can buy in the global market, where the US dollar dominates. When Canadians travel abroad, what one Canadian dollar can buy is determined by the market exchange rate. Depreciation of the Canadian dollar vis-à-vis the US dollar lowers the purchasing power of the Canadian dollar abroad. But the same Canadian dollar may buy the same amount of things within Canada even when the market exchange rate is falling. This happens when the price of things produced within Canada remains unchanged. To capture the purchasing power of a currency within the country, the purchasing power parity exchange rate is used. PPP income indicates how much a country's income

Figure 14.2   Per capita MER GNI relative to US per capita GNI

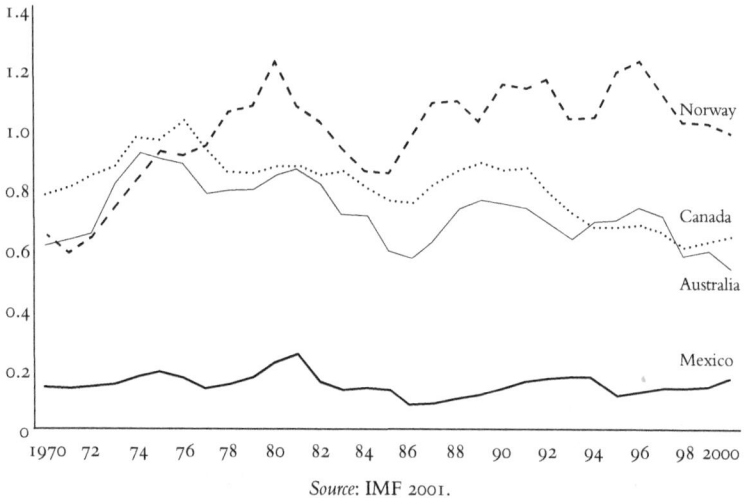

Source: IMF 2001.

can buy in the domestic market, and it is thought to reflect the living standard of a country better than MER income. In other words, MER income represents 'market' income, or how much a given income can buy in the global market, while PPP income represents 'latent' income, or how much the same income can buy in the domestic market.

Per capita MER income varies widely among the four countries, and relative (to the US) per capita MER income puts Canada and Australia in the semi-periphery, Norway in the core, and Mexico in the periphery. There were substantial differences between the 'market' and 'latent' income, as Table 14.2 indicates. Norway's latent income is smaller than 'market' income, while 'latent' income was larger for Canada, Mexico, and Australia. Per capita PPP income is more equal among the four countries than per capita MER income. Since Mexico's income distribution is more unequal than the other three, the number of middle- and upper-middle-class people who enjoy a higher living standard would be comparable to other countries. Inclusion of Mexico in this list can be justified also in terms of relative per capita PPP income. All countries are semi-peripheral if the zonal position is measured by the living standard.

Figure 14.3 Per capita PPP GNI relative to US per capita GNI

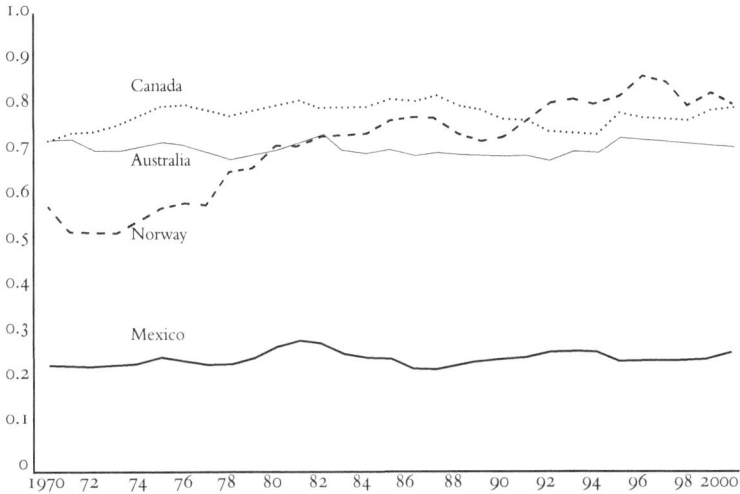

Source: IMF 2001; OECD 2002.

What were the trends of per capita income for the four countries? Figure 14.2 shows relative (to US) per capita MER income between 1970 and 2000 for the four countries. In the figure, the horizontal line at 1 indicates the level of US per capita income. The trends in relative per capita income show that Canada and Australia fell from the core position under globalization and that these countries were relatively impoverished vis-à-vis the US, especially in the 1990s. Canadian relative per capita income was at par with the US in 1976, but the trend since then has been in decline until it reached 0.6 towards the end of the 1990s. Canada took the path of downward semi-peripheralization in the 1990s despite the US–Canada Free Trade Agreement and the North American Free Trade Agreement (NAFTA). Australia also took the path of downward semi-peripheralization. Its relative per capita income stood at 0.9 in 1974, but it has declined with some ups and downs until it reached near 0.5 in 2000. Norway recorded 1.2 in 1980, and it maintained per capita income comparable to that of the US for most years. However, the trend from 1996 is a sharp decline and it fell below 1.0 in 2000. Mexico, on the other hand, took the path of peripheralization under globalization. Mexican relative per capita income stood at the semi-peripheral position of 0.2 in 1981, but it has remained peripheral under the 0.2 line since then.

What were the changes in relative per capita 'latent' income? Figure 14.3 shows per capita PPP GNI relative to that of the US. In contrast to Figure 14.2, relative per capita 'latent' income shows rather steady trends. Canadian per capita income hovered around 0.8 but stayed below 0.8 in the 1990s. In terms of per capita PPP GNI, Canada's fall from the core to the semi-periphery is not as drastic as that in terms of per capita MER GNI. The Australian trend is similar to that of Canada. Australian per capita PPP GNI hovered around the 0.7 line throughout the three decades. Norway, on the other hand, improved its relative income from near 0.5 level in the early 1970s to above 0.8 in the 1990s. Again, Norway's trend is downward in the second half of the 1990s. Mexico's relative per capita PPP GNI was higher than relative per capita MER GNI throughout the three decades, and was about 0.25 (one quarter of US per capita income). The trend in relative per capita 'latent' income shows that neo-liberal globalization did not allow Canada, Mexico, and Australia to catch up with the US in terms of living standards, while Norway did manage to improve in the 1990s.

When real income level is compared between 1980 and 2000, per capita MER income declined by $2,562 for Australia, $315 for Canada, and $31 for Mexico. Norway enjoyed an increase of $2,513, while the US gain was $8,022. Neo-liberal globalization in the 1980s and 1990s resulted in the loss of real income for Australia, Canada, and Mexico, and the gains enjoyed by Norway was less than one-third of the gains enjoyed by the US. The changes in real per capita PPP income were positive for all countries, but the increase was the smallest for Mexico. In twenty years under globalization, Mexican living standard on a per capita basis increased by $1,616 or $81 per year (against a total of $8,022 or $401 per year in the US). Norway's real per capita PPP income increased by $423 per person per year, or about $22 per year more than that of the US, implying that Norway gained over the US. Australia ($289) and Canada ($305), on the other hand, lagged behind the US, even though the gains in per capita real PPP income were positive.

Canada

Economic growth occurred in Canada during the period under examination. Real income in Canadian dollars (GNI at 1995 CND)

Figure 14.4   Real GNI trends, Canada

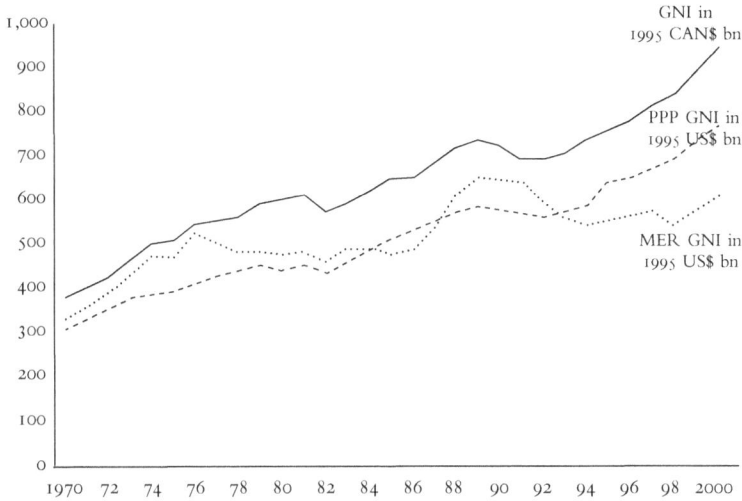

Source: IMF 2001; OECD 2002.

grew by 55 per cent during the twenty-year period (or 2.75 per cent a year), but with declines in the early 1980s and the 1990s. In contrast, real income in US dollars measured by the market exchange rate (MER GNI) increased by only 28 per cent (1.4 per cent on average each year), although by the PPP measurement it grew much faster – a total of 79 per cent or 3.9 per cent a year (see Figure 14.4).

The Canadian policy of integrating its economy with the US economy through the Free Trade Agreement and NAFTA has certainly increased real Canadian GNI since 1993. However, this achievement was accompanied by deepened Canadian external dependency on the US.

As Figure 14.5 shows, the exports/GDP ratio rose from 1993 until it reached 45 per cent in 2000. The imports/GDP ratio also rose in the same period but at a slower rate to reach 40 per cent in 2000. The Assets/GDP ratio is the ratio of outstanding Canadian external assets to GDP. Again, this ratio rose steadily from 1992 until it reached 75 per cent in 1998. The doubling of this ratio in ten years implies that Canadian investors rapidly increased their investment abroad,

Figure 14.5   External dependency, Canada (%)

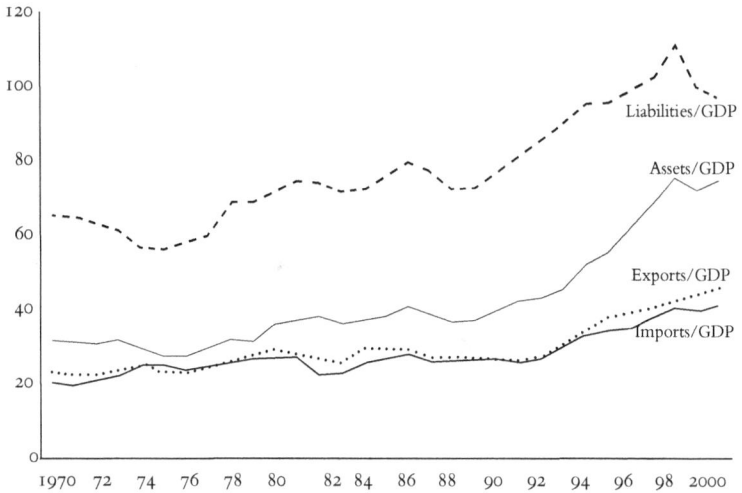

Source: IMF 2001.

including foreign direct investment (FDI), portfolio investment, and loans. Financial globalization certainly emancipated Canadian investors from the constraints of the domestic economy. At the same time, investment flows into Canada increased significantly. The presence of foreign capital has been a constant historical characteristic for Canada (Gray et al. 1972; Laxer 1989). However, Canadian dependence on foreign capital (Liabilities/GDP) increased rapidly from about 70 per cent in 1989 to 110 per cent in 1998. Canadian external liabilities at the beginning of the twenty-first century stood high, at the level equal to total annual Canadian production.

The gap between Liabilities/GDP and Assets/GDP stayed between 30 to 40 per cent until 1998. In the year 2000, the gap narrowed to the 20 per cent level. What does this indicate? A decline in Liabilities/GDP can be interpreted as a sign of lessened dependence, and a rise in Assets/GDP can be interpreted as a sign of increased Canadian participation in global finance. But a completely different interpretation is also possible. A decline in foreign investment in Canada is a sign that the global financial market is signalling a coming crisis for Canada as the US economy stagnates (*Economist* 2001). Also, a rise in Canadian overseas assets may be a sign of Canadian capital flight for a safer container of investor value. Regardless of the

Figure 14.6 Export destination concentration index

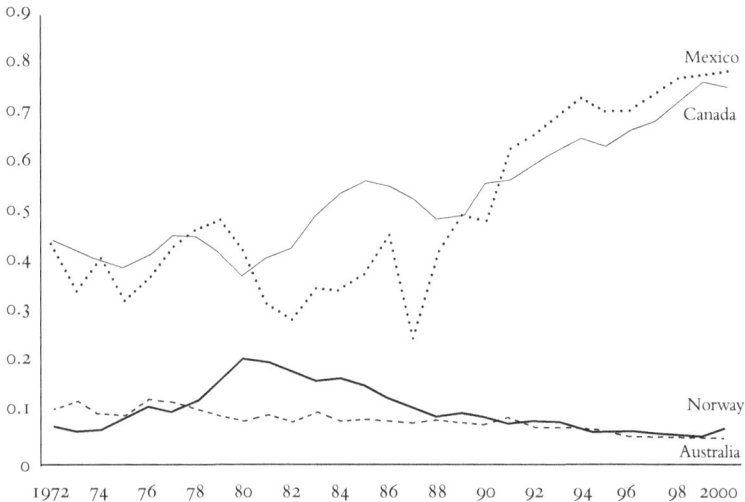

Source: IMF 2002.

unfolding of the latest financial investments, Canadian dependency through international financial activities has certainly increased.

Canadian dependence on the US market for exports increased significantly from 61 per cent in 1980, to 75 per cent in 1990, and to 86 per cent in 2000 (IMF 2002). In order to identify the degree of export dependency on particular countries, the export destination concentration index was derived (Figure 14.6).[5] If a country exports exclusively to one country, the index becomes one. The Canadian index increased from around 0.5 in 1989 until it reached 0.76 in 2000, reflecting the acute concentration of its exports to the US.

The major commodity groups that have been dominating Canadian exports are natural resources, processed materials (intermediate products), and finished products. In the 1970s, 20 per cent of Canadian exports was natural resources, 30 per cent was processed materials, and 30 per cent was finished products (Statistics Canada 2002). Under globalization, Canadian exports increased significantly in the area of finished products (50 per cent) while the shares of natural resources and processed materials decreased (about 10 per cent and 26 per cent, respectively).

While the shift in Canadian exports towards finished goods seems to imply that Canada is reducing the level of external dependency, this may not be the case. This is because Canada has been highly dependent on foreign corporations in various industrial sectors from agriculture, forestry, natural resource extraction and processing to manufacturing. For example, vehicles and parts are the major Canadian manufacturing exports, yet the companies that are producing these products are foreign-owned or -affiliated. The level of FDI into Canada has increased from US$54.1 billion in 1980 to US$194 billion in 2000. Also, portfolio investment into Canada increased from US$62.2 billion in 1980 to US$331.1 billion in 2000 (IMF 2001). These figures indicate that foreign domination in the Canadian corporate sector has risen significantly under neo-liberal globalization. An increase in manufacturing exports without local control and ownership is similar to the dependency that is manifested in Mexican *maquiladora* industrialization along the US border where foreign corporations establish operations to take advantage of the low cost of production. Therefore Canadian dependency is turning from a hinterland type dominated by staple exports to a 'hinterland–*maquiladora* type' where staple exports are complemented by foreign-controlled manufacturing exports.

Mexico

The Mexican economy grew meagrely under globalization and 'market' income in terms of constant US dollars went through turbulence due to repeated financial crises and peso devaluations. Figure 14.7 shows Mexico's real income trends. Real income in Mexican pesos (GNI in 1995 MXP) increased by 43 per cent, or an average of 2 per cent a year, between 1981 and 2000. On the other hand, real income evaluated by the market exchange rate (MER GNI at 1995 US$) only increased by an average of 1 per cent a year. Real income evaluated by the PPP exchange rate (PPP GNI at 1995 US$) increased by 66 per cent in the same period, or 3.3 per cent a year.

Figure 14.8 shows select indicators of Mexican external dependency. Total external debt to GDP ratio (total debt stock/GDP) fluctuated with a peak at 76 per cent in 1986. Since then it has declined to below 40 per cent, with an exception in 1995 and 1996. Total debt service/exports reached nearly 50 per cent in 1986, which means that interest payments for external loans reached a half of the amount of export earnings. This ratio has fluctuated since then,

Figure 14.7   Real GNI trends, Mexico

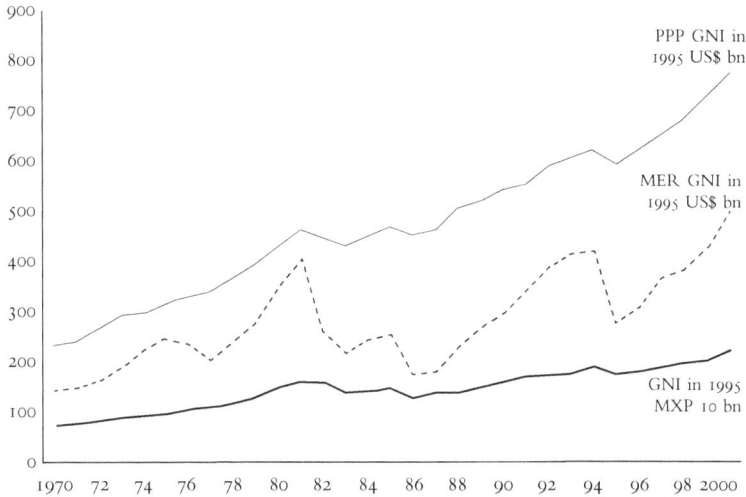

Source: IMF 2001; OECD 2002.

but the burden of international interest payments continues due to a significant level of external debt.

The 'exports/GDP' ratio increased from norms of just under 20 per cent in 1983, and rose to just over 30 per cent in 1995. Each Mexican financial crisis brought about this deepening of export dependency. Between 1981 and 2000, Mexican exports increased more than 600 per cent. However, such a phenomenal increase in exports only increased real 'market' income by 20 per cent and did not affect the level of external debt. The neo-liberal doctrine 'more exports bring in more income' worked only marginally in the case of Mexico.

Mexican trade dependency has characteristics similar to that of Canada. The growth in exports in the 1990s was related to NAFTA exports to the US, which increased from 55 per cent of total exports in 1981 to 90 per cent in 2000 (IMF 2002). Such a concentration of Mexican exports to one market is reflected in Mexico's export destination concentration index (Figure 14.6). From 1990, the Mexican index rose until it reached almost 0.8 in 2000.

Figure 14.8   External dependency, Mexico (%)

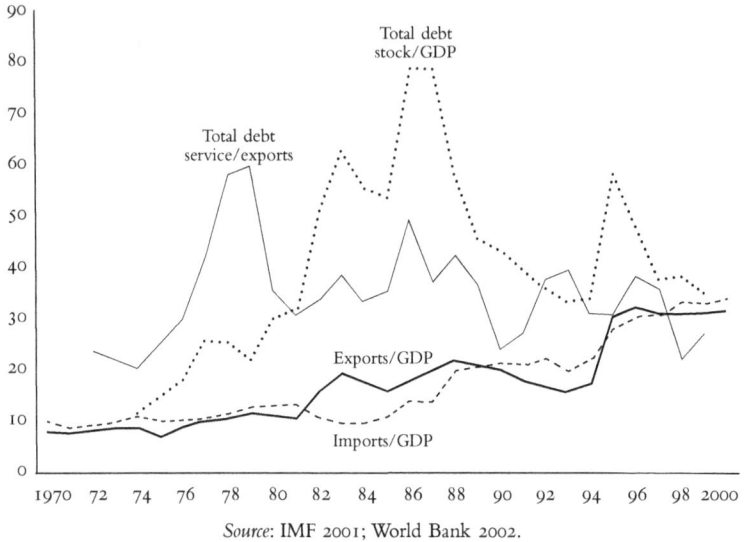

Source: IMF 2001; World Bank 2002.

Mexican exports were dominated by machines and transportation equipment, whose share of total exports increased from 6.5 per cent in 1983 to 58 per cent in 1998. In contrast, the share of petroleum in Mexican exports dropped from 71 per cent in 1983 to 6 per cent in 1998 (United Nations 2000). Mexico's growth under globalization was achieved by deepening export dependency and debt dependency, especially on the US import market in manufacturing and global financial markets. Mexican dependency can be characterized as the 'debt–*maquiladora*' type.

Australia

Real income in 1995 Australian dollars (GNI in 1995 Aus$) grew by 67 per cent between 1981 and 2000, or an average of 3.3 per cent per year (Figure 14.9). Real income in US dollars measured by the PPP exchange rate (PPP GNI at 1995 US$) grew by 73 per cent in the same period. In contrast, real Australian income in US dollars converted by the market exchange rate (MER GNI in 1995 US$) stagnated in the 1990s, and it grew only by 10.5 per cent between 1981 and 2000. The divergent trajectories between

Figure 14.9   Real GNI Trends, Australia

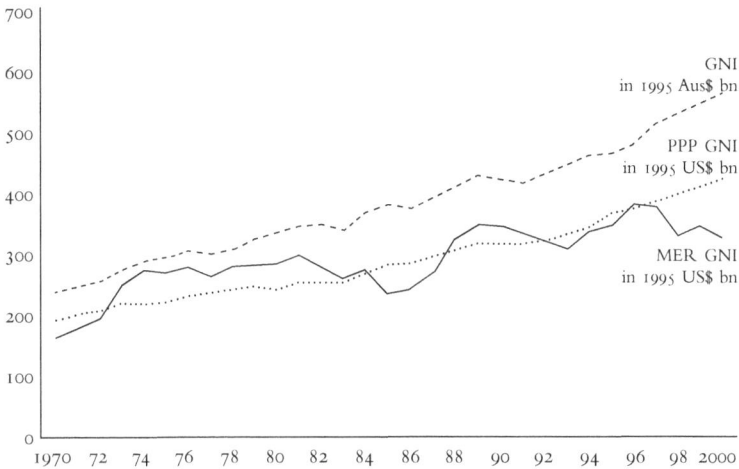

Source: IMF 2001; OECD 2002.

'latent' and 'market' income is a result of Australian dollar depreciation, and this implies that Australians on the average experienced income increase domestically but their income cannot buy much outside the country.

The Australian economy showed a somewhat different pattern from Canada in terms of external dependency, as shown in Figure 14.10. The rise in the Exports/GDP ratio was gradual and modest as compared to Canada. In terms of financial dependency, the Liabilities/GDP ratio reached 60 per cent in 1996, reflecting a surge of portfolio investment. But investment inflow is sluggish at best. The Assets/GDP ratio indicates the activities of Australian investment abroad. It increased in the 1990s to above 20 per cent, but it is not increasing as rapidly as in Canada. These IMF data show that Australian external dependency is limited in comparison with Canada and Mexico.

Australian export destinations have diversified considerably in recent years. After reaching 33 per cent in 1974, Japan's share dropped to less than 20 per cent in 2000, while the share of other East Asian countries increased. The combined share of China, Korea, Singapore,

Figure 14.10   External dependency, Australia (%)

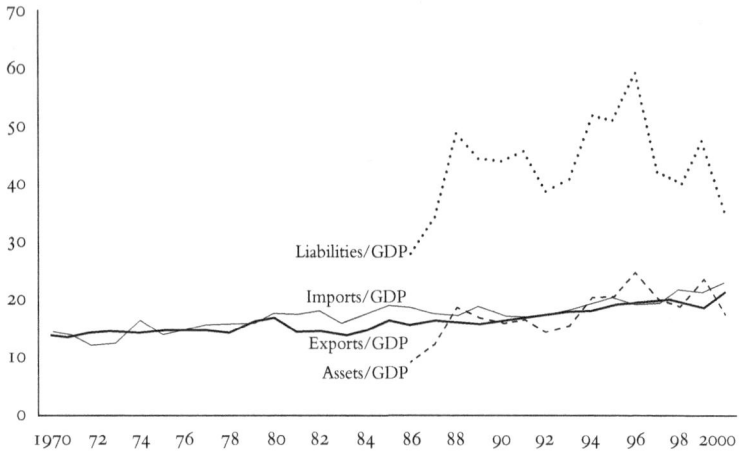

Source: IMF 2001.

Hong Kong, and Taiwan increased from 10 per cent in 1980 to 26 per cent in 2000 (IMF 2002). As Figure 14.6 indicates, Australia's export destination concentration index declined. Also, export commodity composition went through diversification. In contrast to Canada, Australia did not expand exports in manufacturing rapidly in the 1980s and 1990s. Instead, Australian exports have risen in all commodity categories in value terms, but the weight of raw materials and agricultural commodities declined from 78 per cent in 1983 to 54 per cent in 1998 (United Nations 2000).

Although Australia is diversifying its export destinations and commodity composition, such a strategy is not translating into an increase in per capita income when measured by the market exchange rate. From this observation, it is possible to conclude that Australian dependency may be called the 'diversifying hinterland' type. Australia's external dependency is not rising as much as in Canada or Mexico and its 'latent' income is rising steadily. Australia may be showing an example of sustained development with careful selection of external engagement even though its currency takes beatings in the international financial market.

Figure 14.11   Real GNI trends, Norway

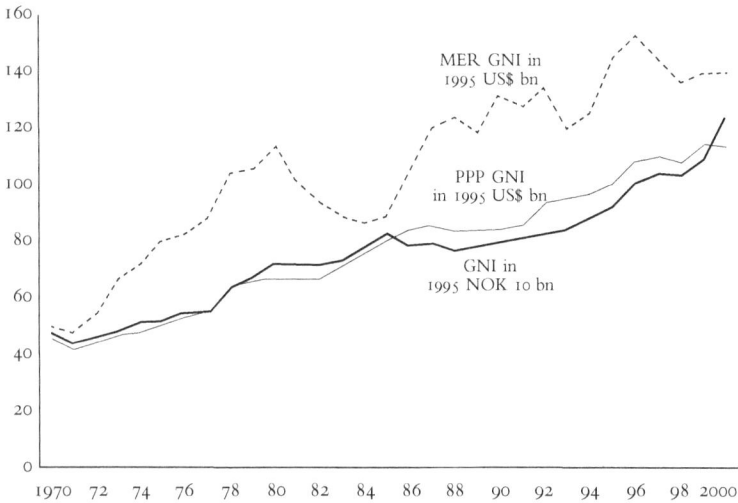

Source: IMF 2001; OECD 2002.

Norway

Real income in Norwegian kroner (GNI at 1995 NOK) increased between 1971 and 2001 with some stagnant years, and between 1980 and 2000 it grew by 73 per cent, or 3.6 per cent a year on average (Figure 14.11). Real income in 1995 US dollars converted by the market exchange rate (MER) showed a sharp rise and fall and the trend in the second half of the 1990s is a decline/stagnation. Between 1980 and 2000, it grew only by 22 per cent, or about 1 per cent a year. Real income converted by the PPP exchange rate showed a pattern similar to real income in 1995 kroner, and between 1980 and 2000 it grew by 71 per cent. These trends show that Norway achieved income gains under globalization, but in terms of what Norwegian income can buy in the global market, the income gain is not that significant (1 per cent annual growth).

These Norwegian achievements in the 1980s and 1990s were accompanied by rising export market dependency. Figure 14.12 shows the Exports/GDP and Imports/GDP ratios. The weight of Norwegian exports in total production was above 40 per cent between 1980 and 1985, declined below 40 per cent between 1986

Figure 14.12   Trade dependency, Norway (%)

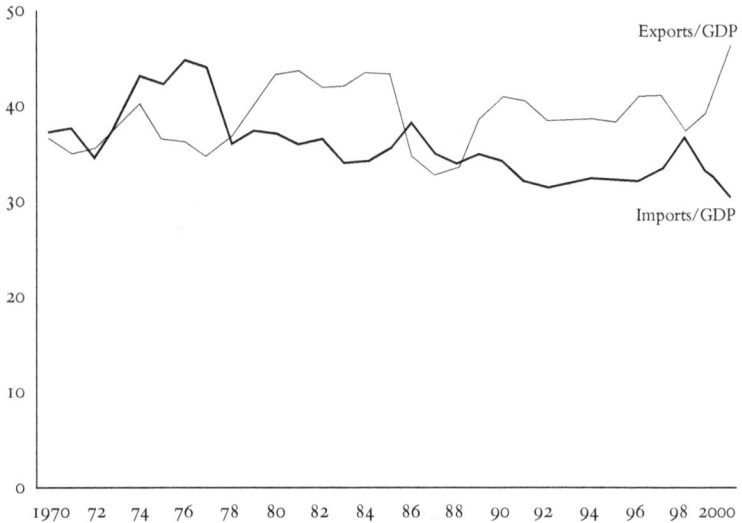

Source: IMF 2001.

and 1988, but was around 40 per cent until 1999. In 2000 and the first quarter of 2001, Norwegian export dependency rose to 48 per cent. This is a ratio similar to Canada's. The rise of Norway's exports was mainly the result of increased petroleum and natural gas exports, and the earnings from such exports made Norway an external capital investor country. Norwegian external dependency in the area of finance manifests itself as an exposure of assets to volatility in global financial markets.

Export destination for Norway took a path of diversification. Great Britain has been the largest export destination, but its share declined from 41 per cent of total exports in 1980 to 21 per cent in 2000 (IMF 2002). The export destination concentration index for Norway declined from 1980 to 1999 (Figure 14.6). This diversification in export destination, however, was accompanied by rather high concentration in terms of commodities. While total exports of manufacturing increased steadily, the exports of crude oil and natural gas increased in the 1980s and 1990s with some fluctuations. In the year 2000, exports of crude oil and natural gas reached 30 billion

kroner, which was more than a half of commodity exports in that
year (Statistics Norway 2001).

   Norway is not a hinterland in the sense that it depends on
foreign capital and corporations for natural resource extraction and
exports. Its natural resource sector is not owned by foreigners, and
the country as a whole is a rich investor in global financial markets.
But crude oil and natural gas are increasing their weight in exports,
reaching about a quarter of GDP in 2000. External dependency in
terms of export commodities and global financial investment suggests
that Norway is becoming a 'hinterland-investor.'

Divergent semi-peripherality, vulnerability, and sustainability

This section examines the sustainability of neo-liberal globalization
in the four countries, considering their differences, similarities, and
specific vulnerabilities. Table 14.3 summarizes the income trends and
the indicators of external dependency. In terms of real per capita
MER income, Australia was the biggest loser, followed by Canada
and Mexico, but it was Mexico that achieved the smallest increase
in real per capita PPP income between 1980 and 2000. Australia is
the country that has been least dependent externally in terms of
exports since the export/GDP ratio was the smallest with diverse
commodities and destinations. In terms of the exposure to global
financial markets, Canada, Mexico, and Australia are more dependent on foreign capital inflow, and Canada and Norway are exposed
to global financial markets due to larger capital outflow relative to
GDP.

   Canada's expanding reliance on the US market for exports makes
it vulnerable to changes in the condition of that market, and Canada's
increased capital outflow makes Canadian investment subject to
global financial fluctuations. The corporations operating in Canada
are increasingly foreign-owned or -controlled. Also, Canada has been
experiencing foreign exchange depreciation, making the country
poorer in terms of the global currency, the US dollar. Policies to
integrate the Canadian economy with that of the US have so far
resulted in deepened dependency with limited gain in terms of
latent income. Canadians on average (per capita basis) have lost
market-evaluated real income.

Table 14.3 Income performance, external dependency, and
vulnerability

	Canada	Mexico	Australia	Norway
Real per capita MER income 1980–2000	Medium loss −$315	Small loss −$31	Large loss −$2,562	Modest gain $2,513
Real per capita PPP income 1980–2000	Medium gain $6,107	Small gain $1,616	Medium gain $5,789	Large gain $8,460
Export/GDP 2000 (%)	48	30	20	48
Export destination	Concentrated on US	Concentrated on US	Diverse – mainly East Asia	Concentrated on EU
Export commodity concentration	Concentrated (manufacturing, resource-based manufacturing)	Concentrated (manufacturing)	Diverse	Concentrated (petroleum and gas)
Capital inflow	Heavy	Heavy (debt)	Medium	Limited
Capital outflow	Heavy		Limited	Heavy
Vulnerability	Dependency on US and global financial markets, depreciating currency	Dependency on US markets, external loans and IMF/WB	Depreciating currency	Dependency on EU markets, resource price and global financial markets
Semi-peripheral typology	Hinterland-*maquiladora*	Debt-*maquiladora*	Diversifying hinterland	Hinterland-investor

Source: Above tables and figures.

Mexico has also deepened its dependency on the US market
for exports while its level of external debt remains high. Debt
service (interest payments for loans) eats up one-third to one-half
of export earnings, creating the situation of permanent debt en-
slavement. Income gain was modest in terms of latent income, but
market-evaluated per capita real income declined. Norway shared a
similar vulnerability to Canada. It deepened its export dependency
on petroleum and natural gas and on European markets. Expanding
Norwegian investment abroad exposes the country to fluctuations in
global financial markets. These added vulnerabilities under neo-liberal
globalization could be justified in the case of Norway, however,

since its gains in both market and latent income were substantial. Its choice of not joining the EU while deriving maximum benefit from being practically integrated into the European economy has enabled it to escape from a decline in its zonal ranking.

In contrast to Canada, Mexico, and Norway, Australia's external dependency did not expand as much. In return, the country experienced a significant devaluation of its currency, resulting in the substantial reduction in market evaluated per capita real income. This reduction contrasts with the gains in terms of latent income. How can we interpret these seemingly contradictory developments? The main feature of Australia as compared to Canada, Mexico, and Norway is its geographical distance from large markets such as the US and EU and the lack of regional economic integration. Not being integrated into the larger economy lowers the market evaluation of the Australian economy, but Australia's rich natural resource endowment allows it to maintain a higher living standard.

Where will these economies go as neo-liberal globalization progresses? In order to answer this question, it is necessary to examine sustainability at the world-system level since what happens to these economies depends on the future of the system as a whole. As discussed earlier, the world-system has gone through further peripheralization of the periphery (most African and South Asian countries), peripheralization of the semi-periphery (Latin American, former socialist, and petroleum-exporting countries), and semi-peripheralization of the core (Western and Northern European and rich petroleum-exporting countries), especially in the second half of the 1990s. These changes are due to the continued growth of the US economy at the expense of the rest of the world mainly through the formation of the global financial order dominated by the US dollar. Global financial surplus flowed into the US in the 1990s, creating capital gains, and the surplus transferred from the poor to the rich was completed through rising exports from the periphery and semi-periphery to the US at discount prices (Ikeda forthcoming). This situation, however, is reaching its limit as indicated by stagnant and falling US stock prices. Finance-driven US growth in the 1990s is over.

This 'slowing down' of the US economy further devalues the currencies of Canada and Mexico as their exports to the US drop and capital flows out due to future economic insecurity. As their currencies are devalued, Canada and Mexico may further expand exports so as to compensate for lost export earnings. But expanded exports under globalization have so far brought limited gains. Canada's and Norway's enlarged exposure to global financial markets may add the further risk of losing income as the world economy experiences US bubble deflation. It is, therefore, not difficult to speculate that deepening external dependency under global economic stagnation will bring the end of whatever 'prosperity' globalization brought. Canada and Mexico achieved meagre income growth at the cost of deepened dependency on the US. Norway achieved modest gain through deepened dependency on oil exports and on the European markets. Australia is losing in terms of global currency. The economies of these countries are becoming either increasingly unstable and vulnerable or poorer.

Notes

1. These countries are selected based on the availability of IMF 2001 data, which include balance-of-payments and national income statistics. The countries not included are those that are not members of the IMF (e.g. Taiwan), those small developing countries from whom the IMF does not receive reports, and those that are not capable of reporting due to war, etc.

2. The purchasing power parity (PPP) exchange rate is derived as a ratio of the local currency and US dollar amounts that can buy the standard basket of consumer goods. When the price of non-traded goods is cheaper in a country than in the US, the PPP exchange rate tends to be higher (stronger) than the market exchange rate. Local income converted into US dollars using the PPP exchange rates is a better measure of the living standard of a country.

3. Gross national income (GNI) is used here partly due to the availability of data. Also, when foreign enterprises and migrant workers stay in the host country, location-based GNI captures better than nationality-based GNP the importance of a country as the locus of activities and its command over the global accumulation process.

4. The above characterization of the changes in the zonal structure depends on the criteria used here – that is, per capita GNI evaluated at the market exchange rate. This analysis can be complemented by other criteria such as military strength, living standard, and the degree of sovereignty for a better understanding of the zonal structure of the world-system.

5. The index is the sum of the square of export destination shares.

References

Arrighi, G. and J. Drangel (1986) 'The Stratification of the World-Economy: An Exploration of the Semi-peripheral Zone', *Review*, vol. X, no. 1: 9–74.

Bullard, N., W. Bello, and K. Malhorta (1998) 'Taming the Tigers: The IMF and the Asian Crisis', in K.S. Jomo (ed.) *Tigers in Trouble: Financial Governance, Liberalisation and Crisis in East Asia*, London and New York: Zed Books: 85–136.

The Economist (2001) 'The Americas: The Big Chill; Canada's Economy', 24 November.

Gray, H. (1972) *Foreign Direct Investment in Canada* (Grey Report), Ottawa: Supply and Services Canada.

Gowan, P. (1999) *The Global Gamble: Washington's Faustian Bid for World Dominance*, London and New York: Verso.

Hopkins, T.K. (1982) 'The Study of the Capitalist World-Economy: Some Introductory Considerations', in T.K. Hopkins and I. Wallerstein et al., *World-System Analysis: Theory and Methodology*, Beverly Hills: Sage Publications: 9–38.

Hopkins, T.K., I. Wallerstein and Associates (1982) 'Patterns of Development of the Modern World-System', in T.K. Hopkins, I. Wallerstein et al., *World-System Analysis: Theory and Methodology*, Beverly Hills: Sage Publications: 41–82.

Ikeda, S. (forthcoming) 'Japan and the Changing Regime of Accumulation: A World-System Study of Japan's Trajectory from Miracle to Debacle,' *Journal of World-Systems Research*.

IMF (International Monetary Fund) (2001) *International Financial Statistics Yearbook* (CD-ROM), Washington, DC: IMF.

IMF (International Monetary Fund) (2002) *Direction of Trade Statistics Yearbook* (CD-ROM), Washington, DC: IMF.

Jomo, K.S. (1998) 'Introduction: Financial Governance, Liberalisation and Crisis in East Asia', in K.S. Jomo (ed.) *Tigers in Trouble: Financial Governance, Liberalisation and Crisis in East Asia*, London and New York: Zed Books: 1–32.

Korten, D. (1995) *When Corporations Rule the World*, West Hartford, CT: Kumarian; San Francisco: Berrett-Koehler.

Laxer, G. (1989) *Open for Business: The Roots of Foreign Ownership in Canada*, Toronto: Oxford University Press.

McBride, S. and J. Shields (1997) *Dismantling a Nation: The Transition to Corporate Rule in Canada*, Halifax: Fernwood Publishing.

Maull, H.W. (1999) 'Crisis in Asia: Origins and Implications', *Internationale Politik und Gesellschaft* 1: 56–66.

OECD (Organization for Economic Cooperation and Development) (2002) *OECD Statistics*, www.oecd.org/xls/M00009000/M00009295.xls.

Statistics Canada (2002) *CANSIM II*, http://datacentre2.chass.utoronto.ca/cansim2/index.jsp.

Statistics Norway (2001) *Statistical Yearbook of Norway 2001*.

United Nations (2000) *International Trade Statistics Yearbook*, New York: United Nations.

Wallerstein, I. (1974a) 'The Rise and Future Demise of the World Capitalist System: Concepts for Comparative analysis', *Comparative Studies in Society and History*, vol. 16, no. 4: 387–415, reprinted in I. Wallerstein, *The Capitalist World-Economy*, Cambridge: Cambridge University Press: 1–36.

Wallerstein, I. (1974b) 'Dependence in an Interdependent World: The Limited Possibilities of Transformation within the Capitalist World-Economy', *African Studies Review* 17: 1–26, reprinted in I. Wallerstein, *The Capitalist World-Economy*, Cambridge: Cambridge University Press: 66–94.

World Bank (2002) *World Development Indicators 2002* (CD-ROM), Washington, DC: World Bank.

About the Contributors

Alejandro Alvarez is a Mexican labour economist and sociologist who is a Professor in the Economics Faculty at the Universidad Nacional Autónoma de México (UNAM). He is co-editor of the independent weekly magazine *Corre La Voz* and is currently working on Comparative Perspectives of the European Monetary Union and the project of a Monetary Union for North America.

Paul Bowles is Professor of Economics at the University of Northern British Columbia. His research interests include globalization and regionalism. He is currently working on a book, provisionally titled *Endangered Species? National Currencies Under Globalisation*', which examines the future of national currencies in Australia, Canada, Mexico, and Norway.

Janine Brodie is a Professor of Political Science at the University of Alberta and is a Fellow of the Royal Society of Canada. She has written extensively on Canadian politics and political economy, and globalization and governance. Her most recent publication is *Reinventing Canada: Politics in the 21st Century* (edited with L. Trimble) (Prentice Hall/Pearson Educational, 2003).

Ray Broomhill is Adjunct Associate Professor in Labour Studies at the University of Adelaide in South Australia. His research interests are in the fields of political economy, gender studies, and public policy. He is currently engaged in researching the uneven impact of global restructuring on working experiences and gender relations within different socio-economic households in Adelaide.

Dick Bryan teaches political economy at the University of Sydney. His research areas concern the Australian economy, international finance, and Marxian value theory. He is currently researching a Marxian analysis of financial derivatives, and the relationship between international finance and economic nationalism.

Dag Harald Claes is a senior Research Fellow at the ARENA program (Advanced Research on the Europeanization of the Nation-State). He holds a doctoral degree in Political Science from the University of Oslo. His recent publications include *The Politics of Oil-Producer Cooperation* (Westview Press, 2001) and 'The Process of Europeanisation: Norway and the Internal Energy Market' (*Journal of Public Policy*, vol. 22, no. 3, 2002).

Stephen Clarkson teaches political economy at the University of Toronto, where he focuses on Canada's relationship with the United States and on North American governance. His major books are *Canada and the Reagan Challenge* (Lorimer, 1982), *Trudeau and Our Times: The Magnificent Obsession* (co-authored, McClelland & Stewart, 1990), *Trudeau and Our Times: The Heroic Delusion* (co-authored, McClelland & Stewart, 1994), and *Uncle Sam and Us: Globalization, Neoconservatism, and the Canadian State* (University of Toronto Press, 2002).

Marjorie Griffin Cohen is an economist who is Professor of Political Science and Women's Studies at Simon Fraser University in British Columbia, Canada. Her research areas deal with public policy and economics with special emphasis on issues concerning women, international trade agreements, the Canadian economy, and labour. Recent books include *Training the Excluded for Work: Access and Equity for Women, Immigrants, First Nations, Youth and People with Low Income* (UBC Press, 2003), and *Global Turbulence: Social Activists' and State Responses to Globalization*, co-edited with Stephen McBride (Ashgate, 2003).

John Erik Fossum is Senior Researcher at ARENA, University of Oslo (on leave from a permanent position as Associate Professor in the Department of Administration and Organization Theory, University of Bergen, Norway) and past president and current board member of the Nordic Association for Canadian Studies (NACS). He has written books and articles on federalism, constitutionalism, citizenship, and democratic legitimacy in the EU and Canada. Recent books are *Oil, the State and Federalism* (University of Toronto Press, 1997) and *Democracy in the European Union: Integration through Deliberation?*, co-edited with Erik Eriksen (Routledge, 2000).

Teresa Gutiérrez-Haces is Professor of Economic Development and Economic Integration and Free Trade at the Political Science Faculty at the Universidad Nacional Autónoma de México (UNAM). She is currently a full-time senior researcher at the Instituto de Investigaciones Económicas at the UNAM, coordinating a project studying the United States foreign economic policy towards Mexico and Canada. Her main research centres on the debate on free trade and protectionism as well as on the impact of NAFTA on North American countries. Recent publications include: *Orígen de los Procesos de Integración Económica en México y Canadá* (Porrúa, 2002), *Canadian International Economic Policy towards México and Latin America* (UAM, 2002), *Building New Economic Relations inside North America* (Taylor & Francis, 2002), *Territoires et mondialisation: L'ALENA et l'espace local au Mexique* (Université de la Sorbonne, 2002), and 'Quebec and Latin America Reaffirm Economic Priorities' (*American Review of Canadian Studies*, 2002).

Satoshi Ikeda teaches world-system studies and globalization in the Department of Sociology, University of Alberta. He has a Ph.D. in economics from the University of Michigan and a Ph.D. in sociology from the State University of New York at Binghamton. He recently published *Trifurcating Miracle: Corporations, Workers, Bureaucrats, and the Erosion of Japan's National Economy* (Routledge, 2002).

Stephen McBride is Professor of Political Science, Simon Fraser University. He has published widely on political economy and public policy. His current research is focused on the domestic political and constitutional impact of international economic agreements and on the sustainability of neo-liberal globalization. Recent books include *Paradigm Shift: Globalization and the Canadian State* (Fernwood, 2001), and *Global Turbulence: Social Activists' and State Responses to Globalization* (2003), co-edited with Marjorie Griffin Cohen.

Øyvind Østerud has a Ph.D. from the London School of Economics and is a Professor in the Department of Political Science, University of Oslo. His special areas of interest are sovereignty, the state system, and nationalism. His latest books are *Globaliseringen og nasjonalstaten* (Globalization and the Nation-State) (Gyldendal, 1999), and an edited volume on the globalization of Norway (Gyldendal, 2001), both in Norwegian, and he is editor of *Power and Democracy* (Ashgate, 2003).

David Schneiderman is an Associate Professor of Law at the Faculty of Law, University of Toronto. He has authored numerous articles on Canadian constitutional law and history, comparative constitutional law and economic globalization. His most recent edited books are *The Quebec*

Decision (Lorimer, 1999) and *Charting the Consequences: The Impact of the Charter of Rights on Canadian Law and Politics* (with Kate Sutherland, University of Toronto Press, 1997). He is founding editor of the quarterly *Constitutional Forum Constitutionnel* and founding editor-in-chief of the journal *Review of Constitutional Studies.* Professor Schneiderman currently is completing a book manuscript entitled *Investing Authority: An Inquiry into the Constitutional Order of Economic Globalization.*

Index

accumulation, 128–9, 134–8, 139–41,
  149–51; *see also* regulation, deregulation
agriculture, 43, 53–4, 65, 104, 111–13, 122,
  128, 141, 156, 162, 251, 278, 282
Amero, 213; *see also* NAMU and euro
Amin, Ash, 140
America, *see* United States of America;
  model of development, 2; *see also*
  Washington consensus
anti-corporate globalization, xiii;
  movement, xv, 45; *see also* public
  protest
Association pour taxation des transactions
  à l'aide des citoyens (Attac), 45
Australia, x, xii–xiii, xv, 3, 7, 10;
  agriculture, 111–13, 122, 128, 141, 282;
  banks, 120–21; corporations, 127–8,
  132, 146; currency, 118, 121–2, 287;
  economy, 117–19, 127, 132, 140, 149,
  281, 287; globalization, 8, 118, 133,
  139, 143, 150–51, 273–4, 283, 288;
  government, 114, 124, 126–7, 132–3,
  136, 139, 141, 143–6 (John Howard,
  xiii); labour market deregulation, 123,
  138, 141, 144, women's unpaid labour,
  145; manufacturing, 113–16, 119, 123,
  127, 141, 282; mining, 111–13, 116,
  119–20, 128; public sector, 127, 141,
  services, 136, 144; state, 110–11, 113,
  116, 120, 123, 125–9, 132–51 (*see also*
  nation-state); South, 132, 137, 141–2,
  143, 148–9; trade, 111–13, 117–18,
  121–2, 128

banks: Australia, 120–21; Canada, 204, 214;
  Europe, 197, 213–14; Mexico, 208,
  210–12; USA, 208; *see also* World Bank
Bauman, Zygmunt, 218
Beck, Ulrich, 19
Bello, Walden, xv, 15
Bretton Woods, x, 63, 203
Business Council on National Issues,
  206–7; *see also* Canadian Council of
  Chief Executive Officers

COC, *see* Council of Canadians
CSOs, *see* civil society organizations
CUFTA, *see* Canada–United States Free
  Trade Agreement
Canada, x, xii–xiii, xv, 3, 10; agriculture,
  156, 162, 278; corporations, 155,
  177, 188, 199–201, 206–7, 278,
  285; currency, 199–208, 213–14;
  dollarization, 198–208, 212–15;
  economy, 275, 285; electricity, 8, 175–7,
  deregulation, 8, 175–6, 179, 180–82,
  187, 189; globalization, 153, 165–6,
  207, 220, 243, 251, 273–4, 276–8, 288;
  government, 154–6, 164, 166–7, 177,
  184–6, 187–8, 189–90, 191–2, 219,
  225, 231 (Jean Chrétien, 221; Brian
  Mulroney, 81, 207): manufacturing, 278,
  286; National Energy Board, 185–6,
  188; public sector, 176–7, 190–91,
  services, 166; trade, 166, 168–9, 176,
  184, 189, 191–2, 199, 201, 206, 225,
  243, 248–9; *see also* Canada–United

agriculture, 43, 53–4, 65; commons, 47–8; economy, 33, 35, 43, 47–8; electricity deregulation, 64, 66; European Economic Area (EEA), 39, 48, 51, 52, 249; European Economic Community (EEC), 38; European Free Trade Association (EFTA), 39, 51; European Union (EU), 6, 36, 38–9, 40–41, 48, 51, 55, 62, 65, 239, 263; foreign policies, history of, 37–40, 51–5; globalization, 6, 33–49, 51, 65–6, 286, 288; government, 33, 38–9; Jorgen Loveland, 52; manufacturing, 284; oil and gas, 46–8; public sector, 33, 35, 39, 42; state, 33, 35, 46–7, 49, 52–9, 61–5, 67 (see also nation-state); trade, 35, 39, 44, 52-4, 64, 239, 249, 284; welfare policies, 23, 33

Organization for Economic and Community Development (OECD), 36, 113, 125–6
Organization of Petroleum Exporting Countries (OPEC), 46–7

Peck, Jamie, 140
periphery states, ii, xii–xiii, xv, xvi, xvii, 2, 3, 4–5, 28, 53, 70, 73–4, 91, 127, 160, 170–71, 198–9, 264, 267–70, 272, 287; see also nation-states, states, zonal position
Polanyi, Karl, xvi, 16–17, 24, 27, 142, 144, 219
Pope & Talbot, Inc., 220–21, 226–8, 232–3
poverty, 4, 13, 15, 17, 27, 72, 104, 106, 147, 149; under-development, 72, 74; see also periphery states
Prebisch, Raúl, 73
privatization, 14, 22, 25, 95, 99–101, 123, 127, 138, 141, 144, 166, 176, 255, 265; electricity, 8, 106, 177, 187, 189, 209–10; public services, 21, 98, 107
public: protest, 24, 84, 165, 167 (anti-corporate globalization movement, xii, xv; Chiapas, 81; Zapatista indigenous movement, 94); sector, 25, 33, 35, 39, 42, 102, 127, 136, 141, 176–7, 190–91; services, xi, xvi, 21, 136, 144, 166; social policies, 14, 17–20, 22, 26–7, 129
Puebla–Panama Plan, 95

quotas, 83, 129 n2, 156, 162, 226; Canada–US Softwood Lumber Agreement quotas, 226; Pope & Talbot challenge, 226

regulation, 2, 6, 9, 10, 14, 16, 19, 20–27, 43–5, 48, 53, 55–7, 59–60, 63–4, 66, 75, 81, 86, 90, 127, 132, 140–41, 145, 147, 150, 154, 156, 163, 169–70, 175–80, 182, 184–92, 207, 210, 219–21, 123–7, 226, 229, 232–3, 243, 245–8, 250, 252, 254–257; approach, 133–5, 142; defined, 151 n1; framework, 133–4; global, 1, 265; mode of, 134 (Fordist, 134, 136–8, 141, 146, 150, post-Fordist, 136, 144–5, 149–50; Keynesian, 45, 134, 136, post-Keynesian, 136, 145–6); theory, 134–6; role of the state, 137; see also accumulation, deregulation
Risse, Thomas, xiv

S.D. Myers, Inc., 168, 220, 230–33
San Andrés Agreements, 94–5
semi-periphery states, ii, x–xx, 4–10, 28, 165, 198, 219–20, 243, 257, 266, 268–70, 272, 274, 287, 294; see also nation-state, state, zonal position
social, the, ii, 6, 13–14, 16–19, 22–8, 73, 136, 145–6, 148; see also welfare state
sovereignty, x–xii, xvii, 13, 18–20, 23–4, 37–8, 40, 43–4, 48, 51, 54, 65, 78, 86, 156, 160, 213–14, 232, 242–3, 245, 249, 251; see also governance, constitutionalism, new constitutionalism
state, xi, xiii–xv, 2–3, 5–10, 13–14, 16–28, 33, 35, 46–7, 49, 52–9, 61–5, 67, 71, 73, 75–6, 81, 83–6, 90, 93–5, 97–9, 106–7, 110–11, 113, 116, 120, 123, 125–9, 132–51, 153–71, 189, 212, 214, 219–33, 239–40, 242–57, 264–5; core, xiii–xiv, 3, 8, 51, 91–2, 140, 246, 257, 264–5, 266, 268–70, 273–4; periphery, ii, xii–xiii, xv, xvi, xvii, 2, 3, 4–5, 28, 53, 70, 73–4, 91, 127, 160, 170–71, 198–9, 264, 267–70, 272, 287; semi-periphery, ii, x–xx, 4–10, 28, 165, 198, 219–20, 243, 257, 266, 268–70, 272, 274, 287, 294; see also nation-state, welfare state
Stiglitz, Joseph, 12
subsidies, 22, 53, 65, 98, 114, 159, 170, 231, 233, 248–9
supraconstitution, 20, 153, 155, 162, 166–7, 171, 220; constitutionalism, 219; new, xii, 19–21, 23, 26, 241; transconstitutionalism, 20
sustainability, environmental, xvi, 22, 161

tariffs, 82, 103, 114–16, 123–4, 129 n2, 143, 156, 162, 249; see also General Agreement on Tariffs and Trade

www.ingramcontent.com/pod-product-compliance
Lightning Source LLC
Chambersburg PA
CBHW070558270326
41926CB00013B/2353